Intercultural Alternatives

Maribel Blasco & Jan Gustafsson (editors)

Intercultural Alternatives

Critical Perspectives on Intercultural Encounters in Theory and Practice

Copenhagen Business School Press

Intercultural Alternatives
Critical Perspectives on Intercultural Encounters
in Theory and Practice

© Copenhagen Business School Press
Printed in Denmark by Holbæk Amts Bogtrykkeri
Cover design by Morten Højmark
1. edition 2004

ISBN 87-630-0124-1

Distribution:

Scandinavia
DJØF/DBK, Mimersvej 4
DK-4600 Køge, Denmark
Phone: +45 3269 7788, fax: +45 3269 7789

North America
Copenhagen Business School Press
Books International Inc.
P.O. Box 605
Herndon, VA 20172-0605, USA
Phone: +1 703 661 1500, fax: +1 703 661 1501

Rest of the World
Marston Book Services, P.O. Box 269
Abingdon, Oxfordshire, OX14 4YN, UK
Phone: +44 (0) 1235 465500, fax: +44 (0) 1235 465555
E-mail Direct Customers: direct.order@marston.co.uk
E-mail Booksellers: trade.order@marston.co.uk

TABLE OF CONTENTS

textual strategies for the production of 'us' and 'them' 171/ The first boundary: 'we's and Otherness 171/ Giver and receiver – a pictorial narrative 174/ Text and power 177/ Condensation and displacement 178/ Meanings of self and Other 179/ The relational constitution of community 181/ Culture, interculturality and textual analysis 181/ Epilogue 182

Introduction 193/ Interculturality 195/ Ethics and morals: a distinction and the relation 200/ The ethical demand 203/ Ethics and cross-cultural universals 205/ Ethical and moral implications for the intercultural praxis 207/ Intercultural ethics and the professional sphere 210

Foreword

PROFESSOR ANNE-MARIE SØDERBERG
Department of Intercultural Communication and Management
Copenhagen Business School

Many books about intercultural communication have primarily been guided by an interest in prescribing adequate behaviour for communication with strangers in order to avoid noise and miscommunication, manage potential conflicts and improve intercultural effectiveness. However, such prescriptive guides have often neither been based on anthropological or sociological knowledge about the cultures and countries described, nor on linguistic proficiency when it comes to the specific languages used in the intercultural communication situations described. Accounts of intercultural encounters – and interpretations of the underlying communication pattern – could therefore sometimes rather be perceived as Western stereotypical images of 'the Other', whose main function is to confirm the image of the sovereign cultural self.

Another critique to be raised against many popular handbooks of intercultural communication is that the presentation of the conceptual foundations of the dominant theories of interpersonal and intergroup communication – and especially the critical examination and reflection of these – is often sacrificed for the sake of producing guidelines and giving advice to practitioners professionally involved in intercultural encounters. The multiplicity of users of the more prescriptive literature on intercultural communication encompasses such groups as foreign service officers, Peace Corps volunteers, business persons in multinational and multiethnic corporations, social workers and staff members of hospitals, teachers in integrated schools as well as police officers dealing with ethnic communities.

In 'Intercultural Alternatives' the main focus is a critique of some mainstream conceptualisations of communication, culture and intercultural encounters, as well as a presentation of alternative ways of thinking about and analysing interculturality. The critique is founded on the authors' thorough knowledge of specific countries created through studies of communication, culture and societal issues in France, Germany, Japan, Latin America and Spain. This specific research background may open up for empathy with those who did not gain a voice in stereotypical Western representations of 'the Other', and it paves the way for a more complex and sociologically based understanding of existing national or regional images of and narratives about 'us' and 'them'.

The approaches to interculturality presented in 'Intercultural Alternatives' have been generated within broader theoretical frameworks such as cognitive theory, hermeneutics, identity theory, mentality theory, narratology and semiotics. Reflections on intercultural understanding and intercultural ethics draw on these theories, which also create adequate frames of reference for the analyses of texts, interviews and concrete intercultural encounters.

I welcome the editors' initiative to collect these research-based contributions from area studies offering a multidisciplinary perspective on interculturality. I am convinced that this book can add value to courses in intercultural communication and broaden the students' perspective as well as providing a useful reference for scholars working on intercultural encounters.

Introduction –
Intercultural Alternatives
Critical perspectives on intercultural encounters in theory and practice

JAN GUSTAFSSON AND MARIBEL BLASCO

Introduction

The idea of making a volume about 'interculturality' was probably for most of the participants the result of being inserted as teachers and researchers in the field of 'intercultural communication', an area of enormous interest and immense potential for study, but also an area in which teaching and sometimes also scientific research can find itself engaging in questionable practices. These include taking for granted certain assumptions about culture, cultures and differences, turning empirical studies – such as Hofstede's (2001) study of cultural differences within IBM – into theory or 'hard facts', or even a tendency to create what might paradoxically be termed 'scientific' stereotypes of cultural 'Others'. These approaches are criticised by an increasing number of scholars working within the field of intercultural communication, including most of the contributors to this volume. In some of the chapters this critical stance is expressed explicitly as a starting-point for an alternative theory or method, while in others it is a silent travelling partner.

This does not mean that the main aim of this book is to criticise or 'settle accounts' with other real or imagined paradigms of 'intercultural communication'. Neither is it our ambition to suggest a new paradigm. The intention is, rather – in keeping with the title – to point out the validity of a number of different theoretical or methodological approaches, and to broaden our definition of intercultural communication beyond what is typically understood by the term, i.e. encounters between individuals and/or groups from 'different cultures', with an idea of culture almost automatically identified as 'national culture'.

Being an anthology, this book does not privilege or represent a sole theoretical or methodological current. But the contributors share an awareness of the need for a conscious approach to the field. 'Interculturality' and 'intercultural communication' should be considered a truly interdisciplinary field, a web woven of threads from anthropology, sociology, ethnology, linguistics and other disciplines. This means that the philosophical, theoretical and methodological resources available are virtually – and perhaps disturbingly – unlimited. It also means that an atheoretical or purely empiricist approach to the field is unsatisfactory. One might as well limit intercultural theory to an idea of 'culture as mental programming' or 'culture as an immense computer' without further discussion of the limits, possibilities and assumptions implied in reducing human culture and mentality to a computer metaphor. Similarly, for the authors of this book, limiting the concept of communication to the sending and receiving of a specific message that ideally has identical meaning both for sender and receiver, with culture seen as 'noise' on the channel, is an inadequate stand-point that can lead to a number of perilous assumptions about human subjects and their relationships.

Hence, most of the contributions contain a theoretical dimension. In some cases, this takes the form of a discussion which deploys more questions than answers, in a search for openness and possibilities rather than prescriptions writ in stone. In other cases, this search produces an answer that, although not definitive, offers some viable theoretical and methodological paths for the study of intercultural phenomena. The main theoretical perspectives represented are phenomenology, hermeneutics and semiotics. More specifically, we find concepts such as 'dialogue', 'mentality', 'stereotype', 'ideology', and 'narratives' as well as ideas borrowed from linguistics.

The theoretical intention and the critique of an atheoretical stand do not mean, however, that the contributions steer clear of the empirical. Whilst a couple of the chapters are mainly engaged with theoretical questions, the others contain an important empirical component. In some cases this forms the point of departure for a theoretical discussion, whilst in others a construction of theory and (or) method precedes an empirical study.

A further important point is that in spite of questioning the conflation of 'national culture' with 'culture' per se, this book does in no way reject the validity of 'nation', 'national culture' or 'nationness' as objects of study. In fact, the majority of the empirical cases do contain a 'national' dimension in their analysis of socially constructed 'narratives' or 'discourses' of national self and Other. One of the reasons for this is, undoubtedly, the fact that several of the contributors do their research and teaching in departments of modern languages, traditionally oriented toward national cultures. But this very fact constitutes a challenge in itself: how do we deal with 'national culture(s)' in our scientific practice – including teaching – whilst avoiding blind acceptance of national culture as a natural, given empirical 'fact'? At the same time, how do we account for the equally important – and to some surprising or paradoxical – fact that national and ethnic-national 'culture' is a fundamental and perhaps increasing source of identification in an ever-more globalised world? Several of the chapters accordingly address the problem of the configuration of national identity in a globalised context.

So how can we pin down the elusive term 'interculturality' that binds together the different contributions to this book? What associations does the term evoke, and does it not in itself already imply yet another perilous assumption: that 'culture' is a kind of solid essence of predetermined entities whose meeting entails a kind of 'clash'? There is no doubt that the majority, if not all, of the chapters of this book see culture as a question of differences, of boundaries and of meanings that do not conform to any simple pattern, and that trace symbolic maps considerably more complex and contradictory than can be represented in a simple idea of interculturality as the 'meeting between people of different national cultures'. The 'inter' in intercultural implies a meeting or encounter as something inherent in 'culture'. To talk about the human subject as a cultural subject – whether this 'culture' be national, ethnic, gender, or of any other kind – is to talk about an 'intercultural subject'. This intercultural dimension of humanity is by no means limited to a cosmopolitan, globalised middle class subject, but refers to the idea of 'culture' being not something in itself, but something that is and gains significance in relationships. If culture is about collective identification, then such identification depends on the existence of something other, against which the self can be posited. Interculturality, thus, is about an 'us' and an 'Other', it is about approaching difference as something that gives meaning when interpreted across a boundary.

All the contributions explore these boundaries by relating to three key and interlinked themes: i) difference ii) distance and iii) the commodification of the cultural Other. Some of the contributions touch upon all three themes, while others have a heavier focus on one or two of them.

i) The first theme deals with the idea of difference in various guises: first, as a problem or a threat; second, in terms of strategies for managing or 'taming' difference; and third, by exploring the power relations involved in the construction of difference. Several chapters take up the topic of stereotyping through 'national narratives': domestication, anchoring and translation (Clausen, Blasco, Zølner); portrayals of the cultural Other in development aid agencies' mission statements and representations of the non-European Other (Gustafsson); and the construction of group boundaries through prejudices about Others (Rye Møller, Lautrup Nørgaard; Cristoffanini). Stereotypes and prejudices may be seen as a positive point of departure for understanding (the mind needs stereotypes in order to simplify a vastly heterogeneous reality into workable categories) or as rigid mind-sets that prevent exploration of, and openness to, the different. As Cristofanini (this volume) puts it: 'Categories are necessary to understand 'reality', to create order, but they are flexible and they change … [whereas] stereotypes apparently give us a feeling of order and security, but are inflexible and try to cement one meaning'. Lautrup Nørgaard, in turn, uses a methodological distinction between morals and ethics to approach this problem, where morals are understood as immutable and closed 'rules' in contrast to ethics which are seen as a more flexible and open way of approaching the myriad different cultural norms for what constitutes acceptable human behaviour in different societies.

The chapters by Cristoffanini, Blasco and Zølner all deal with the representation and construction of Others in intercultural handbooks and theoretical literature on interculturality as well as historical texts on portrayals of the cultural Other in colonial, postcolonial and global contexts. Recognising that people from all cultures necessarily 'anchor' their dealings with Others in terms of their own categories (though these may then be adapted as a result of dialogue), it is not the intention to imply that all representation does violence to the represented, and that it should not be attempted (see e.g. Blasco's discussion of Segalen), as this implies that representations are but mistaken depictions of some 'real phenomenon' that defies description and understanding. Rather, the chapters point to the need to increase our awareness of the assumptions behind the representations and stereotypes we encounter, the meanings associated with them and the contexts in which they are played out; as well as the strategic uses to which they have been put historically, and continue to be put today. For instance,

Cristoffanini refers to how stereotypes of Mexicans as lazy, ignorant and uncivilised served to legitimise the American annexation of Mexican territories in the nineteenth century in the interests of disseminating what were perceived as American virtues: liberty, chivalry and expansionism. Similarly, Blasco points out how the colonial powers deployed derogatory and degrading representations of the 'native' Other in order to facilitate subjugation. And Zølner uses a phenomenological approach to show how French social actors' self-understandings and actions across a broad spectrum of political interests and sectors are shaped by and constructed through their relationship with a distinct national Other – in this case the US - in debates on globalisation. The self-understanding of France in these debates is that of a nation with a 'messianic mission to liberate the world from oppression and ignorance by bringing values with universal bearing, such as liberty, freedom, equality, fraternity, human rights and democracy' as opposed to the 'savage' style of crass, culture-starved and unregulated globalisation propagated by the US, seen increasingly as Americanisation. This discourse bears striking parallels to the savage-civilised dichotomies referred to in the chapters by Cristoffanini and Blasco. As these chapters show, such discursive struggles over 'good' and 'bad', or 'civilised' and 'uncivilised', national traits have very real consequences. We need look no further than the recent interventions in the Middle East and Afghanistan, purportedly carried out in the interests of 'democracy', to conclude that the type of critical analysis carried out here is not a purely academic exercise, but a necessary source of reflection in a world where communication technologies facilitate the rapid dissemination of representations and images through television, internet and other media.

ii) The second theme, distance, deals with ontological distance and the boundaries between self and Other, seen as 'markers of difference'. The chapters by Gustafsson, Lautrup Nørgaard, Rye Møller and Clausen raise the question of whether understanding is possible despite cultural differences, or do these so profoundly colour our understanding that they are impossible to 'overcome'? Can an idea of 'translation' feasibly be applied to intercultural phenomena? If we reject the idea of culture as a superficial 'layer' that can be peeled off to reveal a universal basis for common understanding shared by all humankind (e.g. through handbooks and 'culture training' courses), then does this then mean that we have to deny the possibility of communication across cultures? The implications of such a standpoint in today's multicultural societies would be untenable. In this regard, Rye Møller takes up the concept of mentality as a tool for improving understanding between people from different cultures, concretely Danish managers working with East and West Germans. He posits that 'mentality gives individuals a disposition to certain behaviour patterns and ways of conduct', and he suggests that a similar historical and institutional development and socialisation can create similar cultural dispositions resulting in smoother encounters between people from different national cultures. Clausen, in turn, looks at strategies for managing cultural distance, concretely the phenomenon of domestication in international news reporting. She shows how foreign cultures are mediated and brought closer to home by skilled Japanese newscasters who consistently anchor 'the foreign' in ideas easily assimilable by a Japanese audience, 'translating' and mediating international events and thereby shaping the audience's 'global consciousness' in a particular way. In this way, she argues, 'national news broadcasters still cater to a national majority of citizens and in this capacity perform a considerable role in maintaining and (re)constructing political and national cultural identity'. To her data Clausen applies a dialogic communication model called double-swing, with roots in Japanese philosophy, that avoids imposing commonplace Western communication paradigms where the sender is typically in a dominant position. Gustafsson turns to semiotics to discuss how identity work – the construction of an 'us' and a 'we' in communities – is sustained by symbolic boundaries that underline differences between groups. From the semiotic perspective that he adopts, the technique of dialogue (as in Clausen's case) enables these boundaries and the distance between people from different cultures to be overcome, since texts may then be understood in relation to one another rather than as isolated, decontextualised entities. Gustafsson deploys the concept of semiosphere, which unlike 'culture' stresses... the use of signs' and the textual dimension. As he puts it: 'the idea of the semiosphere turns out to be a useful concept for the study of culture as a basically semiotic phenomenon, whose empirical manifestation is text in whichever form it might appear'. Lautrup Nørgaard raises the question of whether intercultural understanding is possible in ethics, favouring a hermeneutic approach that sees interculturality as the meeting and mutual understanding of meaning, where both meanings 'gain a 'room' in each other's horizons of interpretation' over a constructivist standpoint which 'has a tendency to advise us not to judge what we (think to) see in the culturally different world, since we cannot and will never be able to understand its culture-specific truth, trapped as we are in our home-world'.

iii) The third theme, the commercialisation and commodification of the cultural Other in literature on intercultural communication, is raised in the chapters by Cristoffanini, Lautrup Nørgaard, and Blasco. This theme looks at how difference becomes commodified and converted into a strategic selling point. Two of the chapters (Cristoffanini and Blasco) take up the concept of exoticism, where Others are seen as 'trustees of virtues and qualities that we lack' or as fascinating by virtue of their very inscrutability (Cristoffanini: 79). This type of representation is no less self-absorbed than negative representation, however, since it is devoid of any real interest in or contact with the Other on his own terms. The Other serves merely as a mirror image of ourselves or is rendered an object for nostalgia or æsthetic delectation. Echoing this, Cristoffanini points out how commercialisation 'implies utilisation, dehistorisation, and depoliticisation and contributes to maintain, unquestioned, racial hegemony and white, Western culture. Commodifying the cultural Other produces encounter without experience and, at worst, knowledge without understanding (see Cristoffanini, Blasco). Finally, Lautrup Nørgaard takes up the ethical implications of intercultural communication and representation. Developments such as globalisation and technological progress cause ethical dilemmas to proliferate, and these often contain an intercultural dimension: '... what characterises late modernity and globalisation as an inherent part of it is that interculturality has become everyone's condition, and... an intrinsic part of our daily life'. In this context, he argues, cultural differences are often seen as parameters in strategic action, with a goal-oriented and rationalistic paradigm often dominating attempts to understand interculturality. Seldom do analysts in the field delve into the ethical implications of this, as he rightly points out.

In Chapter 1, Blasco discusses the intercultural handbooks that have become increasingly popular, particularly among businesspeople working across cultures. She questions the ethical basis of attempting to manage culture for strategic purposes, and draws parallels between the handbooks' role in international business, and the colonial powers' attempts to manage difference in their subjugated territories.

Chapter 2, by Mette Zølner, illustrates how French social actors graft traditional national narratives of France and stereotypical images of the US onto discourses on globalisation. Zølner's chapter underlines the need for a healthy scepticism towards taken-for-granted generalisations in our dealings with the cultural Other, so that misleading national stereotypes are not reified and so that micro-level communications between people are not sabotaged by 'hegemonic national narratives'.

In Chapter 3, Pablo Cristoffanini deals with some basic questions of interculturality, such as stereotypes, prejudice and images of the 'Other'. In a critical approach to some other views of intercultural communication, Cristoffanini discusses the question of stereotypes and images of otherness as a problem of ideology. Furthermore, he engages in a critical discussion of different perceptions and images of 'Latinos' and Mexicans at different moments of American history.

Chapter 4, by Lisbeth Clausen, discusses global news and the production strategies behind it with reference to existing intercultural communication models. She draws on cognitive theory to explain how micro processes and strategies behind the proliferation of visuals and concepts affect our phenomenological world and our 'global consciousness', and shows how newscasters translate foreign news into terms intelligible to a Japanese audience.

In Chapter 5, Henrik Rye Møller proposes that the concept of mentality be retrieved from its somewhat dubious status as a tool for analysing intercultural encounters. With an empirical point of departure in a study of encounters between Danish business people and 'East German' employees, Møller argues that 'mentality' is a more deeply rooted and socially (collectively) produced part of our individual and cultural being, and that it must be distinguished from 'identity', which he sees as more subject to negotiation and change.

Chapter 6, by Jan Gustafsson, proposes a semiotic approach to interculturality. Semiotics, according to this author, offers interesting theoretical possibilities both for a general idea of human subjects (collective and individual) as well as some more specific theoretical and methodological analytical instruments. He applies these tools to the analysis of a Danish NGO-text, showing how intratextual and intertextual mechanisms combine to constitute a cultural self that sees itself as superior to the 'Other'.

Chapter 7, by Jens Lautrup Nørgaard departs, like the first chapter, from a more general approach to interculturality based on philosophical hermeneutics. Taking its point of departure in interculturality as an interhermeneutic experience, the chapter discusses the possibility of talking about intercultural ethics as a way of conceptualizing the demands we meet in the intercultural encounter.

1

Stranger to us than the birds in our garden?

Reflections on hermeneutics, intercultural understanding and the management of difference.

MARIBEL BLASCO

If it is to be held that to be unbiased one should be 'objective' in the sense of depersonalizing the person who is the 'object' of our study, any attempt to do this under the impression that one is thereby being scientific must be vigorously resisted (Laing, 1969: 24).

'When all is said and done, they are stranger to me than the birds in my garden', said the reknowned psychiatrist, Eugen Bleuler, of his schizophrenic patients. According to R.D. Laing, who quotes this remark in his book, *The Divided Self* (Laing, 1969: 28), Bleuler would approach his patients with 'a scientific curiosity', as clinical cases whose condition could be diagnosed by observing the symptoms of their disease (Laing, 1969: 28). His patients were, like the birds in his garden, at once intensely familiar to him – they were after all the stuff of his everyday life – and ineffably strange. Like those birds, they could be observed, described and taxonomised, and then a suitable clinical treatment prescribed – but to understand them would mean attempting to see the world as they saw it, making him to all intents and purposes as insane as his patients themselves. Laing himself departed radically from this clinical tradition, arguing that irrespective of how much clinical information psychiatrists amassed about their patients: case histories, observations of behaviour, tests and so forth, this would not necessarily help them 'to understand one single schizophrenic' (Laing, 1969: 33). Instead, he claimed that in order to help his patients, it was necessary and possible to understand their 'existential position'. Otherwise, one risked making objects of one's subjects of study. As he said: 'the methods used to investigate the objective world, applied to us, are blind to our experience, necessarily so' (Laing, 1982: 9).

These two very different modes of approaching the Other – information-seeking and understanding – provide the framework for the following discussion of the growth of handbook-type literature on 'intercultural communication', i.e. communication among people from different national cultures. The chapter focuses on intercultural hand-books written for a business audience. It is not the intention of the chapter to provide a substantive critique of this literature, as a sizeable body of critical literature already exists.[1] Neither are other types of cultural differences such as gender, organisational or regional cultures dealt with here. The intention is, rather, to reflect upon the mode of knowing and of apprehending difference that is represented by this literature, and upon why interest in the subject is flourishing precisely at a time when it would seem that the concept of 'national culture' is fast becoming obsolete.

On the one hand, the notion of 'bounded cultures' is being contested by theorists arguing that globalisation[2] is leading to cultural convergence or integration (Fox, 1988 in Gessner and Schade, 1990: 259; Kramsch, 2002; Featherstone, 1990: 1). And on the other, we are witnessing the 'weakening of the nation as a source of identity', in favour of cultural complexity and diversity, cosmopolitanism and transnational identities that coalesce around non-national foci, e.g. multinational corporations or indeed transnational social movements (Hannerz, 1996: 81; Serbín, 1997; Sklair, 1999).[3] Concepts such as cultural 'deterritorialisation', 'homogenisation', 'hybridisation' and 'creolisation' have been coined to describe these changes (Gupta and Ferguson, 1992: 9; Escobar, 1995; García Canclini, 1989; Hannerz, 1992). It is indeed curious that 'Western social scientists should be elaborating theories of global culture just when this 'new world order' is breaking down into so many small-scale separatist movements, marching under the banner of cultural autonomy' (Sahlins, 1993 in Friedman, 1994: 13).

Why should handbooks that catalogue and reify national cultural traits be necessary when on the one hand globalisation is wresting explanatory power from the concept of national culture at a theoretical level; and on the other at the level of politics 'national cultures' display a stubborn tendency to fragment into myriad groups all claiming cultural identities of their own? As Fog and Hastrup (1997: 3) put it, just as anthropologists are questioning the very concept of culture, 'it has become embraced by a wide range of culture builders [and] anthropological works are increasingly being consulted by people desiring to construct cultural identities of a totalising sort'. These culture builders have spawned a veritable 'culture shock[4] prevention industry' (Hannerz, 1996: 108).

This paradox is treated in the following as a contemporary reflection of a Western assumption that cultural differences can be explained and managed for strategic purposes. Information about foreign cultures is believed to be an economic imperative in today's global market, where large-scale commercial success is coloured by how well brands travel and businessmen can communicate. Websites and literature on intercultural management offering advice along the lines of 'how to avoid mistakes when doing business in country X' abound.[5] I shall argue that what distinguishes this type of approach to intercultural communication from the other fields that also employ the concept[6] is that its motivation for studying foreign cultures is chiefly strategic: cultural understanding is seen as a means to an end, rather than an end in itself; and as something that can be manipulated to achieve that end. As Lautrup Nørgaard (this volume) puts it: 'Interculturality as a scientific field is still and foremost interested in the instrumental side of insight'. Cultural differences must not be permitted to stand in the way of successful transactions, yet at the same time they must be accounted for and dealt with, and they are part of a flourishing and lucrative 'cross-cultural training industry' in themselves (Jack and Lorbiecki, 2003: 213). As Hannerz indicates: 'Cross-cultural training programmes are set up to inculcate sensitivity, basic rules of etiquette, and perhaps an appreciation of those other cultures which are of special strategic importance to one's goals; for Westerners in recent times, as culture follows business, especially... those of the Arab World and Japan' (Hannerz, 1992: 251-2).

The chapter draws parallels between contemporary attempts to manage difference exemplified by such prescriptive, handbook approaches to intercultural communication; and the colonial powers' efforts to 'manage diversity' by plotting the supposed cultural traits of the colonised peoples. To do this, the author draws on the work of an early critic of these colonial endeavours, Victor Segalen, and his concept of the aesthetics of diversity. Finally, based on the philosophical hermeneutics of Hans-Georg Gadamer, it is proposed that differences should be seen as part and parcel of comprehending people from cultures different to our own rather than as barriers to communication that must be explained away before they are actually encountered. Encounters between people from different cultures cannot be 'managed' by applying general rules or prescriptions learned at a distance without objectifying and doing violence to the subject studied. In this way, the chapter also raises the question of ethics in popular intercultural communication methodologies. Gadamer's hermeneutics is employed with the intention not of criticising the idea of intercultural communication for strategic purposes per se, but rather to point out that its presentation as neutral *knowledge* in the handbook genre must be very carefully distinguished from any notion of intercultural *understanding*.

Managing difference

Communication among different cultures has been 'an obsession of the last century' (Kramsch, 2002: 276). Whereas international communication was accorded a high priority in the aftermath of World War 1, with the creation of the League of Nations, the promotion of Esperanto and a surge in cultural exchanges intended to foment friendly relations and understanding among nations; after World War 2 emphasis shifted to cross-cultural communication as a defence against unhealthy nationalisms (Kramsch, 2002: 276). Literature on intercultural communication, however, is a comparatively recent phenomenon that has emerged in force over the past 20-25 years.[7]

Theorists of intercultural communication have sought to categorise different national cultures in two main ways: by constructing typologies of their values, and by documenting their supposed behavioural traits. The values 'measured' in this way include, for instance: a culture's degree of 'uncertainty avoidance', its 'power-distance' relationship, its degree of masculinity/femininity, whether it has an individualist or a collectivist orientation, its degree of personalness or formality, or even the 'deviation allowed from the ideal role enactment' i.e. how far people's actual behaviour is 'allowed' to deviate from the 'ideal roles' of their society (Hofstede, 1980; Gudykunst and Yun Kim, 1984: 73). Behavioural traits include aspects such as body language, attitudes towards time, and etiquette. The idea is that knowing about these values and traits will help to reduce 'friction', 'uncertainty' and other 'barriers' to communication such as inappropriate modes of address, or the 'wrong' kind of nonverbal communication, which are seen as jeopardising the likelihood of smooth interpersonal communication (Gudykunst and Yun Kim, 1984: 179; Jandt, 2001). Box 1:1 contains examples of this type of recommendation.

Much of this work has been pioneering and influential in that it has served to sensitize the field of management to cultural differences (Søderberg and Holden, 2002; Kwek, 2003). However, it presents some striking features. What immediately stands out in the excerpts in Box 1:1 is the attitude to cultural difference that they reflect, which is at once defensive and adaptive. It is defensive inasmuch as differences are seen as problematic sources of 'misunderstanding, pain and conflict' that must be eliminated if people are to communicate effectively (Kramsch, 2002: 282). Difference is depicted as potentially 'insulting' (Extract 1); a 'source of serious misunderstandings' (Extract 2); breaching certain dress codes is described as a sign of 'bad manners' in Britain, and the female business executive is warned against wearing trousers (Extract 3);[8] and generally the excerpts assume that behaving differently to one's interlocutor will lead to a perilous breach of his 'expectations'. And it is adaptive in that in order to avoid this type of misunderstanding it is solicitously recommended that one match one's behaviour as far as possible to that of one's interlocutors, e.g. the visitor to Mexico is advised to adapt to his host's presumed work pace if he wants to get anywhere (Extract 4). This adaptive strategy is warmly recommended in Gesteland's (2002) volume *Cross-Cultural Business Behavior*, which states on its opening page that adaptation is 'Iron rule number 1' of business behaviour for the seller: 'In International Business, the Seller Adapts to the Buyer'.[9]

The implicit message in this type of recommendation is that difference is a problem, a threat to harmonious communication, and thus to successful business transactions. Rather than cultural difference being seen as a positive point of departure from which to build communication, understanding and intercultural contact, the handbooks tend instead to 'spread the idea that different means bad' (Pavlovskaya, 1999: 114), i.e. that it poses a threat to successful communication. As Søderberg and Holden (2002) point out, it is 'striking how author after author within the field of cross cultural management treats culture as a barrier to interaction and an all-pervading source of confusion'.

The attempt to adapt to and over-identify with other cultures, however, 'often comes at the expense of knowledge of cultures/cultural groups other than one's own' (Huggan, 2001: 17). This is because attempts to adapt to an interlocutor prior to an encounter must necessarily be based upon assumptions about the cultural traits of the interlocutors in question, assumptions inevitably based on generalised, stereotypical beliefs.

Box 1:1

Example 1: Extract from a well-known handbook on intercultural communication:

> Misunderstandings can easily occur in intercultural settings when two people, each acting according to the dictates of his or her culture, violate each other's expectations. If we were to remain seated when expected to rise, for example, we could easily violate a cultural norm and insult our host or guest unknowingly' (Porter and Samovar, 1991: 19).

Example 2: Extract from a website offering tips to US executives working in foreign countries also stresses the pitfalls of different behaviour and body language.

> ... cultural misunderstanding can lead to costly and irrevocable mistakes. Differing concepts of time and punctuality, for example, have been the source of serious misunderstandings between Americans and their counterparts in other countries. The same has been true of different practices related to personal and conversational space, the use of eye contact, male-female relations, personal hygiene, and even the business relationship itself
>
> http://www.tmpsearch.com/research_articles/new_global_exec/3c.html

Example 3: Extract on Britain from John Mole's *Mind your Manners* (1993: 110), a handbook offering advice to intercultural business in the European Union.

> Men will wear old school, arm, university or club ties... Since they are meant to be recognised it is not good manners to ask what they mean. It is also a social error... to wear a tie to which you are not entitled. Women have less of a problem, the more senior and authoritative she wishes to appear, the more her clothes should resemble men's, except that skirts not trousers should be worn.

Example 4: Extract from a webpage offering advice to US businessfolk attempting to enter the Mexican market.

> Rule No. 1: Slow down. Most first-time visitors to Mexico try to crowd in too many appointments per day. As a rule of thumb, make no more than four appointments a day. No. 2: Don't get down to business immediately. "Small talk" is important. It shows that you're not in a hurry and that you are interested in your Mexican host...

Similarly, the extracts in Box 1:1 contain an implicit assumption that people expect foreigners to be well versed in the local cultural codes. This is curious: as anthropologists have attested (Keesing, 1981), foreigners typically enjoy considerably more leeway than locals to commit faux pas without incurring censure precisely because they are not expected to be familiar with the local ways. It is hard to imagine a Japanese businessman, for instance, expecting his American counterpart to be fully versed in and to observe Japanese business protocol and body language, or vice versa. The incongruity of this assumption is fully revealed if one imagines a meeting between two manual readers, both of whom have read up on the other's culture and consequently bend over backwards to mimic what they suppose are the other's norms and behaviour. The resulting scenario would, at best, be baffling for both parties. An anecdote once recounted to this author comes to mind here about a group of Danish businessmen who, prior to a meeting with an English company, tried to adapt their dress to what they assumed was the English business style by wearing very formal suits and ties, only to find the English studiously attired in their shirtsleeves, equally sure that they would hit the correct relaxed tone amongst the informal Danes.

The point here is that the manual concept is designed for use by one party in an intercultural encounter, not both. The extracts quoted above reflect a modern Western worldview whereby linguistic and cultural differences can be reduced to a 'communication' problem' that can be 'managed' and overcome by applying the correct tools (Kramsch, 2002: 283; Kassing, 1996 in Min, 2001). These tools are inevitably greatly simplified, with questions of form (what style of dress and address to employ, how many meetings to hold per day, etc.) replacing more substantive issues: information substituting understanding. As Friedman (1995: 186) puts it: 'How you build a house, or how you distribute food at a party is not the same as knowing how you hate, or how you interpret your own immediate social circumstances'.[10] Culture in the handbook approach is depicted as a variable (Søderberg, 1999: 143) that can be learned away or disarmed through imitation, a communicative wrinkle that must be smoothed out prior to an encounter.

Paradoxically, then, it would appear that the very same handbooks that claim to chart the spectrum of cultural diversity in fact operate with an implicit universal notion of personhood, where only the outer 'layers' of culture are truly different. Once these are revealed or imitated, a common basis for human understanding lies just beneath the surface. Warning against this type of approach to cultural difference, Keesing (1974: 74) points out that 'any notion that if we peel off the layers of cultural convention we will find Primal Man and naked human nature underneath is both sterile and dangerous'.

The defensive/adaptive approach to difference also reflects a more profound assumption that the handbook reader possesses the capacity to transcend his own culture and adapt to the Other's presumed cultural norms, whilst the Other remains unreflexively himself: passive, static, and culture-bound. Behind this adaptive stance lies the presumption that another's culture can be seen through and the threat posed by its differences neutralised under a knowing gaze. That this gaze is assumed to be one-sided discloses all the more clearly how the idea of managing difference presupposes the existence of a culturally-bound object that is amenable to manipulation by a culturally literate subject with a cosmopolitan identity.

The strategic intent behind this modern approach to intersubjective encounters and communication is not limited to the sphere of intercultural communication, but is a more far-ranging contemporary phenomenon, as is adeptly illustrated by, *inter alia*, Hochschild in her book, *The Managed Heart: the Commercialisation of Human Feeling*, which looks at how emotions are managed in the airline industry. 'What is new in our time', she indicates, 'is an increasingly prevalent instrumental stance toward our native capacity to play, wittingly and actively, upon a range of feelings for a private purpose and the way in which that stance is engineered and administered by large organisations'. Hochschild sees the assumption that such responses can be managed as a result of the growth of the service sector, where 'communication' and 'encounter' constitute an increasingly important dimension of today's work relationships (Bell, 1973 in Hochschild, 1983: 9). Others, such as Sennett (1998), have similarly attributed this phenomenon to changing work conditions in the new 'flexible' capitalism, where employment trajectories are fragmented and trust and loyalty downplayed in favour of 'fleeting forms of association' (1998: 24) such as networks which are characterised by brief and instrumental forms of interaction – what he calls 'the team-work 'we' of shallow community' (1998: 147). In this post-Fordist scenario, workers must be able to perform effectively in groups and engage in a more participatory and proactive relationship with management, turning abilities that were not previously involved in concrete work tasks, such as communication, sociability and sensitivity to others, into marketable skills that are sought after in the great majority of white-collar job descriptions nowadays (Fairclough, 1992: 7; Melucci, 1997; Du Gay, 1994).

Thus, 'people's social identities as workers are coming to be defined in terms that have traditionally been seen not as occupational, but as belonging to the sphere of private life' (Fairclough, 1992: 7). This is construed in contemporary management discourse as a positive development leading to more 'human' organisational forms where 'work and leisure, reason and emotion, pleasure and duty are once more conjoined and thus the human subject is again a plenitude – restored to full moral health' in contrast to former, alienating bureaucratic organisational forms where these spheres were strictly separated and where work did not necessarily constitute an arena for individual workers' self-realisation and identification (Du Gay, 1994: 661).

The increasing blurring between private, personal qualities and professional skills, however, 'often ignores the distinction between manipulative and non-manipulative relations among people and, thus, lowers communication to the status of a technique – an instrument used for furthering one's personal or national ends' (Macintyre, 1985 in Abhik and Starosta, 2001). Qualities such as empathy, courtesy, solidarity, good-humouredness, etc. must be simulated (if employees do not already possess them 'naturally') and then harnessed to personal or organisational goals. The point of communication becomes not to promote understanding but to improve productivity and efficiency: as outlined before, it becomes instrumental rather than an end or a desirable form of communication in itself. As Martin (1992: 102) has asked, however, what kind of ethics are at play among those who would 'intrude into people's 'hearts and souls' for the sake of selling more hamburgers'?

When applied to intercultural communication, this type of approach produces a deductive form of knowledge about other cultures based on information about cultural values that is systematised and detached from its bearers, rather than on a context-specific, inductive understanding based on intersubjective communication (Søderberg, 1999; see also Clausen, this volume). The values extrapolated are depicted as anchored not to people but to particular places, usually national territories (Søderberg and Holden, 2002); indeed, the very notion of 'intercultural' communication assumes the prior existence of bounded cultural systems that can be observed as independent scientific 'objects'. However, as Hastrup and Hervik (1994: 9) have pointed out in their discussion of cultural understanding in anthropology, cultural models viewed as de-linked from human subjects can preclude a deeper understanding based on experience:

A central methodological problem in anthropology today is how to deal with the flow of intersubjective human experience without dehumanising it, that is without deconstructing it as experience and transforming it into totalising professional models of knowledge...

In the attempt to explain and manage foreign cultures, the cultural handbooks superimpose categories originating in one cultural context onto another (Kramsch, 2002: 277), making the appraisal of foreign cultures a self-referential exercise, and precluding the possibility of uncovering categories or meanings that may not exist at all in the worldview of the handbook in question. This type of literature may thus actually hinder rather than promote cultural understanding.

The instrumentalism that characterises approaches to communication and cultural differences in today's post-industrial capitalism is, however, not a new phenomenon, as I shall attempt to show in the following section, which looks back at how the colonial powers sought to manage cultural difference through superimposing taxonomies in a way not dissimilar to the 'intercultural' literature discussed above. To do this, I draw upon the ideas of Victor Segalen, a prominent early critic of such attempts to categorise and manage the cultural Other.

Disarming exoticism: managing cultural difference in colonial times

The management of differences through assimilating them into familiar categories long predates the arrival of literature on intercultural communication. Neither is it only Westerners who have tended to interpret what they perceived as exotic or incomprehensible by applying their own categories to it – a technique known as 'anchoring' in social representation theory (Jahoda, 1999). According to anchoring theory, foreign or disturbing elements are integrated into our own system of categories, thus rendering them 'familiar' and less threatening (Moscovici, 1984 in Jahoda, 1999: 10; see also Zølner, this volume). This is thought to be a universal way of reacting to others perceived as different from ourselves (Jahoda, 1999).

In this way, for instance, explorers and conquerors in the Americas attached their own categories to the things they encountered on their travels. For instance, according to the famous explorer, Alexander von Humboldt, travellers to the New World would name unfamiliar plants they encountered after plants that resembled them back home (Jahoda, 1999: 11). This 'anchoring' process worked the other way around too:

in the famous encounter between the Mexican emperor, Moctezuma, and Cortes' soldiers, Moctezuma equated the Spanish conquistadores to gods, 'the men about whom his ancestors had long ago prophesied'; whilst the conquistadores described Moctezuma as 'in every way ... like a great prince' in the manner of the European monarchs (Díaz del Castillo, 1963: 220-21; Bitterli, 1971 in Jahoda, 1999: 10). This 'principle of familiarity' (Jahoda, 1999: 11) was at times so extreme that the Europeans' descriptions had very little to do even with the objective physical characteristics of the peoples they encountered:

> ... the case of the American Indians was an outstanding example of European encounters with hitherto unknown peoples, showing how difficult it was for Europeans to fit them into their pre-existing world view. For at least two centuries, discourse about the Indians, and their pictorial representations, was laden with traditional images often grossly at variance with the physical reality of the Indians and their actual ways of life (Jahoda, 1999: 23).

Thus, for instance, in the initial phases of colonisation, Indians were repeatedly described and represented in pictures as 'hairy' – an image signalling wildness and sexual licentiousness in Europe at that time – despite numerous eye witness testimonies that the opposite was in fact the case (Jahoda, 1999: 24). A similar example concerns the writings of the abbé Cornelius de Pauw, who described[11] the American Indians as 'like idiot children, incurably lazy and incapable of any mental progress whatsoever' (Gerbi, 1973 in Jahoda, 1999: 21). When confronted with contradictory arguments pointing out, for instance, the sophisticated culture of the Incas manifested, *inter alia*, in their fine architecture, de Pauw simply refuted this outright, insisting that the Incas lived in 'crude little huts' (Jahoda, 1999: 21). European representations of the Indians also varied notoriously according to the motives of different categories of Europeans: missionaries, for instance, tended to see them as potentially improveable, whilst the conquering forces classed them as 'irremediably sub-human' (Jahoda, 1999: 24).

Whilst anchoring appears to be a typical reaction to strange elements in most cultures, it took on a particular instrumental purpose in the European colonisations. The colonial powers endeavoured to control the colonies by demystifying them and accumulating knowledge of different kinds about them: the maps, taxonomies, ethnologies, and histories which Said (1995: 40) has referred to as 'the whole series of knowledgeable manipulations by which the Orient was identified by the West'. This classificatory exercise, purportedly carried out from the standpoint of 'universal reason', served to rationalise and explain away differences, so that cultural difference could be reduced 'to the grids of Western conceptual thought'. Otherness 'represented not a challenge to be encountered but rather an object to be classified' to facilitate domination (Michel, 1996: 3). In Said's terms, this 'nexus of knowledge and power' both created 'the Oriental' and in a sense also 'obliterat[ed] him as a human being' (1995: 27).

A contemporary critic of these colonial attempts to dominate through 'objective' knowledge and domestication of cultural traits was Victor Segalen, whose reflections on the exotic, known as the 'aesthetics of diversity', constitutes a radical critique of the assimilationalist, colonial attitude to difference. Segalen was a writer, traveller and medical officer in the French Navy whose work, which includes novels, poetry and prose writings, deplores the way in which otherness was constructed through the Western concept of the subject, and laments what he saw as the loss of genuine diversity resulting from colonialism, modernisation and Westernisation. Segalen was fiercely critical of the colonial invasion of non-Western countries, and of colonialist representations of foreign cultures in the work of his contemporaries writing on the 'exotic', criticising them for focusing more on themselves and their own reactions than on the differences with the cultures they supposedly studied, and neglecting to portray what the people from those cultures actually thought, said and did themselves (Michel, 1996: 2-4; Longxi, 2001). In Segalen's view, traditional portrayals of exoticism were one-sided, representing only the European view of the encounter (Michel, 1996: 4). He belittled the activities of the colonialists and colonial bureaucrats of his time for the way they sought to impose their own obliterating order on the colonies:

> Sweep away: the colonial, the colonial bureaucrat... The former comes into being with the desire for native trade relations of the most commercial kind. For the colonial, Diversity exists only in so far as it provides him with the means of duping others. As for the colonial burcaucrat, the very notion of a centralised administration and of laws for the good of everyone, which he must enforce, immediately distorts his judgement and renders him deaf to the disharmonies (or harmonies of Diversity) (Segalen, 2002: 35).

Instead, Segalen championed a radical attitude to difference involving a sensory experience and enjoyment of it, but at the same time a full acceptance of its Otherness that defied assimilation or imitation:[12]

> Let us proceed from this admission of impenetrability. Let us not flatter ourselves for assimilating the customs, races, nations, and others who differ from us. On the contrary, let us rejoice in our inability ever to do so, for we thus retain the eternal pleasure of sensing Diversity (2002: 21).[13]

In Segalen, distance expresses both the 'essence of exoticism... [and] the philosophical relation between subject and object' (Michel, 1996: 8). Unlike many of his contemporaries, he explicitly rejects any attempt to explain or represent the exotic Other, seeking rather to protect it from being 'assimilated or familiarised' (Longxi, 2001: 4) since any attempt to classify it and thus bring it closer will annihilate it. Equally, for instance, to Segalen tourists are mere 'pseudo-exotes' whose experience of the exotic is simulated and superficial:

> Exoticism is therefore not that kaleidoscopic vision of the tourist or of the mediocre spectator, but the forceful and curious reaction to a shock felt by someone of strong individuality in response to some object whose distance from oneself he alone can perceive and savour. (The sensations of Exoticism and Individualism are complementary)... I call them [tourists] the Panderers of the Sensation of Diversity.[14]

For Segalen, a positive and enriching experience of diversity is dependent upon a strong identity. To domesticate diversity by applying one's own categories to it, or to expose oneself to it only in a superficial way, as tourists do is, for him, a sign of a weak identity incapable of withstanding exposure to difference:

> ... if we increase our ability to perceive Diversity, will we enrich or impoverish ourselves? Will this rob us of something or endow us with something greater? The answer is clear: it will infinitely enrich us with the whole Universe (Segalen, 2002: 20-21).[15]

Segalen did not only apply his notion of the exotic to cultural differences but to many other types of difference as well: gender, nature, time (the past and the future), the experiences of children, the alien (i.e. extra-terrestrial) and moral differences, though he points out that the exoticism of human races is 'the only one which is recognised' in literature (Segalen, 2002: 22).

Like Said, Segalen has been criticised for 'condemning any attempt to represent the Other' (Schlick, 1998: 12; Grossberg, 1996: 95). If Segalen's reasoning is taken to its logical extreme, 'then all knowledge – and the construction of any object of knowledge – must be condemned as inappropriate and oppressive' (Grossberg, 1996: 95). In Todorov's words 'Knowledge is incompatible with exoticism, but lack of knowledge is in turn irreconcilable with praise of others; yet praise without knowledge is precisely what exoticism aspires to be' (1993 in Huggan, 2001: 17). Moreover, critics point out that Segalen's concept of the exotic is ultimately paradoxical, since on the one hand his vision recommends that the exotic should remain as pure, undefiled and inaccessible as possible; whilst on the other he advocates replacing the cognitive approach towards the exotic that he is so critical of with a sensory, poetic experience that preserves the exotic as an abstraction, an object for Europeans' aesthetic contemplation (Schlick, 1998). For instance, his novel, *Les Immémoriaux*, depicts Tahiti in the days before the Europeans settled there, narrating the destruction that their arrival occasioned among the Polynesian indigenous population from the perspective of a non-European narrator (Michel, 1996: 2). *Les Immémoriaux* is dedicated 'To the Maoris of forgotten times',[16] showing that he considered the exotic already wiped out by Western colonialists – but this is clearly an exotic both invented and lost by the Europeans – a self-referential notion (Schlick, 1998: 2).

Thus, in Segalen, the power to construct and preserve the different, the exotic, also lies exclusively with the Western subject. His is more an aesthetic argument than an explicitly political one, unlike the postcolonial and development theorists who were later to level criticisms against Western representations of the Third World.[17]

The new orientalism: ersatz familiarity and consumption

Segalen's position on diversity is undoubtedly extreme, obviating as it does the possibility of apprehending and representing difference in a way that does not merely reify existing power relations and do violence to that which is represented. Nonetheless, it carries an important message: that difference should not be obliterated or taxonomised according to pre-given categories, but must be assumed as the point of departure for encounters with diversity (see also Cristoffanini, this volume). Difference is, in Segalen, never depicted as a problem or as an inconvenience that can be dismissed by applying the correct categories to it, as it is in much of the intercultural literature.[18]

Today, global capitalism has opened the field that can potentially be dominated through managing difference. Now it is no longer a question of dominating 'Orientals', Africans or Americans, but of penetrating as many national foreign markets as possible. The distinction between 'centre' and its dependent 'periphery' that featured in conventional exoticist approaches is no longer current (Huggan, 2001: 15). The market imperative means that even cultures that appear very unexotic to us – say the Swedish, the German, the Dutch – must have their differences, however slight, exposed, managed and exploited. The 'logic of capital works through specificity: a new regime of difference produced by capital' (King, 1991: 14). Thus, global capitalism 'does not attempt to obliterate (local capitals) but operates through them. It has to hold the framework of globalisation in place and police that system' (Hall, 1991: 28-9). This new form of exoticism is 'suitable for all markets' (Gallini, 1996 in Huggan, 2001: 15).

Whilst the familiar is subjected to scrutiny and rendered exotic, the exotic appears to become ever-more familiar. Foreign cultures can now apparently be so easily accessed, sampled and consumed due to commerce, tourism and the media (Hastrup, 1992: 7), facilitated by massive technological advances that enable us to 'reach beyond our senses, and concepts, even beyond imagination... tak[ing] us outside what we know directly' (Laing, 1982: 17). The sheer quantity of instantly accessible information available in the information societies of the modernised 'centre' countries (Hannerz, 1992: 31-33) offers an ersatz familiarity with, and proximity to, far-off places, an apparent dissolution of the boundaries between the spatial and the cultural known and unknown. Distance is compressed: it is no longer necessary to interrupt the flow of our daily lives or encounter foreign cultures in the flesh in order to 'know' about them. Cultural difference is thus subjected to a process of global commodification (Huggan, 2001: vii). We can 'experience' Mexico, for instance, by watching a TV programme, surfing the net, buying a taco dinner in the supermarket or maybe taking a fortnight's holiday in Baja California. Foreign artefacts and 'experiences' are to be had with no challenge to our own cultural premises (Knudsen and Wilken, 1993) – what Huggan has called 'imagined access to the cultural Other through the process of consumption; reification of people and places into exchangeable æsthetic objects' (2001:

19). As Bauman (1996: 29-30) notes in his writing on tourism, in a similar tone to Segalen:

> The tourists want to immerse themselves in a strange and bisarre element (a pleasant feeling, a tickling and rejuvenating feeling, like letting oneself be buffeted by sea waves) – on condition, though, that it will not stick to the skin and thus can be shaken off whenever they wish... In the tourist's world, the strange is tame, domesticated, and no longer frightens; shocks come in a package deal with safety...

As foreign cultures become commodified in the neocolonial global marketplace, cultural understanding is also increasingly conflated with knowledge of a culture's consumable products: its music, its literature, its art, its food. As some theorists have argued, the contemporary global economy increasingly produces and exchanges signs that keep consumers at a distance from the material objects they represent and from their producers, whilst providing an illusion of reality (Lash and Urry, 1994: 4 in Hannerz, 1996: 24; Baudrillard, 1993: 16). As Baudrillard (1998: 34) writes:

> The image, the sign, the message – all these things we 'consume' – represent our tranquillity consecrated by distance from the world, a distance more comforted by the allusion to the real... than compromised by it.

There is an expectation that this abundance of information will unproblematically lead to greater understanding of foreign cultures, or to the gradual erasure of cultural differences: a universal cultural homogenisation. This ersatz familiarity with the strange becomes normality, so that experiences of radical difference become disconcerting, hence attempts to order them into familiar and non-threatening categories rather than to treat them a useful means of learning more about others. Despite an abundance of information, cultural differences between people remain very real and they are not always amenable to 'management', despite the modern cosmopolitan's apparent ease with the exotic. Arguably, in today's Western world difference is dealt with through a paradoxical combination of consumption – 'consuming' the disembodied products of Others – and simultaneously eschewing contact with differences embodied in real human subjects by creating totalising forms of knowledge about them that a priori preclude any real encounter.

It is curious that the very same handbook literature that claims to offer a 'learnable' methodology for communicating successfully with foreigners at the same time often concludes that interpersonal skills are ultimately the most important factor in such encounters. Such skills are, paradoxically, usually precisely those that are hardest to learn, for instance: being an extrovert personality type, being open and reflective, being intuitive, regarding others as basically good, having a positive self-concept, being willing to disclose information about oneself, or being 'secure' in oneself (Gudykunst and Yun Kim, 1984: 192; Jandt, 2001; Hoffman, 1999: 464). These are usually qualities that typically vary just as much within cultures as between them. If culture is understood as a system of meaning intelligible to a given group of people, then it must also be stressed that not all people share all aspects of a culture, and some share characteristics and views with people from other cultures. The focus in much literature on intercultural communication is almost exclusively on nationality, with little attention to the fact that this constitutes but one dimension of cultural difference. As Abhik and Starosta (2001: 14) point out: 'the greatest share of research in intercultural communication assumes pre-existing, consistent differences in populations, and does little with domestic co-cultural variation'. Along similar lines Rosaldo (1984: 141) argues:

> ... it makes no sense to see in culture personality writ large. But neither, from the 'interpretevist point of view, does it make sense to claim that individuals – with their different histories, different bodies, and different ways of being more or less emotionally involved – are cultural systems cast in miniature.

Successful intercultural encounters, then, as in Segalen, depend on the inherent human qualities that enable a dialogue to take place between individuals with strong identities who are unafraid to meet and acknowledge difference. The handbook approach to knowledge about foreign cultures is, however, predominantly cognitive and unmediated by such messy encounters between real human subjects.[19] In the following section, I seek to show how hermeneutics offers an approach to apprehending cultural difference that neither seeks to obliterate it nor denies the possibility of understanding it.

Maribel Blasco

Hermeneutics and the notion of productive prejudice

Somewhere in between the adaptive handbook approach and Segalen's radical recommendation to preserve diversity intact lies the hermeneutic approach to understanding. Although Gadamer's hermeneutics has not been greatly used in discussions of intercultural understanding (though see Abhik and Starosta, 2001), a number of his concepts and reflections can usefully be applied to it, particularly as a counterbalance to the prescriptive and totalising approaches popular in this field of research. Gadamer's hermeneutics offers 'a method to interpret other cultures that transcends seemingly lawful regularities to appreciate the uniqueness of individual cases... [and] offer[s] extensions beyond positivistic views of intercultural communication' (Abhik and Starosta, 2001: 11; see also Lautrup Nørgaard, this volume).

Thus, in contrast to the two positions presented above, Gadamer's hermeneutics does not advocate the imposition of one's own categories in order to understand the Other as in the handbook literature; and neither does it condemn any attempt to depict differences as violence through misrepresentation, as Segalen does. Gadamer's major work, *Truth and Method*, focuses on the problem of understanding in the realms of art, historicity and language. In the chapters on historicity, Gadamer discusses the concept of prejudice from a hermeneutic standpoint. Whereas the handbook approach engulfs and assimilates Others' categories by superimposing its own onto them, in hermeneutics preconceived ideas and prejudices are taken as a means of enabling us to apprehend the differences between our own and another's position, hence gaining greater understanding. Rather than seeing violated expectations as a source of misunderstanding, then (as in the examples cited in Box 1:1 above), hermeneutics would consider these an invaluable insight promoting deeper understanding, since they serve to reveal our own, often implicit, preconceptions. The cognitive psychologist, Jerome Bruner (1986: 46), whose work is also inspired by hermeneutics, describes this approach:

Surprise is an extraordinarily useful phenomenon... for it allows us to probe what people take for granted. It provides a window on presupposition: surprise is a response to violated presupposition.

Applying this idea to the study of texts, Gadamer claims that this sensation of surprise arises when: 'Either [the text] does not yield any meaning at all or its meaning is not compatible with what we had expected', an experience he calls 'being pulled up short by the text' (1990: 26). This positive role played by surprise (i.e. breached expectations) derives from a key premise of hermeneutics: that our prior experiences enable us to apprehend particular aspects of a situation precisely through the distance between our perception and that of the phenomenon we wish to understand. Learning occurs through the juxtaposition and comparison of the new with that which we already know (Strauss and Corbin, 1990). For Gadamer, then, prejudice is not something to be overcome but a precondition for understanding, a point of departure for apprehending difference that is neither positively nor negatively tinged (Abhik and Starosta, 2001: 8). Distance, either in time, language or perception, is seen as enabling understanding, rather than as an obstacle to this.

In this respect, Gadamer's thought has much in common with Segalen's reflections on the need to maintain a vivid awareness of difference through preserving distance, though whilst Segalen explicitly rejects any attempt to understand or portray difference, hermeneutics advocates dialogue amongst interlocutors precisely in order to further understanding: 'the important thing is to recognise temporal distance as a positive and productive condition enabling understanding' (Gadamer, 1990: 297). Thus, in hermeneutics, rather than projecting our prejudices onto others in an attempt to reduce distance, 'other people become a means for us to correct our understanding' (White, 1994 in Abhik and Starosta, 2001: 9; Abhik and Starosta, 2001: 7). Conversely, the handbook approach precludes the need for dialogue by explaining away differences prior to an encounter. It is a strategy driven by the search for efficiency, a closed, unproductive prejudice rather than an open, productive one (Abhik and Starosta, 2001: 9; see also Lautrup Nørgaard's discussion in this volume of closed and open attitudes to cultural difference).

Gadamer's notion of prejudice derives from his critique of the Enlightenment's 'discreditation of the concept of 'prejudice'' (Gadamer, 1990: 277). The Cartesian dictum 'that methodologically disciplined use of reason can safeguard us from all error' leads to the 'subjection of all authority to reason' and the resulting imperative to overcome all prejudices deriving from one's situatedness within tradition. In hermeneutics, however, this constitutes a fundamental error, since tradition is always and inescapably part of human beings (Gadamer, 1990: 277-8):

> Does understanding in the human sciences understand itself correctly when it relegates the whole of its own historicality to the position of prejudices from which we must free ourselves? (Gadamer, 1990: 282).

The Enlightenment's legacy, manifest in the attempt to overcome all prejudices, will thus itself become a prejudice (Gadamer, 1990: 276). The hermeneutic endeavour to locate meaning in its historical context and to take on board the implications of tradition and experience is in stark contrast with the handbook literature, which supplants knowledge of history with immutable descriptions of values and behaviour that seem to exist in an ahistorical universe disconnected from human experience.

Gadamer's emphasis on the importance of historical context in understanding the meaning of others' actions is combined with a focus on the Other as an individual situated within his tradition – what he calls the 'Thou orientation'. In this explicit orientation towards the individual interlocutor hermeneutics also brings an ethical dimension to the problem of understanding, which it sees as a key difference between the nature of understanding in the human sciences and in the natural sciences. According to Gadamer, this difference is not so much one of method, but of the *objectives* of knowledge. The attempt to understand another human being is a moral endeavour since 'the Thou is not an object but is in relationship with us... the object of experience is a person' (Gadamer, 1990: 358):

> There is a kind of experience of the Thou that tries to discover typical behaviour in one's fellowmen and can make predictions about others on the basis of experience... We understand the other person in the same way that we understand any other typical event in our experiential field – i.e. he is predictable. His behaviour is as much a means to our end as any other means. From the moral point of view this orientation towards the Thou is purely self-regarding and contradicts the moral definition of man. As we know, in interpreting the categorical imperative, Kant said, *inter alia*, that the Other should never be used as a means but always as an end in himself (Gadamer, 1990: 358).

To objectify the Other and seek understanding of him with a view to controlling or manipulating him is unethical according to the hermeneutical method. As Abhik and Starosta (2001: 10) put it: 'a relationship, characterised by the author attempting to discover, control, manipulate or predict the text in an involved manner, falls under the rubric of scientific methods in which the text loses its uniqueness as a "being", and instead becomes an "object"' (see also Cristoffanini, this volume). We may amass information in this way, but understanding will continue to elude us.

Concluding remarks

The chapter reflects upon the approach to cultural difference manifest in the growing handbook-type literature on intercultural communication. It is considered a paradox that literature detailing the specifics of national cultures should emerge at a time when the foreign has become an almost banal fixture of our everyday lives. An explanation for this paradox is sought in the workings of contemporary global capitalism, which differentiates ever more sharply between cultures, 'exoticising' the familiar so that it can better be rendered marketable. At the same time, however, this differentiation ensures that these cultural differences become banal due to the ever-increasing global circulation of goods, images and people. Thus, whilst Western identity rests upon the individual's ability to differentiate him or herself from others, at the same time experiences of radical difference are nowadays few and far between. The resulting 'anxiety of contamination by [the] Other' (Grossberg, 1996: 97) produces an ever-subtler differentiation between and taxonomisation of cultures, which effectively neutralises difference as far as possible before it is encountered.

The chapter also reflects upon the ethical basis of literature that treats intersubjective communication as a means to an end, rather than as an end in itself. To construct difference in terms of closed, reductionist systems based on pre-established categories objectifies the Other in order to better manipulate him and obviates the possibility of intersubjective understanding. In this connection, it is suggested that intercultural communication literature designed for business audiences should explore in greater depth the ethical implications of the ways in which it constructs the cultural Other.

A reader might well ask at this point: understanding is all very well but what can such an approach offer business? The hermeneutic approach certainly does not offer an intercultural tool-kit that the business traveller can master on a short-haul flight. Hermeneutics can, however, serve to sensitise those engaging in intercultural encounters to the importance of acknowledging difference and regarding it as a productive resource rather than a barrier to communication. In practice, this means attempting to understand the other *on his or her own terms* – exactly the notion that Bleuler, quoted at the beginning of this chapter, would doubtless have found scandalous. It means trying to gain some idea of the other's self-understanding. In practice, what this means is: drop the culture manuals. Instead, buy a couple of novels or a history book written by an author from your target destination. This will prove a far more illuminating – and pleasurable – route to understanding the foreigners you are about to meet – and just as easy to digest on a plane. The merits of using fiction to further understanding have been well documented by Nelson Philips, who has used this method in management and organisational research, and considers it a valuable resource that does not circumvent or attempt to simplify the complexity of the real world. Rather, 'it creates a space for the representation of the life-world within which individuals find themselves (Bruner, 1992; Ellis and Flaherty, 1992b; Huxley, 1963 in Phillips, 1995: 4). For Philips, then, fiction is tantamount to 'vicarious experience': the closest thing to getting inside somebody else's head (1995: 10).

Otherwise, foreign cultures will remain as strange to us as the birds in the garden: strange by virtue of their very familiarity, creatures that add life and movement and colour to our daily lives, whom we can observe and name and classify, but with whom we would never dream of trying to communicate. They will remain yet another potent reminder of the hegemony of information over understanding that characterises today's information societies, a hegemony that separates supposedly objective knowledge from experience and encounter and thus de-links the process of understanding from human subjects.

References

Abhik, R. & Starosta, J; Hans-Georg Gadamer, Language, and Intercultural Communication, *Language and Intercultural Communication,* 1, 1, 6-20, 2001.

Baudrillard, Jean; *The Transparency of Evil.* London: Verso, 1993.

Baudrillard, Jean; *The Consumer Society.* London: Sage, 1998.

Bauman, Zygmunt; From pilgrim to tourist – or a short history of identity, in S. Hall & P. du Gay (eds), *Questions of Cultural Identity.* London: Sage, 1996.

Bruner, Jerome; *Actual Minds, Possible Worlds.* Cambridge: Harvard University Press, 1986.

Du Gay, Paul; Making up managers: bureaucracy, enterprise and the liberal art of separation', *The British Journal of Sociology,* 45, 4, 655-674, 1994.

Escobar, Arturo; *Encountering Development.* Princeton: Princeton University Press, 1995.

Fairclough, Norman; *Discourse and Social Change.* Cambridge: Polity Press, 1992.

Featherstone, Mike; Global culture: an introduction, in Mike. Featherstone (ed.), *Global Culture.* London: Sage, 1990.

Fog Olwig, Karen & Haastrup, Kirsten (eds); *Siting Culture. The Shifting Anthropological Object.* Routledge: London and New York, 1997.

Friedman, Jonathan; De andres erfaringer, *Tidsskriftet Antropologi,* 31, 185-188, 1995.

Friedman, Jonathan; Simplifying complexity: assimilating the global in a small paradise, in Karen Fog Olwig & Kirsten Haastrup (eds), *Siting Culture. The Shifting Anthropological Object.* Routledge: London and New York, 1997.

Maribel Blasco

Gadamer, Hans-Georg; *Truth and Method*. New York: Crossroad, 1989.

García Canclini, Nestor; *Culturas Híbridas*. México: Grijalbo, 1989.

Gessner, Volkmar. & Schade, Angelika; Conflicts of culture in cross-border legal relations: the conception of a research topic in the sociology of law, in Mike Featherstone (ed.), *Global Culture*. London: Sage, 1990.

Gesteland, Richard; *Cross-Cultural Business Behavior*. Copenhagen: Copenhagen Business School Press, 2002.

Giddens, Anthony; *The Consequences of Modernity*. London: Polity Press, 1990.

Grossberg, Lloyd; Identity and cultural studies: is that all there is?' in S. Hall & P. Du Gay (eds), *Questions of Cultural Identity*. London: Sage, 1996.

Gudykunst, William B. & Yun Kim, Young; *Communicating With Strangers*. London: Addison-Wesley Publishing Company, 1984.

Gupta, Akhil & Ferguson, James; Beyond "culture": space, identity, and the politics of difference, *Cultural Anthropology*, 7, 1, February, 1992.

Hall, Stuart; Introduction: who needs identity?, in S. Hall & P. Du Gay (eds), *Questions of Cultural Identity*. London: Sage, 1996.

Hannerz, Ulf; *Cultural Complexity*. New York: Columbia University Press, 1992.

Hannerz, Ulf; *Transnational connections*. London: Routledge, 1996.

Haastrup, Kirsten; *Det Antropologiske Projekt om Forbløffelse*. Copenhagen: Nordisk Forlag, 1992.

Hochschild, Arlie R; *The Managed Heart: The Commercialisation of Human Feeling*, California: University of California Press, 1983.

Hoffman, Edwin; Cultures don't meet, people do: a system theoretical approach of intercultural communication, in Knapp, K. *et al.* (eds), *Meeting the Intercultural Challenge.* Berlin: Verlag Wissenschaft & Praxis, 1999.

Hofstede, Geert; *Culture's Consequences.* Beverley Hills: Sage, 1980.

Huggan, Graham; *The Postcolonial Exotic: Marketing on the margins.* Routledge: London & New York, 2001.

Jack, Gavin. & Lorbiecki, Anna; Asserting the possibilities of resistance in the cross-cultural teaching machine: re-viewing videos of Others, in A. Prasad (ed.), *Postcolonial Theory and Organisational Analysis: A Critical Engagement.* New York: Palgrave Macmillan, 2003.

Jahoda, Gustav; *Images of Savages*, London: Routledge. 1999.

Jandt, Fred; *Intercultural Communication.* London: Sage, 2001.

Keesing, Roger; Theories of culture, *Annual Review of Anthropology,* 3, 1974.

Keesing, Roger; *Cultural Anthropology.* New York: Holt, Rinehart & Winston 1981.

King, Anthony; Introduction, in A. King (ed.), *Culture, Globalisation and the World-System*, London: Macmillan, 1991.

Knudsen, Anne. & Wilken, L; *Kulturelle Verdener: Kultur og Kulturkonflikter i Europa.* Denmark: Columbus, 1993.

Kramsch, Claire; In search of the intercultural, *Journal of Sociolinguistics*, 6, 2, 2002.

Kwek, Dennis; Decolonizing and *re*-presenting culture's consequences: a post-colonial critique of cross-cultural studies in management, in A. Prasad (ed.), *Postcolonial Theory and Organisational Analysis.* New York: Palgrave Macmillan, 2003.

Laing, Ronald D; *The Divided Self.* London: Penguin, 1969.

Longxi, Zhang; The exotic concept of beauty, *Keynote speech, International Conference of "Esthetique du Divers"*. Peking University, April 10, 2001.

Majid, Anouar; Provincial Acts: The Limits of Postcolonial Theory, http://www.scholars.nus.edu.sg/landow/post/poldiscourse/casablanca/majid1.html, 2001.

Martin, Joanne; *Cultures in Organisations: Three Perspectives*. New York: Oxford University Press, 1992.

Melucci, Alberto; Identity and difference in a globalised world, in P. Werbner & T. Modood (eds), *Debating Cultural Hybridity*. London: Zed Books, 1997.

Michel, Andreas; The subject of Exoticism: Victor Segalen's Equipée, *Surfaces*, 6, 1, 1996.

Min, Eungjun; Bakhtinian perspectives for the study of intercultural communication, *Journal of Intercultural Studies*, 22, 1, 2001.

Mole, John; *Mind Your Manners*. London: Nicholas Brealey Publishing, 1993.

Oberg, Kalvero; Culture shock and the problem of adjustment in new cultural environments, in G. Weaver (ed.), *Culture, Communication and Conflict: Readings in Intercultural Relations*. Neadham Heights, MA: Simon & Schuster Publishing, 1998.

Pavlovskaya, A; Russia and Russians in Western orientation literature, in Knapp, K. *et al.* (eds), *Meeting the Intercultural Challenge*. Berlin: Verlag Wissenschaft & Praxis, 1999.

Phillips, Nelson; Telling organisational tales: On the role of narrative fiction in the study of organisations, *Organisation Studies*, 16, 4, 1995.

Porter, Richard & Samovar, Larry; Basic principles of intercultural communication, in L. Samovar & R. Porter (eds), *Intercultural Communication: A Reader*. California: Wadsworth Publishing Company, 1991.

Prasad, Anshuman; *Postcolonial Theory and Organisational Analysis: A Critical Engagement*, London: Palgrave Macmillan, 2003.

Redding, Gordon (ed.); *International Cultural Differences*. Dartmouth: Aldershot, 1995.

Redding, Gordon & Stening, Bruce (eds); *Cross-Cultural Management, Volume II, Managing Cultural Differences*. Edward Elgar: Cheltenham, 2003.

Said, Edward; *Orientalism*. London: Penguin Books, 1995.

Schlick, Y; On the persistence of a concept: Segalen's René Leys and the death(s) of exoticism', 1998.
http://elecpress.monash.edu.au/french/1998_2/schlick.html

Segalen, Victor; *Essai sur L'Exotisme*. Paris: Editions Fata Morgana, 1978.

Segalen, Victor; *Essay on Exoticism*. Durham and London: Duke University Press, 2002.

Sennett, Richard; *The Corrosion of Character*. London: W.W. Norton & Company, 1998.

Serbín, Andrés; Globalización, déficit democrático y sociedad civil en los procesos de integración', *Pensamiento Propio*, 1, 3, 1997.

Sklair, Leslie; Competing conceptions of globalisation, *Journal of World Systems Research*, 5, 2, 1999.

Søderberg, Anne-Marie; Do national cultures always make a difference? Theoretical considerations and empirical findings related to a series of case studies of foreign acquisitions of Danish companies, in T. Vestergaard (ed.), *Language, Culture and Identity* (Language and Cultural Contact 27). Aalborg: University Press, 1999.

Søderberg, Anne-Marie & Holden, Nigel; Rethinking Cross Cultural Management in a Globalizing World, *International Journal of Cross Cultural Management*, 2, 1, 2002.

Maribel Blasco

Strauss, Anselm and Corbin, Juliet; *The Basics of Qualitative Research*. London: Sage, 1990.

Wallerstein, Immanuel; The national and the universal: can there be such a thing as world culture?, in A. King (ed.), *Culture, Globalisation and the World-System*. London: MacMillan Press, 1991.

Notes

1 See e.g. Søderberg (1999); Søderberg and Holden (2002); Hannerz (1992); Prasad (2003).

2 I.e. the increased movement and mingling of people, flows of commodities, capital and labour, knowledge and images which causes local events to be 'shaped by events occurring many miles away and vice versa' (Giddens, 1990: 64; Wallerstein, 1991: 98)

3 But see, inter alia, Hall (1996); Smith (1991); Fog and Hastrup (1997) and Friedman (1997) for a critique of this position. These authors contend that, in fact, both the national and the local remain key foci of identity for the vast majority of people, and that voluntary cosmopolitanism - 'free migration' as opposed to 'forced migration' (Hall, 1996: 4) - remains the privilege of a small elite.

4 The term 'culture shock' was coined in 1954 by the anthropologist Kalvero Oberg, who defines it as 'the anxiety that results from losing all our familiar signs and symbols of social intercourse" while living in another culture'.

5 See e.g. Redding (1995); Redding and Stening (2003);
http://stylusinc.com/business/india/business_india.htm;
http://www.tmpsearch.com/research_articles/new_global_exec/3c.html;
http://gbr.pepperdine.edu/982/china.html;
http://atn-riae.agr.ca/region/britishcolumbia/e3328.htm#Introduction

6 Such as education (especially bilingual and minority education) and linguistics (notably translation studies and foreign language teaching).

7 Although some literature under this heading has existed since the 1970s, e.g. Condon (1974), and the International Journal of Intercultural Relations launched in 1977. Newer journals on the topic include Journal of Intercultural Studies (launched in 1998), Intercultural Education (2000), and Language and Intercultural Communication (2002).

8 Mole's book however, unlike some of the other references cited, takes pains to avoid recommending specific types of culturally adaptive behaviour to the reader: he limits his task to charting countries' cultural traits and identifying points where misunderstandings might arise.

9 The buyer is recommended to adapt only if 'you want to negotiate the best deal' (2002: 15).

10 Author's translation from the Danish text: 'Hvordan man bygger et hus, hvordan man foretager fordelingen ved en fest, er ikke det same som at vide hvordan man hader, hvordan man fortolker sin egen umiddelbare sociale sammenhæng'.

11 In his *Recherches Philosophiques sur les Américains*, published in 1768.

12 In his later work, Segalen criticises the aestheticist ideal that prevailed during his lifetime, calling it 'sensation without experience', and advocating instead

the sensory experiences of travel and encounters with foreign peoples and difference (Michel, 1996: 8)

[13] Partons donc de cet aveu d'impénétrabilité. Ne nous flattons pas d'assimiler les moeurs, les races, les nations, les autres; mais au contraire éjouissons-nous de ne le pouvoir jamais; nous réservant ainsi la perdurabilité du plaisir de sentir le Divers (Segalen, 1978: 25).

[14] L'exotisme n'est donc pas cet état kaléidoscopique du touriste et du médiocre spéctateur, mais la réaction vive et curieuse d'une individualité forte contre une objectivité dont elle preçoit et déguste la distance... Je les nomme les Proxénètes de la Sensation du Divers... (Segalen, 1978: 34).

[15] ... augmenter notre faculté de percevoir le Divers, est-ce rétrécir notre personnalité ou l'enrichir?... Nul doute: c'est l'enrichir abondamment, de tout l'Univers[15] (Segalen, 1978: 25).

[16] Author's translation of the French: 'Aux Maories des temps oubliés'

[17] E.g. criticising the way in which Western categories such as participation, modernity, freedom, ownership and democracy are transferred to contexts that often operate with very different perceptions of social reality. This ethnocentric approach to development has been criticised by, among others, Escobar (1995); Nanda (2001). Similarly, within postcolonial theory, criticisms have been levelled against writing that is accused of being 'largely oblivious to non-Western articulations of self and identity, and has thus tended to interpellate the non-Western cultures it seeks to foreground and defend into a solidly Eurocentric frame of consciousness. Postcolonial theory thus operates with the paradoxical tension of relying on the secular, European vocabulary of its academic origins to translate non-secular, non-European experiences' (Majid, 2001)

[18] In this sense, Segalen's approach to difference is close to the concepts of différance and alterity employed by, *inter alia*, Derrida and postcolonial theorists

[19] Perhaps to a lesser extent in the case of tourism; however, tourists are also typically shielded from all but the most superficial contact with locals: they are also typically accompanied by friends or relatives from their own culture, and they usually have the option of retreating to an anonymous hotel if things get uncomfortable (too hot, too busy, too poor, etc.). The type of activities carried out is also usually of the 'spectator/consumer' type: sight-seeing, shopping, eating out etc.

2

Making Sense of Globalisation
French Narratives and Anti-Americanism

METTE ZØLNER

In this chapter I will look at how political and economic elites within France of the 1990s and early 2000 reconstruct French narratives in the encounter with globalisation. The question raised is whether we, in the era of globalisation, can still observe hegemonic national narratives that contribute to shaping the way in which groups of social actors within France make sense of the world. That is, how do they through their discourse make sense of the social reality in which globalisation challenges existing taken-for-granted values and, among these, national narratives. Thus, on the one hand, the chapter investigates whether the French nation still exists in the sense of narratives on who 'we' are and on what is believed genuinely to characterise French society, as well as in the sense of narratives on the 'Other', such as anti-Americanism. On the other hand, the chapter looks into the extent to which such traditionally French narratives are reconstructed in the encounter with globalisation.

My argument is that in the end 1990s and early 2000, we can observe a certain 'French touch' when French political and economic elites debate globalisation. This 'French touch' is constituted by a shared frame of traditional French narratives that are carried by various groups of social actors despite conflicting interests and differing political views. It follows that even though globalisation challenges the existence of the nation-state as an economic, political and cultural entity, traditional national narratives on 'us' and 'them' are still widespread, giving discourses on globalisation a 'French touch'. In other words, despite the different social, economic and political standpoints of the social actors that hold these discourses and despite processes of globalisation, I argue that we can observe a 'French touch'. However, by the same token, I also contend that this 'French touch' is the result of a reconstruction process, to which French elites contribute by adapting traditional national narratives to a new social reality.

Looking at globalisation, the French case is particularly interesting, since in few countries has globalisation caused so much debate.[1] To explain this, scholars point to the distinctive socio-economic model, French Statism, which is said to have been particularly affected by processes of Europeanisation and economic globalisation, which are based on a more market-driven socio-economic model (i.e. Boltho, 1996; Boyer, 1997; Meunier, 2000 and 2003; Schmidt, 1999). Moreover, as V. Schmidt argues (1997), when French Statism evolved during the 1980s and 1990s, the political discourse did not follow. As a consequence, one observed an increasing discrepancy between a dominant *statiste* discourse and the available policy instruments of the French state. This is the point of departure of the present chapter, which will focus on how political and economic elites cope with that discrepancy in the end 1990s and early 2000, when the debate on globalisation was particularly fervent in France.

Theoretical approach

On a theoretical level, my analysis will be based on the phenomenological perspective, claiming that human beings need to understand and to make sense of the social reality in which they live and act. Making sense implies ordering social reality and when doing so, social actors build on existing social structures and taken-for-granted values (Berger & Luckmann, 1966). According to the social representation theory and the technique of anchoring, social actors are likely to mobilise such values when encountering the 'Other' and/or the 'unfamiliar' as a way of rendering the situation more familiar and less threatening (see also Blasco in this book). Deep-rooted ideas of how to define 'us' and 'them' are part of such taken-for-granted values. Within the literature on nationalism, scholars use terms such as 'history and tradition' (Hobsbawm, 1983), 'cultural codes' (Giesen, 1998), 'ethnic roots' (Smith, 1986), and 'foundational myths (Stråth, 2000). The French historian, Pierre Nora prefers to speak about 'the repository of images and ideals that constitute a certain social community'. He argues that this repository constrains and enables the way in which a community remembers its past (Nora, 1996, xv-xxiv). In a similar vein, this chapter will argue that such images and ideas do not only frame the memory of the past, but likewise contribute to structuring the way in which social actors, belonging to a certain national community, construct their present social world (Marcussen *et al.*, 1999; Marcussen & Zølner, 2001 & 2003).

In the following, I will use the term 'national narratives' in the sense of a storyline that integrates factual events by relating them to a plot (Czaniawska, 1998). When narrating, social actors make sense of factual events that would otherwise remain meaningless in their eyes. And rather than faithfully reflecting social reality, the power of a narrative depends on its capacity to present a 'plot' that makes sense of such factual events to its social carriers. I will use narratives in plural, because even though there is, in general, one dominating national narrative, in most countries other narratives exist that challenge the hegemonic narrative. Thus, like a hegemonic discourse (Fairclough, 1995), a dominant national narrative is continuously challenged by counter narratives carried by groups of social actors who strive to impose their narrative as taken-for-granted in a given nation. This installs a dynamic that contributes to the continuous reconstruction process of a hegemonic national narrative, which can be conceived of as the result of conflicts and compromises between groups of social actors through history.

It follows that national narratives are socially constructed and therefore change continuously. Yet, national narratives are not devoid of a certain historical continuity. Social actors, consciously or unconsciously, reproduce existing narratives that constrain and enable the way in which they make sense of the social reality they confront. Thus, like institutions, narratives are sticky and difficult to get rid of, as they are collectively constructed and taken-for-granted (Hall, 1993 & 1996). Therefore, an individual has to take them into account when taking part and acting in a given social reality. Consequently, 'Frenchness', or any other 'nationness', is socially constructed by social carriers who, in a never-ending process, re-adapt national narratives to a particular time and place. In other words, existing national narratives serve as categories when social actors order social reality, but, when applied, these categories are also slightly adapted by the social actors in order to make sense of their present social world.

It follows from the above that national narratives comprise only one of the factors that contribute to the patterning of reconstruction processes of national narratives. Social carriers of national narratives will be considered to constitute another factor. Carrying a narrative does not entail being a passive 'cultural bearer' hereof, but on the contrary, actively participating in its reconstruction process (Søderberg and Villemoes, 1994). When doing so, the point of departure is the life-world, in the sense of the life that social carriers live and endure. That is, their past experiences and socialisation, their present difficulties and joys and their future perspectives (Schütz & Luckmann, 1989). On a theoretical level, this adds a micro-sociological and interpretative perspective to the societal level of hegemonic narratives. Thus, though a social actor is likely to mobilise national narratives, he does it in a specific context, which makes it impossible to generalise about how a carrier of certain national narratives will understand and act.

A final factor in the reconstruction process to be mentioned is the situational context in which such narratives are applied. Situational context is here understood to comprise socially determined conditions and prevailing ideas that, at a certain point in time and place, are accepted as facts by social actors. A fundamental aspect of the situational context is the 'Other', since the 'border' defines who we are to an even larger extent that we define the border (Barth, 1969). In an analysis of reconstruction processes of national narratives it is therefore highly interesting to focus on an encounter with the 'Other'. In the present chapter, the debate on economic globalisation has been chosen as it represents such an 'Other' in the French context of the 1990s and early 2000. Put differently, the chapter looks at how globalisation is made sense of, since it constitutes a critical juncture in which national narratives are likely to fall apart or be reconstructed. Consequently, the chapter will not go into the discussion of whether globalisation exists, when it started or the social, economic and political consequences it entails (Drache and Boyer, 1996; Hirst and Thompson, 1999; Keohane and Nye, 2000).

Structure and limits of the argument

To substantiate the argument that traditional French narratives frame French discourses on globalisation, the chapter will be structured in the following way. First, I will introduce traditional French narratives, such as a Republican narrative, including a state and a social narrative as well as narratives on the United States. This presentation will be based on a large historical and sociological literature on French nation-building, its socio-economic model as well as Franco-American relations.

To investigate whether and how these narratives frame discourses on globalisation, I will review a number of speeches, interviews and essays published in the period from 1995-2002, during which debates on globalisation were particularly fervent. In order to investigate the extent to which the existing narratives are widespread, and thereby contribute to the creation of a French entity, I will look at different groups of social actors who actively participate in the public debate on globalisation. I will distinguish between political and economic elites whose perspectives on globalisation are likely to differ. That is, on the one hand, national politicians, and on the other, business leaders. In the era of globalisation, the latter are often presented as having the whole world as their playground, whereas the former act as representatives of the nation-state, which is threatening to fall apart. In the process I will clarify the extent to which French political and economic elites reproduce and readapt traditional French narratives. The analysis will focus on similarities between the various discourses, but it will likewise take into account dissimilarities. These show that, within this overarching narrative frame, we can observe diverging and opposing storylines, which illustrate ongoing struggles and negotiations about how to make sense of globalisation (Smith, 2000). Moreover, the dissimilarities also indicate that when making sense of globalisation, the point of departure of the social actors in question differs.

In the final section, I will conclude on how this single case of the encounter with an Other illustrates processes related to the reconstruction of national narratives as well as on how it may contribute to theories on intercultural communication.

My analysis will leave open a number of questions that I will not be able to go into due to the limits of my data and to the scope of the present chapter. One limitation is that my empirical basis does not allow me to elucidate the question of how French politicians and business elites really think and feel. That is, how sincere are they? Do they identify with and act according to their own discourse? Or do they just frame their discourse in national narratives for pragmatic reasons in order to either appear as legitimate discussion partners in the French debate or as a way of appealing to French public opinion? The present chapter cannot go into this question, since the data analysed is constituted merely by discourses held in public. Consequently, the present chapter will not and cannot deal with this question of social actors' sincerity; it can merely analyse whether we can observe a certain national unity in the way in which French elites mobilise national narratives.

A second limitation is that the chapter does not go into the question of the veracity of the narratives on 'us' or on 'them'. The analysis simply concludes on whether or not social actors mobilise such narratives and to what extent they reconstruct them. That does not, of course, tell us anything about whether these narratives are pure 'stereotypes', in the sense of not being correct, or whether they are actually based on some truth. Thus, the argument of the present chapter is not that the national narratives correspond to reality, or that they faithfully echo political or economic intentions of the social actors who mobilise them. The argument is merely that these narratives contribute to framing the way in which the social actors put forward their ideas and justify their actions. French history provides many examples of how politicians have exploited anti-Americanism out of pure populism (Kuisel, 2001) as well as examples of inconsistencies between political discourses and political, social and economic facts (Kuisel, 2001; Gordon and Meunier, 2001; Meunier, 2003).

A third limitation to be pointed at is that, on the basis of my analysis of the French cases in this chapter, I cannot make any general claims about how other social actors in different situational and institutional contexts make sense of globalisation. It may well be that existing narratives, national or other, frame understandings of globalisation, and that such narratives are reconstructed by their social carriers in the light of globalisation. The present chapter can only posit this hypothesis.

French narratives and traditional anti-Americanism

I will use the term 'French narratives' to mean stories that tell 'what France is' and 'how a good and fair society' should be organised. In his book on French nationalism, Winock identifies two kinds of French narratives that have been mobilised during the 19th and 20th centuries. One is Catholic, presenting France as *repliée sur soi* and Frenchness as being a question of religion. Another is Republican, narrating France as a model of civilisation that achieves *grandeur* from its values (Winock, 1982). Today, Republican narratives dominate, also when the issue is globalisation.[2]

A common thread in Republican narratives is the story of a France that, as a bearer of civilisation, has a Messianic mission to liberate the world from oppression and ignorance by bringing values with universal bearing, such as liberty, freedom, equality, fraternity, human rights and democracy. Thus, French specificity and *grandeur* is to be the stronghold of a universal civilisation, believed to be the only one for all times and for all peoples. The Republican narrative also integrates a specific storyline on the state. It is a story about how a rational state, standing beyond any conflicting political and socio-economic interests, efficiently acts in favour of national interests and hereby counteracts harmful private interests and groups suspected of disuniting the Republic. Thus, the state acts for economic renovation and modernisation and serves the general interest of the nation and its *grandeur*, whereas private economic and industrial activities are selfish and suspected of dividing the nation (Crozier, 1991; Kuisel, 1981; Woronoff, 1998).[3] Along the lines of the state narrative, serving general interests is prestigious whereas private interests and industrial activities are presented in a negative light. Several scholars have commented upon this negative conception of doing business and business leaders regularly voice feelings of lacking social esteem (Berger, 1987; Gervaise *et al.*, 1996; Weber, 1986).

Finally, Republican narratives of national unity have progressively incorporated a story of social justice, progress and cohesion, expressed by the Republican principles of equality and fraternity. During the 19th and early 20th centuries, this story constituted a controversial part of the Revolutionary legacy as it was adopted by emerging working classes and Communist and Socialist parties (Winock, 1999). Yet, in post-war France, the narrative on social justice and progress was to a certain extent institutionalised by the French welfare state, based on the principle that all individuals are equal and should benefit from equal rights and social protection. A major role was attributed to the state, which was to ensure adherence to the doctrine of Republican social solidarity and promote social progress.

Narratives on the significant Other, which, as an inevitable part of any identity narrative, mirrors fears and negative values, complement these narratives on 'what France is and how society should be organised'.[4] Narratives on the 'Other' constitute, thus, an anti-model for who 'we' are and for what a good socio-economic model is. Since the 18th century, positive and negative narratives on the United States have been observable in France (Duroselle, 1976; Kuisel, 1993 and 2001; Mattellart, 1997; Rémond, 1962; Toinet et al, 1986; Winock, 1982). As a positive model, narratives on the United States reflect a criticism of France and serve as an example for what France needs to do. In the

18th century, Rousseau cherished the simplicity of the American life, as opposed to the artificiality of French aristocracy, and in the early 19th century, Lafayette depicted the United States as a land of freedom, tolerance and equality (Rémond, 1962). Later, the United States became admired for its productivity. In the Interwar and post-WWII periods, the idea of the scientific division of labour was adopted; large-scale production and financing through renting became an ideal for how France could catch up with its economic and political partners, and American management and management schools became a model for French managers who went to the United States on study and productivity trips (Boltanski, 1981; Kuisel, 1993; Winock, 1982: 55).

However, alongside this positive image of the United States, a negative one emerged (Rémond, 1962; Roger 2002). From being a model of democracy and freedom, the United States came to incarnate the dictatorship of mass democracy and its culture came to be seen as a lack of 'culture'. The American way of life was considered to be monotonous, materialistic, rude, cruel, and deprived of intellectual pleasures, and Americans were criticized for their worship of mammon (Rémond, 1962). The negative image of a materialistic and conformist United States echoed a traditional aristocratic and royalist criticism of the *bourgeoisie*, but it likewise spread to the other side of the political scene, to liberal Republicans as well as to the emerging Socialist Party (Rémond, 1962; Winock, 1982). This contemptible narrative on a society characterized by consumerism, materialism and conformity, and inhabited by a naive and ignorant people was, subsequent to WWI, transformed into an anti-American narrative, telling the story of a colonizing and dominating United States that threatened to transform French lifestyle and culture. Americanisation implied social conformity, economic savagery and a lowering of culture (Kuisel, 1993; Mattelart, 2000; Roger, 2002; Winock, 1982). In the post-WWII period, the Marshall Plan reinforced this fear, particularly among Communists and Socialists, but likewise among Gaullists, who added a political aspect to French anti-Americanism. The 1960s were, moreover, years when American investments in key economic sectors in particular came to be interpreted as a loss of decision-making power, equivalent to a loss of national pride and influence. Moreover, American economic behaviour was still considered to be less humane than the French one (Kuisel, 1993). To sum up, we can say that, in general, anti-American narratives express a fear of losing French cultural integrity and this fear is closely interwoven with economic arguments. It is the law of the 'dollar' that will ruin French culture, if it is imposed on society as a whole (Gordon & Meunier, 2001; Winock, 1982).

Discourses on globalisation at the turn of the century

Political discourse: savage globalisation equals Americanisation

> Globalisation is inevitable. It brings considerable progress in terms of living standards and economic development... but globalisation, if we are not cautious, may also bring serious dangers, such as exclusion. Exclusion of an increasing number of countries as well as social exclusion of an increasing number of men and women within each country... We need to regulate and humanise globalisation (J. Chirac, European Parliament, December, 12 2000).[5]

> Globalisation constitutes the reality in which we live. But this reality is ambiguous. Globalisation favours economic growth, but it is accompanied by increasing inequalities. Globalisation favours the encounter with cultural diversity, but carries with it a risk of cultural uniformisation... The consequences of globalisation depend on what we make of it.... We need to regulate globalisation in order to benefit from it and prevent its downside (L. Jospin, "Maîtriser la mondialisation", Brazil, April, 2001).[6]

These quotations by the two executives of the French state, the Gaullist President Jacques Chirac and his Socialist Prime Minister (1997-2002), illustrate the way in which most French political actors spoke about globalisation at the turn of the century. Globalisation is negative if economic forces are left unregulated/untamed, allowing social inequalities to deepen and cultural diversity to disappear. On the other hand, globalisation is positive if these forces are 'regulated/tamed' with the aim of ensuring economic development, social cohesion and cultural diversity and enrichment. Thus, one observes a narrative on globalisation, stating that untamed/savage economic globalisation is negative, whereas a 'tamed' and 'civilised' globalisation is positive.[7]

On both sides of the political spectrum, 'savage' globalisation refers to a socio-economic model that, furthering the interests of economic forces at the expense of the general interests of society, deepens social inequalities within and among nation-states. The model is, however, also 'savage' in that it is perceived as letting the competitive logic of the free-market invade all aspects of life, transforming everything into a product and homogenising cultural diversity. These two strands of the 'savage' globalisation discourse come, not surprisingly, most clearly to the fore in the discourse of left-wing political actors. Thus, in 1999, the Communist party leader, Robert Hue, speaks of 'the ultra-liberal globalisation' that reduces everything to an economic question (Hue, 1999: 115), while the Socialist Prime Minister at the time, Lionel Jospin declares a 'yes to market economy, but no a marketised society'.[8]

Yet, the two threads of the savage globalisation discourse also characterise the Right, which denounces a 'brutal' or 'excessive liberalism' that deepens social inequalities and reduces everything to economic logic. One example is President Jacques Chirac's former Prime Minister (1995-1997), Alain Juppé, who, in the aftermath of the 1995 social movement, criticised globalisation processes for letting 'unscrupulous and unpredictable financial markets dominate' and 'for enriching speculators while impoverishing people economically and politically' (Juppé, 1996: 52-61). His predecessor, Edouard Balladur (1993-1995), who was likewise a Gaullist, opposed, a few years later, the French tradition of counterbalancing private property rights with the system of 'liberalism without rules and private propriety without control' which many countries have applied, believing that this was a solution to all their problems (Balladur, 1999: 150-151). And in April 2001, E. Balladur calls for a 'civilised globalisation' on the front page of *Le Monde*. The leader of the umbrella formation, *Union pour la démocratie française* (UDF) and candidate for the presidential election in 2002, François Bayrou, speaks of the need to limit 'the excess of blind commerce', adding:

> We do not think that the aim of society is to make everything marketable; it is, on the contrary, to put things in the right place. The market is for products and services, but values constitute the essential part of society (*Conseil national de l'UDF*, 27 November 1999).[9]

Also, Alain Madelein, the head of the Liberal Party (*Démocratie liberale*), which in 1998 broke with Bayrou's *Union pour la démocratie française* to present a more liberal profile, stresses that being liberal does not imply that 'we reduce man to being an economic subject' (quote from the *Convention Libérale*, 17 October, 1998). Finally, the discourse of both of the two extreme-right-wing parties, the National Republican Movement and the National Front Party, enter into the frame of the savage globalisation discourse. This happens despite the fact that both advocate a national liberalism. Thus, Bruno Mégret states that 'excessive globalisation is anti-social' (Party meeting of *Mouvement Républicain et National*, Baule, 2 October 1999) and he is echoed by Jean-Marie Le Pen from the National Front Party (*Bleu, Blanc, Rouge* meeting, 26 September 1999).

Politicians on the Left and the Right do not only agree to condemn savage globalisation, they also, more or less explicitly, associate this globalisation with Americanisation. For example, in his essay, the Gaullist and former Prime Minister, Éduard Balladur declares that 'globalisation is the world that has become American' (Balladur, 1999: 178). The Eurosceptic Gaullist, Charles Pasqua, is even more explicit, speaking of American colonisation in his article bearing the illustrative title 'The spiral of enslavement' (*Le spiral de l'asservissement*, *Le Monde*, 27 October, 1999). On the Left wing, the Eurosceptic presidential candidate from 2002, Jean-Pierre Chévènement, states that the economic and technological strength of the United States empowers it to colonise the world.[10] Furthermore, the Green politician, Noël Mamère, says no to the imperialism of the American model, as the title of the book he co-authored in 1999 indicates: *No thanks, Uncle Sam*.

By 'Americanisation', political actors refer to the generalisation of an Anglo-American socio-economic model that is too liberal and too little concerned with social cohesion and the preservation of social benefits. This model is considered to be inapplicable in France, as the following quotation exemplifies:

> I reject the excessive liberalisation and globalisation that we see in the Anglo-Saxon countries... France could not go so far in the processes of liberalisation and flexibility as to question fundamental social rights. Consequently, as I have said, I do not recommend that model (President Jacques Chirac, 14 July, 1998).[11]

Thus, globalisation and liberalism are constructed as being something non-French, something Anglo-American. That this idea was widespread is illustrated by the liberal Alain Madelin, who, when aiming at legitimating liberalism, argues that unlike the general belief in France, the origins of liberalism are not American, but French. Referring to authors such as de Tracy, Alexis de Tocqueville and Benjamin Constant, Alain Madelin defines his liberal project as incorporating the values of generosity, fraternity and solidarity.[12]

However, by Americanisation, politicians also refer to the other aspect of savage globalisation, namely cultural homogenisation. On the Right, Éduard Balladur writes, for example:

> Globalisation is a world in which eternal repetition of the same forms, the same lifestyles, same ideas and same ways of thinking and speaking creates disenchantment and arouses the sentiment of a universal banality in which one hardly finds any beauty of diversity (Balladur, 1999: 178).[13]

On the Left, the Socialist Minister of Foreign Affairs at the time, Hubert Védrine, echoes this narrative when comparing the United States to a France characterised by quality and diversity (Védrine, 1999).

It follows from the examples above that the savage globalisation discourse echoes former French anti-American narratives. Savage globalisation is constructed as the generalisation of an excessive liberal socio-economic model that possesses the same weaknesses as the perceived Anglo-American model. Moreover, cultural homogenisation is in essence an Americanisation and therefore a degradation of culture.

Reconstructing the state narrative

The other side of the coin, the 'tamed' and 'civilised' globalisation, is less homogenously constructed. All political actors, on the Right as well as on the Left, call for an instance that, representing the will of the people, counteracts individual and private interests. In this way, their discourse resonates with the state narrative, that is, the idea that when market forces assume supremacy over political power the state can no longer protect and serve the general interests of the political community against short-sighted and selfish individual interests. Political actors tend to agree that despite globalisation and Europeanisation, the state still has a role to play as an organiser of the economic as well as the social environment. Thus, on the role of the state J. Chirac declares:

> Globalisation has, of course, challenged our conception of and the role of states... Yet, it is still the role of the state to organise a legal, fiscal, social, intellectual and industrial environment that favours the flourishing of work (quote from a speech inaugurating a

conference on globalisation and languages 'Trois espaces linguistiques face aux défis de la mondialisation', 20 March 2001).[14]

Also, the Minister of Economy and Finance at the time, Laurent Fabius, who represents the liberal stand within the Socialist party, put forward this view in his article entitled 'The new era of the state'. He writes further that 'France changes. The need for a state remains. But its action forms change' ('Le nouvel âge de l'Etat', *Le Monde*, 23 February, 2000).

This exemplifies the fact that most politicians agree on the need to modernise the economic role of the state. The state is to ensure the well functioning of a free-market economy. For the previous and present governmental and presidential majorities, the state is to exercise that role together with international institutions such as the World Trade Organisation and the European Union. To paraphrase the former Socialist Prime Minister, Lionel Jospin, these institutions should 'direct globalisation towards right and social justice' (quote from "Maîtriser la mondialisation", Brazil, 6 April, 2001).

Yet, there is no full political consensus on this point. On the Left as well as the Right, advocators of national sovereignty wish to re-establish the political independence of the nation-state. In their views, the European Union and the World Trade Organisation only contribute to the acceleration and accentuation of globalisation. Thus, by politicians on the Right, the EU is described as a 'Trojan horse' (W. Abitbol, European deputy, RPF, quoted in *Le Monde*, 15 August, 1999) and the World Trade Organisation as a 'puppet led by forces of globalisation' (B. Mégret, at a party meeting of *Mouvement Républicain et National*, in Baule, 2 October 1999). On the Left, the Communist Party is critical towards the World Trade Organisation and the European Union, which the Party judges to be guided by a too liberal ideology aimed at accelerating financial globalisation. The Communist party is in favour of a different Europe than the EU (Hue, 1999: 333-358).

Reconstructing the universality of France
A final element of the French national narratives that emerges when political actors debate is that France is presented as possessing certain values and having a particular role to play on the international scene. It is mostly referred to as 'the special role of France', or as the 'voice of France speaking to humanity'. One example is the party leader of the

UDF, François Bayrou, who, when presenting his preliminary project for the upcoming presidential election in 2002, stated:

> In an inhuman world, we would like France to be the most human nation. In a world in which the most dominant value too often appears to be financial, we would like the most recognised, cherished and honourable value to be human (*Conseil National de l'UDF*, 28 April, 2001).[15]

Nevertheless, though most discourses echo the 'open' narrative on France, they reconstruct it slightly. The mission of France is no longer to propagate one universal civilisation but on the contrary, to defend cultural diversity. To paraphrase Hubert Védrine (Minister of Foreign Affairs, 1997-2002), France's contribution towards 'civilising globalisation' is to act for the preservation of 'cultural diversity', for example, by promoting 'cultural exceptions', as was done in the GATT negotiations in 1993 and within the World Trade Organisation.[16] On these occasions, France speaks for all cultures with the aim of combating cultural homogenisation (Védrine, 2000: 47), and according to his Prime minister, Lionel Jospin, this is the way to be faithful to French universality in a globalised world:

> Even though globalisation is rich in promises, it threatens national cultural identities... Today, for France, promoting cultural diversity in the world, is a modern way of being faithful to its Universalism of 1789 (Jospin, quoted in *Le Monde*, 19 July, 2000).[17]

President Jacques Chirac goes even further when, in a speech to French artists on the occasion of the WTO negotiations, he states explicitly that 'cultural diversity is the ideal, whereas the idea of one universal civilisation is to be rejected' (J. Chirac, 16 November 1999).

Thus, 21st century France is depicted as a leader that, by possessing values of cultural diversity, remains faithful to its universal and progressive role dating back to the Revolution. France still stands on the side of the people as a defender of universal human rights and individual freedom. However, today the opponents are no longer aristocratic tyrants, but 'the tyranny of uniformity' and the freedom to be protected is the 'freedom to be different', to paraphrase Edouard Ballardur (1999). Moreover, France no longer plays this role alone, but together with Francophone countries (J. Chirac, 16 November 1999) and Europe (L. Jospin, "L'avenir de l'Europe élargie" 28 May 2001).

Summing up the above analysis, we can conclude that political discourses on globalisation are framed by national narratives on 'us' and 'them'. While the two-sided discourse on savage globalisation echoes traditional narratives on the 'Other', namely anti-Americanism, the discourse on how to tame and humanise globalisation tends to reproduce elements of narratives on 'us'. That is, the need for a state, social justice and finally the ideas of an open and universal France. However, the examples above also show that political actors did not merely reproduce national narratives when making sense of globalisation. They readapted and readjusted national narratives in order to adapt them to social reality at the turn of the century. This is particularly the case with regard to the narrative of an open and universal France, which is particularly inappropriate to the situational context. The idea of one universal ideal of civilisation has been discredited by decolonisation and a Third World discourse (Zølner, 2000). Moreover, France is not the superpower it once was, but has been reduced to a mere middle-ranking European nation-state whose language is losing its status as a world language. Thus, as one can no longer view France as representing 'civilisation', French politicians seem to put forward the ideal of cultural diversity. This ideal likewise appears as a defensive discourse against what is feared, namely, American cultural and economic domination. Finally, the above analysis also indicates that within the common narrative framing of globalisation discourses, there were disagreements on how to redefine the economic and social role of the state. Though the analysis does not allow us to go into these divergences, the examples given seem to indicate that the social actors' differing ideologies can explain the disagreements.

Business discourses

The two strands of the savage globalisation discourse, analysed above, likewise characterise the discourse of the social partners. It is definitely not surprising to note that the savage globalisation narrative frames the discourse of the trade unions, despite their differing strategies and divergent attitudes to social dialogue. After all, this globalisation discourse seems perfect for mobilising their fight to preserve and to improve social rights. The economic and financial interests that this discourse denounces have always been the opponents of trade unions, politically engaged on the Left.

What is more surprising to note is that business leaders of large corporate companies also distinguish between a savage globalisation, associated with an Anglo-American capitalism and a civilised and tamed globalisation respectful of French socio-economic values. This is despite the fact that the French public designates precisely Chief Executive Officers (CEOs) as the new masters of the world who benefit most from globalisation.[18] Numerous examples of the savage globalisation discourse are found in interviews with French CEOs of large companies published by Ockrent & Séréni in 1998. Some merely remark that globalisation imposes an Anglo-American business culture on their sector,[19] others regret exactly this,[20] but many CEOs also include criticism of the Anglo-American socio-economic model. Just like the political actors, CEOs praise the preservation of a French or European social responsibility that differs from the American one, making the socio-economic model of the latter inapplicable in Europe.[21] Moreover, they disapprove of a society that lacks social coherence and has pronounced social inequalities.[22]

Even the reputed liberal head of the employers' organisation, Ernest-Antoine Seillière, states not only that the French socio-economic model has a stronger human and social dimension than the Anglo-American one, but also that the French specificity in that respect needs to be preserved.[23] This is particularly interesting since the election of Ernest-Antoine Seillière as president of the employers' association and its subsequent change of name into MEDEF has marked a move towards a more offensive and liberal discourse. Ernest-Antoine Seillière's political line has been interpreted as a break with a tradition of family capitalism with paternalistic employers (*patronat*), which demanded a certain moral obligation towards its employees (Dubois, 1999).

In addition to the criticism of the lack of a social dimension, CEOs, implicitly or explicitly, disapprove of a socio-economic model in which economic results are the only concern. This view is particularly strong within the Christian organisation *Les Entrepreneurs et Dirigeants Chrétiens*, which, in 2000, decided to work to 'turn globalisation into a sign of hope for social justice for all human beings' and to avoid globalisation that implies a moral that makes profit the aim of everything (www.cfpc.org/Strasbourg2000/message_mondialisation.htm).[24]

This view also appears to be regularly voiced by individual business leaders of large as well as small and medium-sized companies (Zølner, 2002a & 2002b). Likewise, the secular movement the Centre for Young Business Leaders (*Centre des Jeunes Dirigeants d'Entreprise*), expresses a similar concern. They state that globalisation should not be governed exclusively by the market, but also by an overall concern for humanity. Their conviction is that companies should not win at the expense of society and humanity (*Centre des Jeunes Dirigeants d'Entreprise*, 1996: 28-30).

Despite their criticism of the Anglo-American socio-economic model, CEOs admire its economic efficiency and productivity. They wish to incorporate these elements into a European model of capitalism, while ensuring social coherence,[25] a view that likewise seems to be widespread among managers in small and medium-sized companies (Zølner, 2002a & 2002b).

To this, we should add that in their ideal European model of capitalism, the CEOs would like a state that is stronger than that found in the United States. Thus, one CEO declares that he personally would prefer to preserve a European model in which the state has a regulative role that is unknown in the United States.[26] Another says that he is not in favour of reducing the role of the state, but that he wishes it were more efficient.[27] Though these quotations do not present a precise picture of the kind of state French business leaders wish for, they do indicate that they are far from claiming a minimal state, but rather a French conception of state, albeit modernised and more efficient.

This short presentation of French business discourse illustrates that it is shaped to a certain extent by national narratives. According to these, good and ethical business behaviour is respectful of social solidarity, and the state is not an evil but, on the contrary, assumed to regulate and control business in order to defend the interests of the public. Moreover, business leaders apply both positive and negative American narratives. That is, their ideal socio-economic model is less state-directed than the traditional French model, but the economy is not, nevertheless, relinquished to the invisible hand of the free market, since the role of a reformed state is to set out general directions for the development of France and to ensure social cohesion through an efficient social policy. In other words, they present their ideal model as tempered liberalism with a strong social model that combines positive components of their constructed Anglo-American and French socio-economic models. One can, of course, question whether this business discourse expresses a profound wish to retain certain French or European values or whether their discourse simply follows the general worldwide trend of ethical enterprise and investments. Ethical behaviour and social and environmental responsibility have indeed become crucial for the image of almost any company.[28] Though this is a very likely interpretation it does not affect the argument that traditional national narratives frame the CEO discourse, as well as that of political actors.

Reconstructed French narratives

The above analysis has illustrated that, when debating globalisation publicly, the discourse of political and economic elites has a certain 'French touch'. It is provided by deep-rooted Republican and anti-American narratives that frame the way in which these actors make sense of and present globalisation in a legitimate way. Whereas the civilised globalisation discourse resonates the Republican narrative on how society should be organised and what the role of France should be in the world, the savage globalisation discourse echoes traditional anti-American narratives. Nevertheless, as we saw above, when reproducing the deep-rooted narratives, social actors reconstruct these slightly in order to fit a new social reality. For politicians, it was in particular the case with regard to the role and mission of France being reduced to a middle-ranking European nation-state with a culture that is no longer considered to be 'the' Culture. For business leaders, as well as some politicians, it was the need to modernise state narratives.

The reading of the public debate on globalisation also illustrates that the United States is to a large extent still narrated as a counter-model for what France should be and as a model for what France's future is feared to become. Thus, the anti-American narrative is still that of a materialistic and money-oriented society, characterised by lack of culture and a societal organisation that appears to be rude and cruel. Nevertheless, the focus is slightly different. In the 21st century, the consumer society is a French reality and the issue at stake is the French socio-economic model in terms of a balance between political and economic power. Thus, Americanisation refers to 'unrestricted rule of the market', excessive liberalisation and deregulation that leads to social inequality and injustice. Also, the imperialistic fear has a new face: it is less the fear of losing Culture with a capital 'C', than culture in the sense of lifestyle and national identity. In that respect, anti-Americanism follows the reconstruction of the national narratives presenting France as the advocator of cultural diversity rather than of one universal civilisation. Moreover, as has happened previously in French history, the United States functions as a model for how France is to improve its performance. This positive American narrative is mobilised by business elites, who just like the author of the well-known essay from the 1960s, 'The American Challenge' by Jean-Jacques Servan-Schreiber, put forward the need to learn the American way of being flexible, innovative, and better managers. In addition, today's business leaders point to corporate governance and pension funds. We can therefore conclude that as both a negative and a positive significant Other, the United States still occupies a key position in French public debates.

Reconstructing national narratives and the intercultural encounter

The fact that the discourse of French political and economic elites has a French touch indicates that France still exists as an entity of shared values and narratives in the era of globalisation. Despite supposedly different interests, a common point of departure for making sense of globalisation seems to be taken-for-granted narratives. Like institutions, these appear to be sticky and difficult to do away with, even when the economic, political and social reality tends to make them obsolete. Rather than disregarding existing narratives, the social actors in question reconstruct them, making them fit a new reality and investing them with new meaning.

However, they do not mobilise any national narrative, but the narratives that are meaningful in relation to at least two elements. The anti-American narratives illustrate this. They were picked on the one hand in relation to a situational context in which the social actors confronted a globalisation that appeared to uphold the American socio-economic model. Thus, processes of globalisation seemed to have an American face and hereby recall existing ideas and images of the United States. On the other hand, the life-world of the social actors in question, and in particular the here-and-now, tends to determine whether or not they mobilise both negative and positive narratives on the Unites States.

Similarly, they do not reconstruct the national narratives in just any way. To further our understanding of the reconstruction processes of national narratives, a look at the situational context and life-worlds of the social actors is illustrative. The social actors adapted narratives to the political, economic and social reality of the situational context they lived and acted within. Yet, in doing so, their point of departure was their life-world. Politicians tended to speak about societal issues of globalisation coloured by their ideological standpoints, whereas business leaders focused on changing business models and ethics and the need for more efficiency.

Mette Zølner

These concluding remarks take me to the question of whether this French case on how political and economic elites make sense of globalisation can tell us anything about intercultural communication in general. That is, about how we best encounter and communicate with the Other.

One point to bear in mind is that we tend to mobilise the knowledge that we believe we have on the Other in question and on what we relate to it. Consequently, we need to increase our awareness of the narratives and categories that we take for granted and which contribute to shaping the way in which we make sense of the world in general, and in particular, when encountering the Other. Without such cultural awareness, well-internalised narratives that constitute an obstacle to constructive and successful communication will continue to be applied. Thus, successful communication requires going beyond internalised categories and being able to revise these according to what is observed and experienced in a concrete context.

A second point is that we also need to consider divisions, that is, differing opinions among various social groups. Belonging to a nation and sharing national narratives does not imply uniformity; it never has, and it does so even less in the era of globalisation. Also, communication normally takes place on a micro-level, between two individuals or two collective actors. In such a situation, knowledge of the hegemonic national narratives are indeed useful and helpful, but not sufficient. Yet, as pointed out by other chapters in this book (see particularly Blasco on the handbook literature on intercultural communication; and Gustafsson), our supposed knowledge of the Other may actually hinder successful communication between two individuals because if we are too eager to act according to knowledge generated on a macro-level, we may forget to take into account the micro-level on which the actual communication takes place (Søderberg, 1999). Thus, to enter into a successful intercultural dialogue, one needs to take into account the nature of the person in front of us and the situation in which the communication takes place. Doing that implies a thorough knowledge of the diversity within a language and cultural area, as well as what one may call communication skills in general.

References

Arnault, Bernard; *La passion créative*. Paris: Plon, 2000.

Balladur, Edouard; *L'avenir de la différence*. Paris: Plon, 1999.

Barth, Fredrik; *Ethnic groups and boundaries: the social organisation of culture difference*. London: Allen and Unwin, 1969.

Berger, Peter & Thomas Luckmann; *The Social Construction of Reality*. London: Allen Lane, 1966.

Berger, Suzanne; Libealism Reborn: The New Synthesis in France, in Jolyon Howorth and George Ross; *Contemporary France: A Review of Interdisciplinary Studies*. London: Frances Pinter, 1987.

Boltanski, Luc; America, America... Le plan marshall et l'importation du 'management', *Actes de la recherche en sciences sociales*, 38, 1981.

Boltho, Andrea; Has France Converged on Germany? Policies and Institutions since 1958, in S. Berger & R. Dore (eds), *National Diversity and Global Capitalism*. US: Cornell University Press, 1996.

Boyer, Robert; French Statism at the Crossroads, in C. Crouch & W. Streeck, *Political Economy of Modern Capitalism. Mapping Convergence & Diversity*. London: Sage, 1997.

Centre des Jeunes Dirigeants d'Entreprise; *L'Entreprise au XXIe Siècle*. Paris: Flammarion, 1996.

Crozier, Michel; *État modeste. État moderne*, Paris: Seuil, 1991.

Czarniawska, Barbara; *A narrative approach to organisation studies*. California: Sage, 1998.

Desportes, Gérard & Laurent. Mauduit; *La Gauche imaginaire et le nouveau capitalisme*. Paris: Grasset, 1999.

Drache, Daniel & Robert Boyer; *States against markets: the limits of globalisation*. London: Routledge, 1996.

Mette Zølner

Dubois, Jean; Le Patronat en quête d'identité, *Études*, no 3903, 1999.

Duroselle, Jean-Baptiste; *La France et les Etats-Unis, des origines à nos jours*. Paris: Seuil, 1976.

Fairclough, Norman; *Critical Discourse Analysis. The Critical Study of Language*. London: Longman, 1995.

Forrester, Vivien; *L'horreur économique*. Paris: Fayard, 1996.

Forrester, Vivien; *Une étrange dictature*. Paris: Fayard, 2000.

Gervaise, Yves, Bernard Quirin & Elisabeth Crémieu; *Le nouvel espace économique français*. Paris : PUF, 1996.

Giesen, Bernhard; *Intellectuals and the German Nation: Collective Memory in an Axial Age*. Cambridge: Cambridge University Press, 1998.

Gordon, Philip H. & Sophie Meunier; *The French Callenge. Adapting to Globalisation*. Washington: Brookings Institution Press, 2001.

Hall, Peter A.; Policy Paradigms, Social Learning, and the State: The Case of Economic Policymaking in Britain, *Comparative Politics,* 25(3).

Hall, Peter A.; Political Science and the Three New Institutionalisms, *Political Studies*, 1996, 44 (5).

Hanley, David; French Political Parties, Globalisation and Europe, *Modern & Contemporary France*, 2001, 9 (3), August.

Hirst, Paul & Grahame Thompson; *Globalisation in Question :The International Economy and the Possibilities of Governance*. Cambridge: Polity Press, 1999

Hobsbawm, Eric; Introduction: Inventing Traditions, and Mass-Producing Traditions: Europe 1870-1914, in E. Hobsbawm & T. Ranger, *The Invention of Tradition*. Cambridge: CUP, 1983

Hue, Robert; *Communisme un nouveau projet*. Paris: Stock, 1999.

Izraelewicz, Erik; *Le Capitalisme Zinzin*. Paris: Grasset, 1999.

Jacquard, Albert; *J'accuse l'économie triomphante*. Paris: Calmann. Lévy, 1995

Juppé, Alain; *Entre nous*. Paris: Nil éditions, 1996

Keohane, Robert O. & Joseph S. Nye; Globalisation: What's new? What's not? (and so what?), *Foreign Policy*, Spring, no 118, 2000

Kuisel, Richard; The Gallic rooster crows again: the paradox of French anti-Americanism, *French Politics, Culture and Society*, , 19 (3), 2001.

Kuisel, Richard; *Capitalism and the State in Modern France: Renovation and Economic Management in the Twentieth Century*. Cambridge: Cambridge University Press, 1981.

Kuisel, Richard; *Seducing the French. The Dilemma of Americanisation*. California: University of California Press, 1993.

Mamère, Noël & Olivier Warin; *Non Merci, Oncle Sam*. Paris: Ramsay, 1999.

Marcussen, Martin & Mette Zølner; The Danish EMU-referendum 2000: Business as Usual, *Government and Opposition*, 36 (3) Summer 2001.

Marcussen, Martin & Mette Zølner; Monetarism and the Masses. Denmark and Economic Integration in Europe, *Cooperation and Conflict,* 2003, 38 (2), 2003.

Marcussen, Martin, Thomas Risse, Daniela Engelmann-Martin, Hans Joachim & Klaus Roscher; Constructing Europe? The evolution of French, British and German Nation-State identities, *Journal of European Public Policy*, 6 (4), 1999.

Mattelart, Armand; La nouvelle idéologie globalitaire, in Cordellier, S. (ed), *La Mondialisation au delà des Mythes*. Paris: Découverte, 1997.

Mette Zølner

Meunier, Sophie; France's Double-talk on Globalisation, *French, Politics, Culture and Society*, 21 (1), Spring 2003.

Meunier, Sophie; The French Exception, *Foreign Affairs,* July-August, 79, (4) 2000.

Minc, Alain; *La Mondialisation Heureuse*. Paris: Plon, 1997.

Noiriel, Gérard; Français et étrangers, in Pierre Nora (ed.). 1992. *Les Lieux de Mémoire. La France: 1. Conflits et Partages*. Paris: Gallimard, 1992.

Nora, Pierre; *Realms of Memory*. New York: Columbia University Press, 1996.

Ockrent, Christine & Jean-Pierre Séréni; *Les Grands Patrons : Comment ils Voient Notre Avenir!* Paris: Plon, 1999.

Passet, René; *L'illusion Néo-Libérale*. Paris: Fayard, 2000.

Rémond, René; *Les Etats-Unis Devant l'Opinion Française*, 1815-1852. Paris: Colin, 1962.

Roger, Philippe; *L'Ennemi Américain*. Paris: Seuil, 2002.

Schmidt, Vivien A.; Economic Policy, Political Discourse, and Democracy in France, *French Politics and Society*, 15 (2), Spring, 1997.

Schmidt, Vivien A.; La France entre l'Europe et le monde. Le cas des politiques économiques nationales. *Revue Française de Science Politique*, 49 (1), February 1999.

Schütz, Alfred & Thomas Luckmann; *The Structures of the Life-World*. Vol. II. Evanston: NorthWestern University Press, 1989.

Servan-Schreiber, Jean-Jacques; *The American Challenge*. New York: Atheneum, 1968.

Smith, Anthony D.; Towards a Global Culture?, in David Held & Anthony McGrew (eds), *The Global Transformations Reader*. Cambridge: Polity Press, 2000.

Smith, Anthony D.; *The Ethnic Origins of Nations*. Oxford: Blackwell. 1986.

Søderberg, Anne-Marie and Anette Villemoes; *Undervejs. Sprog, Kultur og Kommunikation i den Erhvervssproglige Medarbejders Perspektiv.* Copenhagen: Samfundslitteratur, 1994.

Søderberg, Anne-Marie; Do National Cultures always make a Difference? Theoretical Considerations and Empirical Findings related to a Series of Case Studies of Foreign Acquisitions of Danish Companies, in T. Vestergaard, (ed.): *Language, Culture and Identity.* Aalborg: Aalborg University Press, 1999.

Stråth, Bo (ed); *Myth and Memory in the Construction of Community.* Brussels: P.I.E.-Peter Lang, 2000.

Toinet, Marie-France, Denis Lacorne and Jacques Rupnik (eds); *L'Amérique dans les Têtes : Un Siècle de Fascinations et d'Aversions.* Paris: Hachette, 1986.

Védrine, Hubert & Dominique Moïsi; *Les Cartes de la France à l'Heure de la Mondialisation.* Paris: Fayard, 2000.

Weber, Henri; *Le Parti des Patrons.* Paris: Seuil, 1991.

Winock, Michel; *La France Politique.* Paris: Seuil. 1999

Winock, Michel; *Nationalisme, Antisémitisme et Fascisme en France.* Paris: Seuil, 1982.

Woronoff, D. *Histoire de l'Industrie en France du XVIe Siècle à Nos Jours.* Paris: Seuil, 1998 [1994].

Zølner, Mette; Cultural Change and Continuity: The Case of French E-managers, *Sociale Wetenschappen*, 2002(b), 45 (2).

Mette Zølner

Zølner, Mette; French E-Managers: A Generation in the Making. *French, Politics, Culture and Society*, 20 (3), 2002(a).

Zølner, Mette; *Re-Imagining the Nation: Debates on Immigrants, Identities and Memories*. Brussels: P.I.E – Peter Lang, 2000.

Notes

[1] This debate is illustrated by numerous essays written by journalists and academics (such as Desportes & Mauduit, 1999; Forrester, 1996 & 2000; Izraelewicz, 1999, Jacquard, 1995; Minc, 1997, Passet, 2000) as well as by chronicles and speeches given by politicians. To be added is also the strength of anti-globalisation movements, such as ATTAC, and the presence and popularity of a figure like José Bové.

[2] To be noted is that recent debates on immigration illustrate that the Catholic narrative may still be reactivated either as a counter-model or in a recomposed version onto which Republican aspects are grafted (Zølner, 2000).

[3] The roots of state-interventionism can, of course, be dated back to Colbert and, the view of economy serving national interests on the international scene reflects to a certain extent mercantilism. Yet, inscribed into the Republican narrative the state acts for the benefit of the sovereign people and Republican France represents a generous and universal message rather than promoting economic and political interests of an absolute king.

[4] Similar to the concept 'the significant Other' are the concepts 'the affective Other', 'the generalised Other' or simply a 'reference group'. Within the area of social psychology, a 'significant Other' signifies a heterogeneous social group whose imagined value systems, attitudes and/or behaviours constitute an important element in the studied object's external environment and therefore serve as a basis for action (Marcussen & Zølner, 2001). The significant Other may have different faces depending on the issue in question. For example, in French history, we can observe an immigrant 'Other', who were/are constituted by respectively Italian, Polish, Portuguese, North African and African workers (Noiriel, 1992; Zølner, 2000), but also an economic 'Other' incarnated by the United States (Winock, 1982; Kuisel, 1993).

[5] "La mondialisation est inévitable, elle est porteuse de progrès considérables, en termes de niveau de vie, en termes de progrès social, en termes de développement économique... mais la mondialisation, si l'on n'y prend pas garde, est porteuse également de dangers très lourds, comme l'exclusion, l'exclusion de certains pays et, l'exclusion, dans les pays, d'un nombre croissant d'hommes et de femmes... on est obligé à la fois de maîtriser et d'humaniser la mondialisation" (J. Chirac, European Parliament, 12 December 2000).

[6] "La mondialisation constitue la réalité dans laquelle nous évoluons. Mais cette réalité est ambivalente. Elle favorise la croissance globale, mais s'accompagne d'inégalités croissantes. Elle favorise la découverte de la diversité humaine, mais porte en elle le risque de l'uniformisation. Elle libère des énergies, mais

entraîne aussi des forces négatives qu'il faut maîtriser. Le sens de cette mondialisation dépendra de ce que nous en ferons... Elle suit un cours que nous devons maîtriser, pour en tirer les bénéfices et pour en prévenir les revers" (L. Jospin, "Maîtriser la mondialisation", Brazil, April, 2001).

[7] This narrative is expressed by the commonly used terms – a 'untamed/savage' (sauvage or débridée) versus a 'tamed/civilised' (maîtrisée or humanisée) globalisation.

[8] 'Oui, à l'économie de marché, non à la société de marché' (L. Jospin, op.cit.)

[9] "Nous pensons que le but de la société n'est pas de tout rendre marchand, mais de remettre les choses à leur place. Le marché est fait pour les produits et les services marchands, mais les valeurs forment l'essentiel de la société" (Conseil national de l'UDF, 27 November 1999).

[10] "Ne soyons pas naïfs : l'administration Reagan a financé, à travers un énorme déficit budgétaire, un secteur de haute technologie sans équivalent dans le monde. C'est au moyen de cette "rente technologique", acquise dans les années 80, que les Etats-Unis ont pu nourrir leur croissance dans les années 90 et sont aujourd'hui en position de coloniser le reste du monde (J.- P. Chévènement, quoted by L'Expansion, no 620, 27 April 2000).

[11] ... je refuse les excès que l'on voit dans les pays anglo-saxons, de la libéralisation, de la mondialisation... la France ne pouvait pas aller aussi loin dans ce que l'on appelle la libéralisation, la flexibilité, en quelque sorte la remise en cause des garanties et des acquis sociaux. Donc, je ne propose pas ce modèle-là, je vous l'ai dit" (President Jacques Chirac, 14 July, 1998).

[12] "Par formation, par tradition, les Français ne seraient pas faits pour un libéralisme qui, par nature, nous dit-on, correspond beaucoup mieux aux particularités historiques et sociologiques du monde anglo-saxon qu'aux nôtres. Il s'agit-là d'une idée reçue. Nous avons perdu de vue le rôle central joué par les auteurs libéraux français des 18ème et 19ème siècles dans la formation, la conceptualisation et la diffusion des idées libérales" (A. Madelein, quoted from 'La modernité de la pensée libérale', Spring 1999).

[13] "La mondialisation, c'est le monde... où l'éternelle répétition des mêmes formes, des mêmes rites de vie, des mêmes modes de pensée, des mêmes tics de langage et d'attitude, crée le désenchantement, suscite le sentiment d'une banalité universelle où le rêve de la beauté qui exprimait la personnalité de chacun n'a plus guère de part" (Balladur, 1999: 178).

[14] "Bien sûr, la mondialisation a bouleversé la conception et le rôle des États... comme elle estompe les frontières physiques et les souverainetés. Mais il revient à l'État d'organiser un environnement juridique, fiscal, social, intellectuel ou industriel qui favorise l'épanouissement des œuvres" (quote from

a speech inaugurating a conference on globalisation and languages "Trois espaces linguistiques face aux défis de la mondialisation", 20 March 2001).

[15] "Dans un monde inhumain, nous rêvons que la France soit le pays le plus humain. Dans un monde où trop souvent on laisse croire que la seule valeur est financière, nous voulons que la première valeur reconnue, protégée et honorée soit la valeur humaine.... La France humaine, c'est un projet pour les Français et cela parle aussi à notre Europe et à toute l'humanité" (F. Bayrou, *Conseil national de l'UDF*, 28 April, 2001).

[16] "Il y a plus de deux ans, des ministres latino-américains, sensibles à cette question, m'ont convaincu que le terme de "diversité culturelle", qui parle au monde entier, serait plus mobilisateur que celui d'"exception culturelle", trop défensif, même si c'est devenu chez nous un mot fétiche. Disons que la diversité est l'objectif, et l'exception, le moyen" (H. Védrine quoted by *L'Express*, 25 November 1999).

[17] "La mondialisation, si elle est riche de promesses, menace les identités culturelles nationales... Aujourd'hui, pour la France, être le moteur de la diversité culturelle dans le monde est sa façon, moderne, d'être fidèle à l'universalisme qui est le sien depuis 1789" (L. Jospin, quoted by *Le Monde*, 19 July, 2000).

[18] When asked to indicate who are the beneficiaries of the globalisation 55% designated multinational companies, 47% financial markets and 32% the United States (Sofres, 18 July 2001).

[19] Such as Bernard, in Ockrent & Séréni, 1998: 55; Lagardère, in ibid: 143; Mestrallet, in ibid: 226.

[20] Examples are: "Je le trouve moralement choquant que les Anglo-Saxons nous imposent des règles de gestion d'entreprise" (Bourguignon, in ibid: 75) - "Au lieu de la dictature du prolétariat, on aura le diktat de l'actionnariat anglo-saxon" (F. Pinault, in ibid: 250).

[21] Examples are: "Le capitalisme global, dont l'archétype est le capitalisme américain, s'imposera. Par contre, sur le plan social, le poids du passé est tellement fort qu'on ne peut pas aller vers un modèle simplement américain" (Richard, in ibid: 293) ; "Il est vrai que nous ne sommes pas des Anglo-Saxons, nous tenons beaucoup à une certaine cohésion sociale; cet aspect clan, au fond, est un peu latin, il y a presque là du client, au sens latin du terme (Bernard, in ibid: 52).

[22] One example is : "Le modèle européen... doit allier l'efficacité économique de type anglo-saxon sous peine d'échouer, et en même temps éviter les excès que l'on peut rencontrer outre-Atlantique, ces zones déshéritées, cette partie de la société abandonnée au bord du chemin" (Pinault, 1998: 244). Another is : "Je ne suis pas prêt, comme de nombreux autres dirigeants, je crois, à renoncer à de

nombreux aspects que nous a apportés le capitalisme anglo-saxon. Mais c'est vrai qu'il existe une dimension sociale qui fait partie de notre culture européenne et qui n'est pas prise en compte chez les Anglo-Saxons" (an anonymous CEO, quoted in *Le Monde*, 27 April, 2001).

[23] ... il y a incontestablement une manière très française caractérisée par l'attention plus forte qu'ailleurs portée à la dimension humaine et sociale, avec un sentiment de responsabilité plus aigu à l'égard des acteurs de l'entreprise. Il faut sauvegarder cette originalité par rapport à la méthode anglo-saxonne qui donne la priorité absolue à la réussite financière des propriétaires de l'affaire. Il est certain que quand une entreprise bascule dans le monde américain ou anglais, elle tend à perdre ses bases unionistes pour être plus un instrument de profit. Il me semble que la réussite du groupe doit pouvoir s'accompagner du maintien de ce regard particulier, à la française (E.-A. Seillère, in Ockrent & Séréni, 1998: 317).

[24] Also the employer's organisation for small and medium-sized companies, CGPME, opts for a moderate liberalism (Audition de D. Barbey, Secrétaire général de la Confédération Générale des Petite et Moyennes Entreprises et du patronat réel", in Rapport fait au nom de la commission d'enquête sur certaines pratiques et groupes nationaux et multinationaux industriels, de services et financiers et leurs conséquences sur l'emploi et l'aménagement du territoire, Assemblée National, 2 June 1999).

[25] "... le plus important défi aujourd'hui, notammment en Europe continentale, est de mener de pair efficacité économique et cohérence sociale..." The reason being the wish to ensure social cohesion and hereby a social climate of confidence without conflict (J.-L. Beffa, Ockrent & Séréni, p. 15).

[26] "Je souhaite, personnellement, le maintien d'un modèle culturel propre à l'Europe, où l'État gardera un rôle de régulateur inconnu aux Etats-Unis" (P. Richard, Ockrent & Séréni, 1998: 293)

[27] "Je ne suis pas partisan d'une réduction du rôle de l'État, je souhaite qu'il soit efficace. Le secteur privé n'a pas à se substituer au secteur d'État, le mécénat des entreprises n'a pas à remplacer l'État pour moderniser les musées nationaux' (J.-L. Beffa, Ockrent & Séréni, 1998: 24).

[28] One example is the CEO, Bernard Arnault, who writes in his book "Il s'agira de donner plus de sens à la vie des gens, en soutenant, par exemple, des causes humanitaires, ce qui permettrait, par ailleurs, de donner un sens à la consommation de certaines marques" (Arnault, 2000: 129-130).

3

The Representation of 'the Others'
as
Strategies of Symbolic Construction

PABLO R. CRISTOFFANINI

Introduction

A central problem concerning communication between people of different cultures is the representation of 'the 'Others' as different from 'us'. Many of these representations have a long history: they feed upon images created in the encounter between Europeans and non-Europeans – indigenous Americans, Asians, Africans, products of the expansion of European powers (in turn Spanish, Portuguese, English, and French) – and other continents. This history also covers the encounter of Anglo-Saxon Americans with people of other 'races', for example, Mexicans in the SouthWestern United States. When we speak of Others different from 'us' we are not referring exclusively to 'exotic' peoples, but rather in general to all those marked by their differences from a racial, sexual, social, national, or ethnic perspective.

Some frequently cited works in the field of intercultural communication in Denmark are based on the representation of the Other.[1] Although these representations are subjective constructions, they attempt to make us believe that they deal with the 'reality' of the Other, since the descriptions are supported by graphs, statistics, and computational models.[2] Nevertheless, they deal with ultra-simplifications based on the cultural values of researchers anchored specifically in Northern European culture, where methodological and critical separation are not applied. Mexicans, Venezuelans, and Chileans, for example, are represented as people who are distanced in relation to power (authoritarian), who have a great tendency to avoid uncertainty (control and hierarchies), and collectivists (not individualistic), and therefore not modern.[3] One must ask, with respect to whom are they collectivists, authoritarians and hierarchical? Who is the evaluating subject? The main problem with this sort of ultra-simplification, presented otherwise as a scientific one, is that the characteristics of certain groups are shown as the true nature of that nation's citizens.

Representations of Others that are more or less partial, distorted, selective, ultra-simplified, or deformed persist, at times, in spite of education, travel experiences, or information received from individual people. On a collective level, in certain social and economic circumstances (for example, in today's Europe with considerable immigration coming from Arab countries and Africa) sociopsychological scenarios appear in which negative representations of the Others become sharper, returning to the stigmatisation of entire groups because of their religious beliefs. Our beliefs and attitudes toward Others, the images that we emphasize, and the words that we use when referring to them have consequences and they are an important factor in our communication.

A current of cognitive sociology – to which Scandinavian experts in intercultural communication such as Øyvind Dahl[4] adhere – affirm that the selective and ultra-simplified representation of Others is necessary and inevitable as it is a product of the mental mechanisms found in the processing of stimuli. This perspective leaves us defenceless against partial, distorted and instrumental representations of the Others. For this reason it is necessary to examine some central suppositions and presuppositions as well as to confront the cognitive approach with alternative conceptions of this problem, such as those inspired by semiotics, rhetoric and social psychology, where not only the limitations, but also the possibilities of choice in the representation of the Others are realised. New research in social psychology and rhetoric has seriously questioned the cognitive comprehension of the thought process and representation and is sowing serious doubts about the inevitability of prejudice and stereotypes in the process. If these *figures of representation* cannot be attributed to a 'cognitive iron cage' (in the sense that we are talking about psychological mechanisms from which we cannot escape) how can we explain the fact that the majority of the representations of the 'Others as different from Us' might be negatively or positively exaggerated? To answer this question I think that it is necessary to see the attitudes, beliefs, prejudices, and stereotypes in the broadest context as tied to ideologies. Symbolic constructions permit us to learn, evaluate, or communicate a reality. Often, this occurs as ideological creations and arguments, in other words, helping to legitimise dominance, exploitation and inequality.

These are some of the reasons for the persistence of stereotyping and prejudice. There are also reasons of a psychological nature, such as our fascination with exotic peoples.

Representation and meaning

Representation is narrowly tied to meaning. In effect, we give sense and meaning to things through usage: that which we say, think, and feel about them. On the other hand, we give meaning to events, people, and objects by means of interpretive maps in which we place ourselves. Therefore, our evaluation of these people, events, and objects may be very different, although we may be referring to the same 'reality'. Yet, we also give meaning to things, people, and objects through the manner in which we represent them, the feelings that we associate with them, the images that we use, and the stories that we tell. In order to represent these things, people, and objects we make use of signs, i.e. words, sounds, or images that replace a concept or something in reality with something else.

Culture deals precisely with the production and exchange of meanings and that is why we can say that the members of one culture tend to see the world in a similar manner, which does not mean that a culture must necessarily be unitary. We must recall that Nero and Seneca were members of the same culture as Pinochet and Allende. In fact, in any culture there is more than one meaning associated with people, events, and objects; moreover – and this is important – that significance is contested.[5] The way in which we categorize the world and the significance we give to things influence our behavior. Therefore, those who are interested in influencing our behavior fight to make their meanings dominant. Thus, culture is not only a matter of ideas and concepts, but rather also a matter of feelings. Jews under Nazism experienced this after the Nazis succeeded in giving a specific significance to the word 'Jew'.

Meaning is also tied to identity in the sense that the demarcations made by the culture to which we pertain allow us to distinguish between those who are 'within' and those who are 'outside'. Representations of personal identity and national culture also perform in this sense since we can know what it means to be Danish, Mexican, or

Spanish just by the representations that have been made of Danish-ness, Mexican-ness, or Spanish-ness.

As I have indicated, we represent with the help of semiotic systems, which stand for our concepts, ideas, and feelings. For this reason, in the current study of the question of the mimesis or representation of the Other, the semiotics of theory, concepts, and methods constitutes a principal discipline.[6] Another central approximation involves theories of discourse. I understand discourse as a form of talking about a topic and the images, ideas, and practices associated with it.

From stereotypes as necessary and inevitable to stereotypes as ideology and fascination

Stereotypes and prejudice
The study of representation is not exhausted. Nevertheless, it is the problem that concerns me here. The relationship between representations and behavior is neither direct nor simple. Two Danish businessmen, for example, might share a similar representation of Muslims, but one of them, in spite of this, and for reasons of profit, might decide to employ workers of the same ethnic group, while the other, because of the strong feelings of aversion that his representation provokes in him, does not do it, despite possible losses. On the other hand, there is no doubt that there is a graduation from less to more violence in our behavior toward negatively represented Others. This graduation ranges from speaking badly about someone to, at the other extreme, torture and extermination.

Representations are tied to beliefs and attitudes. Because of this, it is reasonable to turn our attention to social psychology which, through studies of stereotypes and prejudice, offers us some explanations as to how and why distorted or generalised images of groups and individuals – and the attitudes and behaviors tied to them – persist and resist change.

One of the methods of clarifying the question of negative representations and attitudes is through the cognitive process. This approximation has been based in great measure on the ideas of Gordon W. Allport, developed in his classic work, *The Nature of Prejudice* (1954).

The context for Allport's ideas come from his lived experience of World War II and subsequent efforts to avoid a similar catastrophe. Researchers' efforts are focused on how to better human relationships. On the one hand, technical and scientific conquests and dominance over nature were indeed impressive, confirms Allport. But, from the point of view of human relations, the situation was quite different. His description of the animosity between Muslims and non-Muslims, of the situation of the Jews and the refugees that arrived in inhospitable countries are disturbingly similar to the current situation. The experience of World War II and the tragedy of the Jews led him to search for the roots of prejudice, which are seen as an obstacle to human relationships and an impediment to the development of human abilities. What is prejudice? asks Allport, offering various definitions, including: 'Thinking ill of others without sufficient warrant', with 'thinking ill' understood as both feelings of rejection and hostile behavior. Allport distinguishes between prior judgment with a sound basis, and prejudice. Thus, the negative representation and feelings of rejection toward the Nazi leadership by the great majority of the North American population, according to him, did not constitute prejudice as they had a solid knowledge of the theory and practice of the Nazi leaders.

Prejudice is also described as a hostile attitude and shunning of a person because he belongs to a group with criticisable characteristics. The 'erroneous' and 'inflexible' character of the representations contained in prejudice are emphasized in all of these definitions. The definition of prejudice from the *Oxford Dictionary* summarises the essence of the different definitions presented by Allport:

> Dislike or distrust of a person, group, custom, etc. that is based on fear or false information rather than on reason or experience, and that influences one's attitude and behaviour towards them. (Oxford: 909)

Where does prejudice come from? According to Allport, certain mental characteristics and aspects of human nature such as the tendency to generalise and hostility, which, to a lesser extent, causes us to group ourselves with people of our own ethnic group. The process of categorisation is fundamental to the formation of prejudice and stereotypes: we think with the help of categories and in the process a) the mind forms groups and classes to guide our daily actions; b) it assimilates as much as possible from each group; c) the categories allow us to quickly identify an object; d) we call the purely intellectual categories concepts, but generally the concepts are added to a feeling, for example 'School, I like school'; e) categories can be more or less rational, the former are based on a nucleus of truth; the latter are not. A fundamental aspect of the prejudice-category relationship, from the perspective of the consequences that it has had for the concepts just mentioned, is Allport's idea that categorisation carries with it an erroneous simplification:

> Man has a propensity to prejudice. This propensity lies in his normal and natural tendency to form generalisations, concepts, categories, whose content represents an oversimplification of his world of experience.[7]

Allport's conception about stereotypes was ambivalent. Influenced by Adorno, he distinguished from the outset between category and stereotypes. Thus, for example, *black* is the category, and stereotypes are the images that add a bias to the category: musical, good runners, sexually well-endowed, rhythmic, etc. However, he later underlined the idea that categorisation implied generalisation and distortion and that this was the basis of prejudice and stereotypes. This last idea impregnated all cognitive psychology that has seen categorisation as a cardinal cognitive process that allows us to structure and give coherence to our knowledge of reality and to the social world. In this approximation, from a biological perspective, categorisation implies distortion and simplification. Just like other living creatures, human beings organize the world on the basis of stimuli from various perspectives – edible/inedible, dangerous/not dangerous, etc.

This rationale leads to some scholars' assertion about the need for stereotypes. Effectively, if categorisation is a function of thought and if all categorisation implies generalisation, the stereotype is an inevitable derivation of the same function of thought.

Dahl, a Scandinavian expert in intercultural communication, arrives at similar conclusions in *'The Uses of Stereotypes in Intercultural Communication'*, where he affirms that the predictions we make about Others (foreigners) will inexorably be based on stereotypes and that this is a necessary and inevitable process. Furthermore:

> We must recognize that we cannot communicate with people from our own or another culture (or talk about them) without stereotypes (Dahl, 1995: 17).

The same concept of the stereotype, based on suppositions about how thought functions, runs the risk of converting itself into a legitimisation of them. Not only this, but also the study of stereotypes and representations of the Others loses interest and leaves us impotent in the face of racism, xenophobia, and sexual discrimination. So in effect, if stereotypes are an inevitable product of universal cognitive mechanisms and therefore necessary and inevitable, they have no importance other than that of being an illustration of how cognition functions and, even worse, they cannot be changed, questioned or countered. Nevertheless, we know that representations of Others are modified (Jews, blacks, Arabs, women, homosexuals, Russians) to different degrees from society to society, and at different rates, but one thing remains certain: they change. Stereotypes not only change, but at times certain representations of them disappear as a result of historical context: they are politically specific and are discerned in a new way, i.e. European Jews post WWII versus today's European Jews.

In addition, this manner of understanding stereotypes is rather boring if we do not consider – in light of the supposed universal character of cognitive mechanisms – the historical and cultural contexts that mold and contribute to the development of stereotypes.

Criticism of the concepts that see prejudice and stereotypes as a derivative of a so-called *iron cage* built by universal laws of cognition have made the social, historical, and collective sides of the figures of representation of the Others visible.

From the outset, it is important to note the essential difference between the processing of stimuli by human beings and by other living beings. The peculiarity of human beings resides precisely in the fact that their access to the world depends on hugely complex symbolic and semiotic systems, depending on how one understands the concepts of sign and symbol.[8]

Categorisations of human beings are made principally through a key semiotic system: language. Language allows us to represent people, groups, and happenings in simplified or enriched forms, in prejudiced or tolerant ways. Language can be used to group details and to generalise, particularize or argue special cases.

For these reasons, authors such as Michael Billig (1985) have suggested that instead of applying the bureaucratic model which uses categorisation to make things malleable and predictable, it is much more appropriate to see this process from the perspective of rhetorical metaphor: i.e. the individual can argue, critique, and persuade. Thus, even racists and fascists often argue their points of view in a complicated manner.[9]

Authors such as Dahl equate the concept of category with that of stereotype; whilst for others, the processes of thought and communication are made possible thorugh categories. But, as Allport indicates, category and stereotype are not the same. Categories are necessary to understand 'reality', to create order, but they are flexible and they change. It might suffice to simply remember which categories are used to recognize social groups in a determined society today compared to fifty or three hundred years ago. On the other hand, stereotypes apparently give us a feeling of order and security, but are inflexible and try to cement one particular meaning over others.

When we think and communicate we are not only using categories but we are also making distinctions among them, observing generalities and discussing concrete cases. We see collective attributes and individual ways of being (Pickering, 2001). The same categories are elastic, as concepts like 'democracy' and 'violence' demonstrate.[10] Moreover, if categorisation is a necessary element of thought, then communication is also particularisation. The former cannot exist without the latter.[11]

Stereotypes constitute an inadequate way of representing Others. First, because they isolate certain aspects, behaviors and inclinations, which are removed from their historical and cultural context and attributed to all the individuals in a social group. Second, they ignore or put a slant on certain central aspects of the identity of victims of stereotyping, or on their culture and social life. Finally, they 'cement' representations of Others, impeding alternative ways of seeing and understanding them. In this process, the press plays a central role in contemporary Western societies. It represents metonymically certain ethnic groups, demonizes them, contributes to their marginalisation, and ignores others. Finally, we can add that stereotypes about an ethnic group can be contradictory, as illustrated in the following paragraph by Argentine writer and essayist Ernesto Sábato about Jews and anti-Semites:

Nevertheless, and violating the principle of contradiction, a basis for Aristotelian logic, the anti-Semite will say successively – and yet simultaneously – that the Jew is a banker and a Bolshevik, greedy and squandering, limited to his ghetto and with a finger in every pie. It is apparent that in these conditions Jews have no escape: whatever he says, does, or thinks will fall under the jurisdiction of anti-Semitism. It doesn't matter if he is generous or miserly, dirty or clean, elegant or unkempt, shy or bold, religious or atheist (Sábato 1991: 30-31).

This underlines that the key to stereotypes as a form of representation is not the 'reality' of the image of the person or group, but rather in how the aversion is justified.

We represent Others using language or images, which give us the means to represent in ways that can be generalised or particularized, prejudiced or tolerant, rigid or flexible.

If we are not obliged by strict laws of cognition to choose the first category of these opposites, the question arises as to why groups within a nation or group of nations adhere to partial, rigid, metonymic representations of Others.

Ideology and symbolic constructions

Representations of Others can be seen as ideologies. Because this concept has many meanings, it is necessary to define it in order to make it operative. Two main ways of understanding ideology may be discerned.[12] One is the non-evaluative conception, represented by, among others, Mannheim and Clifford Geertz. This defines ideology as beliefs and ideas, or as symbolic systems.

Therefore, from the perspective of anthropology, Clifford Geertz has thought of ideology as cultural schemes that attempt to offer us orientation *vis-à-vis* a problematic reality. Geertz (1973: 216) states that:

Culture patterns 'religious, philosophical, aesthetic, scientific, ideological' are 'programs'; they provide a template or blueprint for the organisation of social and psychological processes, much as genetic systems provide such a template for the organisation of organic processes.

A further contribution of Geertz is that he highlights the rhetorical character of ideology. Ideologies, according to him, move away from the moderate language of science and utilize figures of speech such as metaphors, metonymy, and hyperbole. Here we can recall, for instance, the metaphor of Muslims in Denmark as 'invaders', or the metonymy of the Muslim as a macho religious fanatic, or hyperbolic images of them as rapists and bloodthirsty.

The second key way of conceptualising ideology is as an illusion, a deceit, a distortion or a falsehood. This is an idea already contained in Marx and developed by many authors inspired by him. Here I will limit myself to presenting a few studies that examine ideology from this angle.

From a semiotic perspective, Ronald Barthes (1999 and 1971) developed the idea of various levels of meaning.[13] It is said that a sign can, on a second level, comprise itself in the meaning of a new sign derived from the first. This idea of new levels of meaning is important, because it allows understanding of mythologies of modernity and (why not?) of post modernity. Barthes' intuition can be illustrated with the example of the car or automobile that on the first level means a self-propelled vehicle used to travel, and on the second (depending on the type of car), it can mean prestige, wealth, youth, sportiness, good taste, etc. On the third level, and in certain social contexts, it can be associated with the idea of technical sophistication, comfort, speed, saving time, the ability to travel in diverse terrain, protection and comfort that permit one to become independent of rain and wind (control over nature), etc. We enter directly here into the *mythology of modernity*. The themes, plots, and characters of the ancient myths open the road and manage to express themselves as events and spectator sports, in film or in literature: the good and the bad, 'Us' and 'Them', David versus Goliath, the just sacrificed, nature against man, etc.

Concepts can also convert themselves into myths. Therefore, childhood has been seen as a depository for innocence, uncorrupt, uncontaminated and good only in modern times (Danesi and Perron, 1999). Modern mythologies can therefore be connected with ancient symbols filled with meaning.

Another vision of ideology is that of the semiotician and writer Umberto Eco (1977). For Eco, ideology is a partial and unconnected vision of the world that is characterized by concealing alternative meanings and relationships through one's choice of words and argumentation, which do not take account of the complexity and at times contradictory character of semantic fields. Eco offers the example of the maximum adjective in relation to a mechanical apparatus and the calculations of /pressure/ /heating/ and /production/. While a maximum has positive connotations in the calculations of 2 and 3, it has a negative connotation in 1 = danger. An ideological reasoning in which heating and production are the supreme values and equated with general happiness, conceals the ultimate meaning, and with it, the incompatibility between these values and general security.

Thompson's (1990: 59) approximation is within the same perspective, but with a clearly different nuance that highlights situations in which ideology is united with power so that concepts, ideas and beliefs are used to establish and sustain dominance. Dominance exists when we find ourselves faced with a systematic asymmetry of groups and individuals in relationship to power:

> When particular agents are endowed with power in a durable way which excludes, and to some significant degree remains inaccessible to, other agents or groups of agents, irrespective of the basis upon which such exclusion is carried out.

It is important to point out that dominance does not limit itself – as the Marxist tradition tends to – to relationships between classes. It goes much further, and includes, in the world in which we live, relationships between the sexes, between ethnic majorities and minorities, between nations, etc.

Ideology can also operate in five additional ways to strategies tied to symbolic construction. These, with certain adjustments and interpretations, seem to me to be adequate to analyze the question of the representation of Others.

Before discussing these, I would like to point out two important aspects of ideology in Thompson's approach. One is the special role of ideologies in modern and secularized society as substitutes for myths and religion, which used to give sense to social organisation and life in pre-industrialised societies.[14] The other is the importance of the press in the diffusion of these ideologies. The impact of ideas, stories, and images in societies with newspapers, radio, television, and film, is immense and regarding the questions at hand, it is obvious that the representations of other ethnic groups in the press, television, and film are of decisive importance.

Any domination, as indicated by Max Weber, needs *legitimisation* in order to be stable; in other it needs words, ideas and images that make the domination acceptable and valid. A legitimising ideology can be validated by the symbolic construction of strategies such as: a) *rationalisation*, or reasonings that justify determined social relations and institutions and that present them as worthy of support; b) *universalisation*, that is, the interests of an institution, group, or nation are presented as the best and most advantageous for all other individuals, nations, etc.; c) *narrativisation*, which includes the stories, legends, and myths associated with a timeless past and ideal that confers unity and cohesion upon a nation or ethnic group despite social, economic, situational differences, etc.

Pablo R. Cristoffanini

Another function of ideology that makes it possible to establish and maintain dominant relationships is dissimulation, which operates through denying and concealing these relationships. The strategies of symbolic construction tied to this method are: a) *displacement*, when a term that is typically used to refer to a person or object is employed to refer to another, moving toward positive or negative connotations, from one to the other: for example, 'the allies' to refer to the United States and England in the war against Iraq; b) *euphemism*, the selective representation of relationships of power with the goal of obtaining a positive evaluation, as when the torture, execution and exile of political opponents is termed the 'restoration of law and order', or concentration camps are termed 'rehabilitation centres'; c) *tropes* (metonymy and metaphor): metonymy in which the veil represents all women who come from nations where the religion is Islam; or metaphor when for instance immigration is referred to as 'the Muslim invasion'.

A third mode of operation is *unification*, which attempts to elude differences in economic, social or other types of power by building a symbolic unity, for example, speaking a determined language or being a member of a national Church.

A fourth mode is *fragmentation*, which operates by emphasising the differences between groups and people and obviating the similarities. The supposed differences that stand out can refer to attitudes, beliefs, or appearance. In extreme cases, one can arrive at the elimination of the different Others: 'the eradication of the Marxist cancer' (Constable and Valenzuela 1991: 47).[15]

A fifth mode is reification, which, following Thompson (1990: 65), allows that:

> Relations of domination may be established and sustained by representing a transitory, historical state of affairs as if it were permanent, natural, outside the time. Processes are portrayed as things or as events of a quasi-natural kind, in such a way that their social and historical character is eclipsed.

Reification works through the *naturalisation* of certain situations that are the product of historical, social, and cultural factors, which are presented as the result of inherent characteristics. Dominance over women, for example, has been supported by the idea that the psychological and biological characteristics of women have made them suitable only for certain professions and jobs, excluding them from others.

Another strategy is *eternalisation*. Relationships of power in certain societies cause certain sectors to see their superior identity confirmed by eternalising messages such as 'things have always been this way'. This is the case of tea advertisements that show the pride and the magnificence of the Empire. Or tourist brochures that offer an exotic 'Other' as a perpetual theatrical backdrop against which the lives of white tourists can be represented (Ferguson, 1998: 53).

Anglo-Saxonism and the American representation of Mexicans

If we examine strategies of symbolic construction we can observe that the form in which we represent Others has been and is utilized to legitimize the oppression of certain groups to the detriment of others. Thus, the legitimisation of the expansion of the United States by means of the strategies of *rationalisation* and *universalisation* has its roots in Biblical motives about (white Protestant) man's right to subjugate and exploit nature (Pike, 1992).[16] The English Puritans that conquered and colonized North America understood themselves to be the personification of civilisation and regarded uncultivated nature with suspicion and contempt. They associated the chaos and disarray that they were observing in nature as work of the devil as well as his dwelling place. Dominance over nature was a metaphor for the internal conquest of their passions and desires.

This illustration, with its emphasis on material progress as well as the rationale that demanded control over nature, was later united with the religious legitimisation of this conquest and dominance, and had Darwinist motives. The domestication of nature was seen as a 'heroic war'. The mission of the white man was to better and correct nature, eradicate evil, and promote good among living beings. The racial motive emerged, and a series of legitimising oppositions were established by the Puritan colonial mission:

Pablo R. Cristoffanini

Table 3:1

Civilisation

Progress	Primitivism
Christianity	Paganism
Whites (Protestants)	Redskins and blacks
Light	Shadow
Good	Evil

Nature

In the same way that the Americans understood themselves as the personification of civilisation, they saw indigenous peoples as the personification of uncultivated nature. Virtue and its fruits – private property and economic greatness – depended on the continual and systematic exploitation of nature. Indigenous Americans had, according to the Puritan colonizers, been incapable of exploiting natural resources. Doing this and imposing civilisation were a divine mandate that legitimised the appropriation of indigenous property.

The American expansion to the West and South was justified by their belief in the superiority of their civilisation and the right to subdue nature and groups seen as slaves of nature: women, Indians, blacks, Latin Americans. Many of the stereotypes and mythologies about Indians and blacks were later attributed to the inhabitants of the other America, largely populated by people of color, who were considered effeminate for being closer to nature. Likewise, women were considered people of feelings rather than reason since they adhered to a religion that celebrated feminine mysticism as opposed to rational, intellectual explanation, purportedly causing them to lack self-control and tend towards submission, etc.

A clear example of how representations of Others can be tied to ideologies is the *Anglo-Saxonising* of the United States in the 1830s and 1840s.[17] This ideology came from the encounters and conflicts between Americans and Mexicans in the American Southwest in connection with the rebellion of Texas and the Mexican-American War. From the first encounters and conflicts it became clear that American and Mexican interests were not the same and that the imposition of American interests would entail suffering for the Mexicans. Americans were also anxiously looking for explanatory models for their apparent success as well as the apparent failure of Spanish-speaking America. The explanation for this failure as well as the legitimisation of the suffering inflicted on the Mexicans are achieved through the creation of a series of beliefs about their racial inferiority and about a mythology surrounding the supposed virtues of the Anglo-Saxon 'race'. It was much easier to attribute the plundering of the Mexicans and their suffering to their racial inferiority than to accept that it could be the result of the merciless search of power and wealth on the part of the Americans.

In the descriptions of Mexicans by Americans in the above-mentioned contexts, one of the factors that stands out the most as representative of inferiority is the *mestizo* character of the Mexican 'race', in which one finds, according to American commentators, all the 'poisonous' combinations possible of colour and blood. Another motive for criticism was of the heterogeneous character of the Mexicans that 'speak more than twenty languages' (Horsman 1981: 215-216).[18]

Mexicans are depicted as people that consistently try to do things with the least physical and mental effort possible, as 'uncivilized', scarcely above the masses of barbarians that surround them. They are associated with adjectives such as: lazy, dirty, ignorant, dishonest, and cruel (Horsman, 1981: 213).

The dehumanisation of the Mexicans made their plundering and abuse acceptable. Snatching land from them was not a crime, but rather a fulfilment of the divine mandate to make it fruitful.[19] The destiny of the Americans was to populate the continent with industrious Anglo-Saxons, cultivate it, and expand civilisation. Facing the Anglo-Saxon push, the other races that populated the continent vanished (a euphemism for extermination), just as the North American Indians had. A *narrativisation* arose praising the virtues of the Anglo-Saxon race as chivalrous, expansionist lovers of liberty. This ideology should be understood in the context of economic depression and the increase of German and Irish immigration, which created insecurity that Americans tried to alleviate through a racial mythologisation and accompanying attempt to generate feelings of solidarity.

The expansionism of England and the United States was seen as a realisation of the destiny of the Anglo-Saxon race to spread liberty and commerce to the most remote regions of the planet for the good (*universalisation*) of the whole world. Therefore, when England attacked China during the opium war, the aggression was celebrated in the *New York Herald* with the following lines:

Another movement of the Anglo-Saxon spirit in the remotest East, against the barriers of semi-barbarians and a half-civilized race, who have been stationary for twenty centuries or more (Horsman, 1981: 208).

Pablo R. Cristoffanini

The ambiguous representation: rejection and fascination

Up to this point I have outlined the more negative representations of Others. Nevertheless, we can confirm that through travel writing, literature, paintings, film, music and dance styles, pro-Indian movements and so on, the exotic and primitive Others have exercised and continue to evoke a sense of fascination in Europeans and Americans. The fascination for the non-Western Other has a long history and has been termed *exoticism*. In this form of representation, Others are supposedly trustees of virtues and qualities that we lack. However, this is not necessarily the case. For example, in the 'exotic' representation, the Other is utilized as allegory to criticise aspects of society that the subject it represents wants to transform. In this manner, American Indians or other primitive peoples were portrayed as the antithesis of the deficiencies and vices of Western society that they sought to criticize: among the (good) savages there was no private property (seen much before Marx as a principal cause of the evils of European society), no social hierarchies or subordination – but there was sexual liberty (Todorov 1993: 208).

In these and other ways of representing the Other, there was no interest in getting to know them more closely, or to find out what they thought about, felt, or longed for. This attitude is expressed in travel and experiential narratives where the narrator is a white European or American male who tells of his relationships with exotic women and countries. The exotic woman is doubly Other: exterior and strange because of her sex, and furthermore (from the perspective of the white, Western male), because of her race. The motives behind the desire for a relationship with the exotic woman are varied, but one of them in the past and in the present has been that of giving flavor and colour to a life considered boring and insipid by Western societies. Thus, the French naval officer Pierre Loti, who published books in the 1870s that were half fiction and half travel narrative, wrote: 'I have come to the conclusion that I have the right to do as I please, and that this insipid banquet of life requires all the spice that one can lend it' (Todorov, 1993: 352). And more recently, bell hooks (1992: 21) affirmed:

> The commodification of otherness has been so successful because it is offered as a new delight, more intense, more satisfying than normal ways of doing and feeling. Within commodity culture, ethnicity becomes spice, seasoning that can liven up the dull dish that is mainstream white culture.

In Loti's works the capacity of giving oneself over to actual sexual pleasure is attributed to the black woman, a product of a natural sensuality associated with a closeness to animals. In general, in order to represent people of other races (black, and yellow in the vocabulary of the time period), animal-like images recur, e.g. the Japanese are compared to monkeys (Todorov, 1993: 313).

Loti not only wrote exotic narratives, but was also interested in the opposite case, that is, that the European citizen of a European colonial power who sees himself obliged to remain in the colony when he longs to return to his home country. So the figures are inverted from exoticism (the Others and the Other are the best) to nationalism (those which are ours and that which is ours is the best): xenophilia transformed into xenophobia. Apparently a paradox, but as Todorov writes, the common theme in both cases is that Others are seen and treated as objects, as are their national nature and culture. The only subject is the white man. There is only interest in what he feels, experiences, and thinks; the Others are simply objects and statistics. Here we must emphasise the representations that Loti presents of Turks, Senegalese, Tahitians, and Japanese, who were tied to a situation of dominance: that of French colonialism.

One of the current expressions of this fascination with primitive and/or exotic[20] Others is expressed as *nostalgia* for their ways of life, cultures, and traditions that the expansion of Western economies has destroyed. Consider films about the redskins made by Americans, such as *Dances with Wolves*. For some members of white, Western, hegemonic culture, the body of the Other of color would still be the trustee of the *primitive spirit*.

The current desire for the Other of color then also has to do with projecting ideas of plentitude, exuberance and corpororeality onto him/her which we lack. As with ancient religious ceremonies, the Other is devoured to take possession of their virtues and spirit:

Today, one wants to sexually possess the Other not only for the pleasure of the act, but also because of the belief that this will bring with it a transformation (hooks, 1992: 23).

It is indubitable that the nostalgia for the desire for the different Other is commercialised, as seen with cigarettes such as *Ducados* with round-bodied, soft, sensual, young black women as a metaphor for the cigarette. Or how the nostalgia of romanticism, erotic longing and corporal plasticity have been used to promote the group *Buena Vista So-*

cial Club. (Valerio-Holguín, 2000: 79-86).[21] Commercialisation is justly criticised, because it implies utilisation, dehistorisation, and de-politicisation and contributes to maintain, unquestioned, racial hegemony and white, Western culture. For example, the production of cultural objects related to the phenomenon of *Buena Vista Social Club* (compact discs, video, DVD, photo book) has brought the flavor of Cuban music to the European public, but without references to social and political contexts: that of the musicians in their youth and that of Cuban music today. The incorporation of these contexts carries with it a critical reflection that is lost in the mere tasting of cultural morsels.

Conclusions

Stereotypes and prejudice as forms of representing Others are not as simple and innocent as the theories currently in vogue in the field of intercultural communication might suggest. The research of academics like Michael Billig and Michael Pickering show the need to distinguish between categories (necessary to understand and order the world) and stereotypes as figures of representation that are inadequate because of their inflexibility, tendency to cement a meaning, dehistorisation, and the way that important traits of stereotyped groups are concealed.

One of the causes of the persistence of stereotypes and prejudice, in spite of better information and apparently better education, is that they are useful in constructing a positive self-image in the groups that regard Others with disdain through the use of stereotypes and prejudice.

Another perhaps even more important factor is the negative representation of Others which has been and remains tied to ideologies. These representations of Others can be seen as strategies of symbolic construction that share the rhetorical style of ideologies and that, upon representing Others, utilise figures such as metonymy, metaphor, hyperbole, euphemism and displacement. Ideologies legitimise the dominance of one group over another, and lead to discrimination, inequality, and that scandalous word of our postmodern times: exploitation. Innumerable cases in the relationships between men and women, ethnic groups and even nations can illustrate the role of these ideologies. In this chapter, I have tried to demonstrate how ideology, Anglo-Saxonism and negative representations of Mexicans tied to this ideology were justified, making acceptable the appropriation of half of the Mexican territory by the United States as well as the suffering of Mexicans derived from this act of expansion. Representations of

Mexicans and, in fact, of Latin Americans in general (the authors studied maintain that Americans tend to see Latin Americans based on the image that they have of Mexicans) evident in that time period have lasted. This is not difficult to confirm based on the innumerable American films in which Latin Americans are represented as ignorant, dirty, corrupt, violent, superstitious, inefficient, cruel, etc. We will have to examine how these representations have been used to sanction American intervention with the aim of establishing regimes that insure the economic and geopolitical dominance of the United States in the region.

At the other extreme, we find representations of Others that are, apparently, markedly positive. In these, the culture or the body of the Others is depicted as in harmony with nature. In this last case, the Others have been or are instrumentalised with a utopian end: the non-existence of private property or the absence of social hierarchies and sexual restrictions. In more recent times, the Others are represented as in harmony with nature. But how these exotic Others live, think, feel, and desire or the nature of their institutions and history is of little importance.

The need to give colour and flavour to life in programmed, disillusioned societies where instrumental knowledge is appropriated from the public and private spheres, carried a desire for a more harmonious contact with the body and nature that stemmed from a longing for romanticism, eroticism or magic that is projected upon the exotic Others that are imagined as trustees of a great need to enjoy, dance, rhythm, passion, feelings, etc. The body and culture of the exotic Others are utilized to satisfy these deeply-felt feelings. They are commercialised, dehistorised, depoliticised, and converted into objects. The latter is what gives meaning to the apparent contradiction of negative and positive representations. When the Others have been reduced to objects, it is secondary that they are denigrated or exalted in the process: the important thing is that they are stripped of their condition as integral human beings. The unique feelings, emotions, thoughts, and life experiences that count are those of the ones that have the power to make their representations the dominant ones.

Pablo R. Cristoffanini

References

Allport, Gordon W; *The Nature of Prejudice*. Cambridge, Massachusetts: Addison-Wesley Publishing Company, 1954.

Barthes, Roland; *Elementos de semiología*. Madrid: Comunicación, 1971.

Barthes, Roland; *Mitologías*. Madrid: Siglo Veintiuno, 1999.

Billig, Michael; "Prejudice, categorisation and particularisation: from a perceptual to a rhetorical approach". *European Journal of Social Psychology,* Vol. 15, 79-103, 1985.

Billig, Michael; *Arguing and thinking. A rhetorical approach to social psychology*. Cambridge: Cambridge University Press, 1996.

Cassirer, Ernst; *Las ciencias de la cultura*. México: Fondo de Cultura Económica, 1982.

Cassirer, Ernst; *Esencia y efecto del concepto de símbolo*. México: Fondo de Cultura Económica, 1989.

Cobley, Paul; *The Communication Theory Reader*. London: Routledge, 1996.

Constable, Pamela & Valenzuela, Arturo; *A Nation of Enemies. Chile Under Pinochet*. London: W.W. Norton & Company, 1991.

Dahl, Øyvind; "The Use of Stereotypes in Intercultural Comunication". In: "Essays on Culture and Communication" (edited by Torben Vestergaard). *Language and Culture Contact 10*. 1995.

Danesi, Marce & Perron, Poul; *Analyzing Cultures. An Introduction and Handbook*. Bloomington, Indiana: Indiana University Press, 1999.

Eco, Umberto; *Tratado de semiótica general*. Barcelona: Lumen, 1997.

Ferguson, Robert; *Representing 'Race'. Ideology, identity and the media*. London: Arnold, 1998.

Geertz, Clifford; *The Interpretation of Cultures.* New York: BasicBooks, Harper Collins Publishers, 1973.

Gilman, Sander; *Inscribing the Other.* London: University of Nebraska Press, 1991.

Gottdiener, Mark; *Postmodern Semiotics. Material Culture and the Forms of Postmodern Life.* Oxford: Basil Blackwell, 1995.

Gustafsson, Jan; *El Salvaje y nosotros. Signos del latinoamericano: Una hermenéutica del otro.* Frederiksberg: Institut for Fransk, Italiensk og Russisk. Handelshøjskolen i København, 2000.

Hall, Stuart (ed.); *Cultural Representations and Signifying Practices.* London: Sage Publications, 1997.

Halperin, Donghi Tulio; *Historia Contemporánea de América Latina.* Madrid: Alianza Editorial, 1977.

Hofstede, Geert; *Culture's consequences: international differences in work-related values.* Bevery Hills, Calif.: Sage Publications, 1997.

Hooks, Bell; *Black Looks. Race and Representation.* Boston, MA: South End Press, 1992.

Horsman, Reginald; *Race and Manifest Destiny. The Origins of American Racial Anglo-Saxonism.* London: Harvard University Press, 1981.

Kristensen Kærgaard, Erik; *Kulturforskelle og den internationale markedsføring.* København: Samfundslitteratur, 1993.

Langer, Susanne K.; *Menneske og symbol.* København: Gyldendals Uglebøger, 1969.

Pike, Fredrick B.; *The United States and Latin America. Myths and Stereotypes of Civilisation and Nature.* Austin: University of Texas Press, 1992.

Pablo R. Cristoffanini

Pickering, Michael; *Stereotyping. The Politics of Representation.* New York: Palgrave, 2001.

Ricoeur, Poul; *Ideología y Utopía.* Barcelona: Gedisa Editorial, 1999.

Sábato, Ernesto; *Apologías y rechazos.* Barcelona: Seix Barral, 1991.

Thompson, John B.; *Ideology and Modern Culture.* Oxford: Polity Press, 1990.

Todorov, Tzvetan; *On Human Diversity: Nationalism, Racism, and Exoticism in French Thought.* Cambridge: Harvard University Press, 1993.

Valerio-Holguín, Fernando; Buena Vista Social Club: Canibalismo cultural y nostalgia imperialista, in Sara Zas (ed.) *Actas del Coloquio Internacional de la Asociación Europea de Profesores de Español.* Colorado: Colorado State University, 2000.
http://lamar.colostate.edu/~fvalerio/buenavista.htm

Notes

1. For example, Hofstede (1984).

2. See Hofstede (1984) and the innumerable articles and academic works based on his ideas and beliefs

3. These simplistic categorisations can be questioned from many angles. I mention only two. The categories depend on the culture of the subject that creates them. Would a studious Frenchman, Mexican, or Chinese consider the Chilean culture as having a great power distance? The Danish culture in the schemata of Hofstede is associated with individualism. But how is it that in an individua-listic society one must pay 50% and more of one's salary for the welfare of the society as a whole? A culture can be individualistic and collectivist, depending on the sphere being discussed. For this reason, I view the schemata of Hofstede as an ultra-simplification bordering on stereotypes.

4. Øyvind Dahl (1995).

5. Consider, for example, the controversy about how to categorize the Chechens that fight against the Russian invasion. Are they terrorists or resistance fighters? Categorisation has a series of serious political and legal consequences.

6. Examples of the use of semiotics are found in works like those of Gustafsson (2000) and Hall (1997).

7. Gordon W. Allport (1954). The Nature of Prejudice, p. 27. Addison-Wesley Publishing Company: Cambridge, Massachussets.

8. Those that have been mentioned, among others, by Cassirer, Langer and Geertz. Ernst Cassirer (1982).

9. See Billig (1985).

10. What is the common element, for example, of the American, Scandinavian, and Indian model of democracy? Is violence only physical aggression or is it also the tremendous social differences that condemn children to sickness, hunger, and illiteracy?

11. See Billig p. 86. Also, "Arguing about categories", in Billig (1996). *Arguing and thinking. A rhetorical approach to social psychology*, pp. 176-182.

12. On the different ways of conceiving ideology, see Ricoeur (1999) and Thompson (1990).

13. See also the Introduction by Cobley (1996) and Gottdiener (1995).

14. Idea already mentioned by other authors such as Goddenier, and Barthes in works cited above.

15. This is how the persecution and murder of political opponents of the dictator-ship of General Pinochet was justified.

16. These affirmations of the character of the English colonists in America and about the stereotypes and prejudices of Americans regarding Indians, Afro-

Americans, Mexicans and Hispanic Americans in general are based on the book by the North American historian Pike (1992).

[17] The presentation of this ideology and its relationship to Mexicans are based on the work of Horsman (1981).

[18] Quote from Mississippi senator Robert J. Walker, who became leader of the Democratic Party in the mid-1840s.

[19] México lost half of its territory to the United States. See Tulio Halperin Donghi (1977). *Historia Contemporánea de América Latina*, p. 180. Alianza Editorial: Madrid.

[20] This can also take the form of super-modern exoticism: the fascination that today's Japan exercises over the United States is considered to be more technologically than Western Europeans.

[21] Fernando Valerio-Holguín's article can be downloaded at: http://lamar.colostate.edu/~fvalerio/buena-vista.htm

4

Intercultural encounters in the global transmission of news
The perception and production of cultural images

LISBETH CLAUSEN

News communication in some form has always been a source of knowledge about other cultures but the development of technology and news distribution infrastructures has enabled immediate access to any corner of the world at any time. News permeates every social space (Cottle, 2000) and greatly influences our perceptions and mental images of other cultures.

The dynamic flows of media images, texts, sounds and graphics across countries, cause processes of communication across cultures to entail an increased awareness of other cultures while heightening the awareness of one's local culture and much more immediate experience of the world as a whole (Hjarvard, 2001).

The present chapter presents a framework for the study of micro processes and strategies in mass media organisations behind the proliferation of visuals and concepts that affects our phenomenological world or our 'global consciousness' (Robertson, 1992). It takes a specific look at the perception and considerations of news producers at national broadcast stations who chose and give meaning to the visual images and texts that are disseminated with great impact on national audiences. Despite theories of fragmentation and assessments of the uncertainty of national institutions in a globalising post-modern society (Fiske, 1997), national news broadcasters still cater to a national majority of citizens and in this capacity perform a considerable role in maintaining and (re)constructing political and national cultural identity (Clausen, 2003).

Lisbeth Clausen

This chapter thus studies intercultural encounters in international news production through a study of the sense-making of news producers through interviews. The main questions in the chapter are: what cultural knowledge and perception do news producers have, and how do they use this perception and their experience of the strategies of international news production in the production of news images and texts? The primary purposes of the chapter are as follows: (1) to present a theoretical framework that enables analysis of intercultural encounters in news communication as a reflexive process of negotiation between the global and the local culture on the part of professional news producers (2) to discuss existing theories of intercultural communication and models and argue for a complex dialectic model of perception and production rather than a linear communication process model (3) to present a model representing the global (event) professional (broadcaster) and the local (audience) of communication, based on theories of cognitive and social psychology, (4) to apply the proposed model to an empirical study of global news output and the production strategies behind it.

What is culture?

'Culture' is a problematic concept. The notion of culture originated in anthropology in the 1950s and 60s. In 1952, the American anthropologists Kroeber and Kluckhohn registered 152 different definitions of culture (Holden *et al.*, 2002). Definitions of culture were mainly used by anthropologists in their ethnographic studies or in different fields in the humanities. Culture was introduced in media, organisation and management studies during its heydays in the 1970-80s. Many studies are still inspired by the classic definition in which culture is understood as being relatively stable, as an internal system of assumptions, values and norms that are carried by an organisation or nation collectively. The present study is inspired by recent views of culture as 'based on shared or partly shared patterns of meaning and interpretation. In this view, these patterns are produced, reproduced and continually changing by the people identifying with them and negotiating them' (Holden *et al.*, 2002). As described in this chapter, people identify and affiliate with a multiplicity of different cultures e.g. *national*, *organisational* and *professional*.

Culture in this chapter is furthermore seen as being made up of relations, rather than as systems of form and substance (Holden *et al.*, 2002) This implies that culture only comes into existence in relation to and in contrast with another culture, be it national, organisational or professional. Cultural meanings are in this perspective *contextual*.

Against this backdrop, the present study presents a context-sensitive qualitative case study that explores the notion of culture as an analytical concept as it emerges at different levels of interaction in the study of micro processes in international news production.

Data and design

The empirical exemplifications of information processing are based on observations of and interviews with 40 news producers at Japanese national broadcast stations in 1997. The findings of this fieldwork were presented in the book *Global News Production* (Clausen, 2003). However, the present study elaborates on the intercultural aspect of news production through an in-depth analysis of the on-location deliberations made by the news desk (editorial position) at the Public Service Station NHK and by the programme director at the commercial Station TV Asahi. The programme director is Swiss born and the only foreign news producer at the station (or any national station). His non-Japanese world views and his Western cultural background allow for cultural reflection in his professional practices and in his statements.

The empirical case chosen for analysis of the presented model is the production and presentation of the French Nuclear Testing in Mururoa. This piece of news was considered a 'global' news event in the corporate study of 'International News Flow in the 1990s'.[1] It provides an exemplary case of the complexity of 'intercultural encounters': meetings of perception at the global, national and organisational/professional levels of analysis. The prime time news programmes at NHK News 7 and the TV Asahi's News Programme are analysed in a comparative perspective with the prime time news programmes on the Danish Public Service DR1 and commercial station TV2. This analysis is not systematic as it merely serves to provide a comparative perspective on the Japanese transmission of the event.

Perception and production of images and texts

News producers who work in the space between the *global* and the *national* have, as stated above, developed special competences in intercultural communication. They have included a *reflexive* hunch in their strategy for the selection and production of international stories.

Their competence of both knowing about international affairs and knowing about elements of identification themes of their receiving audience is essential in the selection and production of international news information, and an important element in the process of 'translating' and mediating international events to national audiences. The chapter is thus concerned with their perception and their production of images.

News producers are, just like other professionals, members of several cultures. They deal with national cultural issues, their corporate culture, the industry culture, and the professional culture. This chapter explores the different cultural layers of influence that news producers encounter in their professional practices, which ultimately influence the way they perceive the world in the final output.

Culture and communication models – an overview

The point of departure and aim of this section is to describe the move from the linear model of communication through the dialogic process to a more complex model of communication as presented in this chapter.

The standard model of communication, known as the process model, was introduced by Shannon and Weavers in *Mathematical Theory of Communication* in 1949. A similar model for *linear* communication was developed at the same time by the American sociologist Lashwell in his studies of propaganda. Lashwell was concerned with the *effect* of communication and described the process from the original idea of the sender, with emphasis on the noticeable change in values and behaviour of the receiver.

Later, linguistic and cultural conventions were integrated in communication models. Various researchers have suggested modifications of process models, taking into account the cultural basis for the codes and the complications when cultures differ. Dahl & Habert, (1986 cf. Søderberg, 1995) include the notion of 'cultural filters' in their model of communication. The cultural filter refers to the knowledge, attitudes and interests of the sender and receiver that may affect their understanding of the message. Individuals interpret the message through this cultural filter of values and norms. The message of the sender and the message received may therefore differ.

Leiniger (1997) is critical of the process models of communication exemplified above. She presents a model for business use that includes the global mission, global management strategies, international communication approaches, and individual rhetorical strategies. Her model shows the relationship between the different variables and emphasises the *business* context of intercultural communication. Yan (1997) likewise has criticised the transmission models. She argues that the notions of linear communication based on Western premises place the sender in a dominant role. Communication in her view is thus distorted and manipulated. Yan argues for a consensus approach inspired by Eastern philosophy as an alternative to the process models that have originated in Western scholarship. The Japanese scholar Muneo Yoshikawa, introduced below, has developed a dialogic communication model inspired by Japanese philosophy.

Cultural uniqueness

In the field of intercultural communications, the difference between Japan and the US is a pivotal issue. Today, there are more studies of Japanese/American communication than of intercultural communication between any two other cultures, according to media and communications scholar Youichi Ito at Keio University (1993). When American and Japanese intercultural communication scholars began studying US/Japanese communication behaviour in the 1970s, they stressed differences in individualism/collectivism, low context/high context cultures, self-disclosure, and other values.

Their findings and conclusions have consequently served to illustrate the *uniqueness* of Japanese culture and communication behaviours. Hall's concept of high- and low-context communication (Hall, 1959; 1976) was particularly useful for Japanese scholars to explain Japanese communication through cultural concepts. Therefore, according to Ito Youichi, many have used these polar concepts to solidify their theories and reify the theories of 'Japanese uniqueness' *nihonjin-ron* (Ito, 2000). They have attempted to capture Japanese communication psychology, a phenomenon that cannot easily be translated into English. Japanese scholars have clung to the indigenous concepts of *amae* (psychological dependence), *ma* (time space), *wa* (harmony) and *nemawashi* (consensus-building before decision-making), and have thus reinforced the idea of uniqueness (see also a critique of the Japanese uniqueness theories in Clausen, 2003).

Although international news production involves the 'translation' of international information into national cultural terms, professional practices are in many respects similar to professional journalistic practices in other industrialised countries. Although the analysis below shows Japanese traits and perceptions related to national and organisa-

Lisbeth Clausen

tional/professional culture, these are considered specific to the situation rather than unique.

From linear to dialogic communication

The 'classic' communication models above rely on the premise that communication is a linear process of transmitting information from A to B. The 'double swing' model introduced below allows for a continuous reciprocate action and importantly, it includes the notion of self-reflection in the communication process.

It is generally asserted in intercultural communication studies (see Samovar and Porter, 1997) that people from Western and Asian cultures have the greatest chance of misunderstanding each other. Much of this misunderstanding comes from the fact that Western and Asian cultures have two very different views of communication. Western cultures, especially the United States, give higher status to the speaker or 'source' of information than to the 'receiver', the person who pays attention to the information. Asian cultures view communication as communicators cooperating to make meaning. This model of communication reflects Confucian collectivist values in which the relationship through communication can be more important than the information exchanged. The double swing model is presented by the Japanese scholar Muneo Yoshikawa.

Figure 4:1 Dialogic communication. The 'Double Swing' model (Yoshikawa 1987: 321)

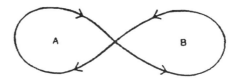

Yoshikawa's model is the result of his search for new ways of interpersonal, intercultural, and international relations within which people of diverse cultures can respect their cultural differences as well as their similarities. The Möbious strip, or the infinity symbol, signifies the idea of a twofold movement and the Buddhist idea of the paradoxical relationship:

The model is not to be constructed as a fixed entity or principle but in fact has much to do with the ways we perceive, think, and relate to whatever we encounter. It is essentially related to our basic attitude and life stance. (Yoshikawa, 1987: 327)

Yoshikawa's model illustrates that the processes of intercultural communication continue even when both parties (in face-to-face or virtual communication) leave the encounter. The model can be applied to the whole spectrum of human existence – interaction between individual human beings, communication between countries, and dialogue among different religions, and, as here, in intercultural encounters of communication between countries and between people. The assumptions behind the model are as follows:

- The actors in Yoshikawa's simple communication model are not senders and receivers respectively, but are ongoing co-producers of the communication process.
- The awareness of *identity* of self and other is created in the communication process.
- Difference and otherness, which are commonly conceived as problematic in intercultural communication are viewed as positive factors and as essential ingredients for growth.
- The model illustrates the act of meeting without eliminating the otherness or uniqueness of each culture and without reducing the dynamic tension created as a result of meeting.
- The dialogic communication process creates not a homogeneous, but rather a diversified pluralistic world.

While the linear process model views communication as a transition of information from sender to receiver (the 'hypodermic needle' approach), communication in the double swing model is an ongoing dialectic process of meaning creation. As we try to make sense through a dialogic communication process *we strengthen the consciousness of our own identity* while strengthening our consciousness of the identity of others. *This reflexivity and mental negotiation of cultural knowledge is the focus of this chapter.*

The strength of the 'double swing' model is that Yoshikawa Muneo considers the effect of the face-to-face (or virtual) communication. A weakness is the fact that he does not consider context. (See Jensen, 1998: 195 for a critique). Yoshikawa is inspired by the Enlightenment Buddhism and the Western Philosopher Martin Buber's theory of dialogue. Buber and other Western colleagues such as Bakhtin and Levinas represent a strong 'Western' dialogical tradition (Jewish thinking, Continental philosophy, current American pragmatism) which is also beginning to gain ground in the intercultural paradigm (cf. Blasco, Lautrup Nørgaard and Gustafsson, this volume).

A perception model of communication

The perception model of communication presented in the following illustrates information as processed by viewers and news producers alike. Theories of information processing and perception form the basis of the framework and proposed communication model introduced below.

It is assumed in cognitive theory and elaborated below that we attribute meaning on the basis of what has been meaningful to us in past experience. People from similar cultures or from similar professional backgrounds may have a similar store of past experiences and knowledge in their 'data banks', and that usually leads to an attribution of meanings that are close. If we share common experiences and values with others, it is easier to interpret the meaning behind their messages.

The definition of communication in relation to the proposed model is inspired by Beamer and Varner.

> Communication is the perception of verbal (worded) and non-verbal (without words for visuals) behaviour and the assignment of meaning to them. Communication takes place whether the sending of signals is intentional or unintentional. It even takes place when the verbal or nonverbal action is unconscious as long as it is observed and meaning is assigned to it. (Beamer and Varner, 2001).

Beamer and Varner explain that messages or signals can be either verbal or visual. The perception process is explained as follows: when you encounter something unfamiliar you have several choices: you can assume it is nothing, since it fits no category known to you, or you can assume it is simply a variant of something familiar that is already in a mental category. Another option is that you can choose to perceive the signals as unfamiliar and therefore not to be matched with existing mental categories; thus, you will reject them or retain them until you can relate them to something already familiar. However, it is hard to keep the uncategorised and unmeaningful in mind for very long unless you have learned to do so. Finally, you have the option of altering your mental category to accommodate the new information and assigning it a new meaning. This is how categories are constantly reviewed and increased, as shown in the model (cf. Beamer and Varner, 2001: 22-23).

Figure 4:2 Perception Model of Communication

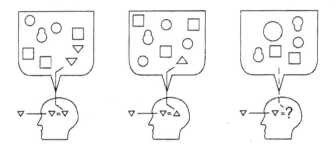

From Varner, I. and L. Beamer. Intercultural Communication: The Global Workplace, 2001. Reproduced with the permission of the McGraw-Hill Companies.

This model may be used to explain the perception processes of news producers and audiences alike. The task of the news producers is to process their perceived version of the global event to the mental scripts and models of their audiences.

Cultural imprints on information processing

Information processing in this chapter is inspired by the political scientist Doris Graber. In *Processing the News* (1984) she examines the ways in which people seek out, understand, and utilise political information presented in news. She employs *schema theory*, 'an integrative and particularly context-sensitive extension of social psychological analysis, to chart the patterns of recognition and the retention upheld in news audiences.' (Graber, 1984: 26). Schema theory is applied in this project to explain how news producers process, recognise, retain and retrieve information.

The theory behind Graber's cognitive approach is based on the detailed description of information processing given in an 11-stage model. It may be summarised as involving the following steps: first, there is the message reception. Next, the integration process starts with a series of questions to determine whether and how the new information relates to stored concepts, and whether it is worth processing.

Such questions would include: does it cover a topic about which the receiver already has information? Is it a familiar or predictable consequence of familiar knowledge? Does it make sense in the light of past experience? Or does it convincingly contradict past experience? Is it worth considering? Is it redundant?

If the answers to such questions indicate that the information is both worthwhile and reasonably well related to established thought schemes readily brought to mind, it is integrated into them. If, however, the answers do not indicate this, the information or its source may be discredited and rejected. Alternatively the new information may alter or replace the previous schema that has been called into question. In order to summarise the information processing, schemes perform four major functions. (1) They determine what information will be noticed, processed, and stored so that it becomes available for retrieval from memory. (2) They help individuals organise and evaluate new information so that it fits into their established perceptions, thereby making it unnecessary to construct new concepts whenever familiar information is presented. (3) Schemes make it possible for people to go beyond the immediate information presented to them and fill in missing information, thereby allowing them to make sense (inferences) from abbreviated communications. (4) Finally, *schemes help people solve problems because they contain information about likely scenarios* (referred to below as social scripts and models) and ways to cope with them (Graber, 1984: 24, my emphasis). In this way, schemes explain the evaluation, storage and retrieval of information and are thus a strategic tool for problem solving and social action. It is noteworthy, as stated by Graber, that emotions are important when accepting or storing information (Ibid: 172). The incorporation of an affective dimension in cognition, according to Graber, helps to delineate the difference in previous research between emotion and information. The notion of emotions is elaborated upon in a section below.

Cognitive psychologists have described schemas as pyramidal structures 'hierarchically organised with more abstract or general information at the top and categories of more specific information nested within the general categories' (Graber, 1984: 23). Put more simply, this means that most schemas contain conceptions of general patterns, along with a limited repertoire of prototypical examples to illustrate them. The general patterns are usually common-sense models of life situations that individuals have either experienced personally or encountered vicariously. They may be embedded in an overarching ideological conception that helps structure the subordinate levels of the schema, or they may exist side by side with only casual connections (Graber, 1984: 23).

Schema acquisition may bear the imprint of the particular culture in which learning takes place. Thus, children raised in the same culture learn the schemes common to their culture and the processing strategies that lead to them. The cultural imprint is deepened further throughout life because information sources usually reflect general cultural or sub-cultural values. Ultimately, the schema system is an

> ... enormous brain-filling, painfully learned store of principles, doctrine, dogma, premises, values, theories, prejudices, habits, codes, defences and the like developed and passed on by people who share common experiences and processing rules. (Graber, 1984: 148).

Cultural schemes, according to Graber, are imprinted in the early years of childhood and more than a decade before professional training begins. Cultural schemes are developed and form the cognitive bases for one's perception of the world. News impressions and knowledge acquisition are also based on these schemes, as well as the professional schemes elaborated below. Schemes that are culture bound include ideas about the appropriate time and place for an event to occur and ideas about the minutiae of behaviour expected from the participants. They encompass ideas about the causes of what is good and what is evil, and ways of coping with the everyday questions of life. They also include ideas about the purpose of life and broad norms of behaviour to be followed by people in a variety of social roles; be it singly or in a group. They may learn which dimensions of a given situation are worth noting and which can be safely ignored.

> There is a culturally given metaphysics, an ethics, an epistemology, and a value scheme. (Graber, 1984: 149).

National culture is thus included in basic cultural schemes, which again influence information acquisition throughout life, including the professional lives of, for instance, news producers, as studied here. Cultural schemes in this framework may be defined as information about appropriate behaviour in given situations. Inferences about other cultures may be made and news information stored. However, the opposite tendency is also a likely scenario. Early acquisition and hardening of schemes may explain why people retain social consciousness

Lisbeth Clausen

norms throughout life. To quote Lippmann (1922), an American political scientist:

> For the most part, we do not first see, and then define, *we define first and then see*. In the great blooming, buzzing confusion of the outer world, we pick out what our culture has already defined for us, and we tend to perceive that which we have picked out in the form stereotyped for us by our culture. (Lippmann, 1922: 81, my emphasis).

Most people, in cognitive terms, rely primarily upon culturally provided explanations because they lack the interest, and often the capacity, to break out of the cultural norms and think independently. They also lack the stimulus unless they are directly confronted with different cultures. On the whole, according to Graber, 'people tend to be conventional and conformist' (Graber, 1984:150). This may, of course, be said about news producers to a certain extent. However, as seen below, interest is a main motivator for acquiring new knowledge and may lead to independent thinking and change of perceptions.

Some cognitive psychologists have viewed schemes only in cognitive terms (as 'factual' information, without taking emotions into consideration), but Graber argues that schemes also contain memories of feelings and evaluations about the concepts in question (Graber, 1984:180). The picture that emerges from Graber's survey is one of a people (the Americans) who deal with a potentially overwhelming flow of information more successfully than one might think. They trim, skim and simplify, but for the most part, people get enough news to function effectively in their particular socio-political location. Moreover, they are capable of *taking news items that lack background and positioning them in contexts that are both cumulatively and personally meaningful*. While general understanding more than factual detail is most effectively retained through this process, Graber argues that over time, general understanding is enough to create a relatively well-informed public, which is central to the functioning of a democratic political system. 'Information overload' and the notion of 'noise' in communication theories is similarly a work condition that news producers cope with.

In short, Graber's study shows that the schema concept is applicable when studying political thinking and understanding through news. It presents evidence that the schemes used for political thinking possess the characteristics that cognitive psychologists have described for schemes dealing with simpler types of knowledge. The schema concept is appropriate for studying the process of dealing with information about international political events from the perspective of *both* audiences *and* news producers.

Box 4:1 Cognitive theory and perception in news production[2]

- *Schema theory* provides a framework which explains meaning production in media texts and in social practices as individual *and* as socially shared knowledge: inner scripts of individuals (models in the mind) and outer world scripts (models in the world).
- It helps explain how news events can be particular kinds of *cultural* models, and can be related explicitly to other cultural phenomena. Thus, news items must be considered an informational as well as a cultural product.
- It provides scripts and models for professional interaction.
- It provides models for emotions and senses.
- It may be conceptualised as context sensitive and functions by integrating dichotomies of macro and micro levels, thus providing a framework to explain human experience and the processing of social information.

Models and scripts in news communication

The notions of models and scripts are described by the Dutch discourse analyst Van Dijk in his study of the working practices and perception of journalists (1988). According to Van Dijk, our shared, social knowledge of scripts of, for instance, eating out, travelling, etc. provides the so-called 'missing links' between the concepts and propositions we encounter. In news communication we rely on shared information to make sense of visuals and texts. A text, to use an analogy, is described as a semantic 'iceberg' of which only the tip is actually expressed. The remaining information is, by presupposition, already known by the sender and receiver. This dependence on world knowledge and beliefs, in the view of van Dijk, can render coherence subjective, ideological or both.

Event models in memory, according to Van Dijk, feature not only knowledge, but also opinions or evaluative beliefs about events and their participants. The evaluative implications of news stories may be

Lisbeth Clausen

explained by spelling them out in a description of the mental models of the journalist. If a news report is 'biased', this is usually because the mental model of the journalist embodies structures and opinions which favour a particular perspective on an event. It follows that critical analysis of the meaning of discourse (the approach taken by van Dijk) will often involve a tentative reproduction of these beliefs. If social cognition about different social groups and social events is similar (in van Dijk's case, minorities; in the present study, political actors and international events), then, van Dijk insists, they are being monitored by the same fundamental interpretation framework, i.e. by the same *ideology*. Ideology features the basic norms, values, and other principles geared towards realising the group's interest and goals, as well as towards the reproduction of and legitimisation of its standpoints. A main point in the research of van Dijk is to show the transition of ideology from journalist to reader. Against this backdrop, the present project assumes that audiences are active in meaning construction (Dahlgren, 1992) and not passive receivers of ideological 'injections'.

In sum, *models* and *scripts* serve to explain knowledge (discourse) in society, in texts and in the minds of actors.

Perception and production of news images – a model

The proposed model illustrates the reflexive process of perceiving and producing news. A synthesis of ideas form the bases for the assumptions about perception and communication behind this model.

Figure 4:3 Cultural influences on strategic news communication – communication as on-going dialectic processes

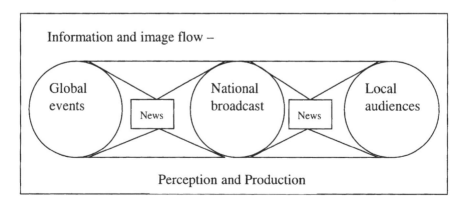

It is inspired by the schemata and perception models described above and by Muneo Yoshikawa's double swing model, which emphasises the cultural reflexivity and expanded awareness about self that comes from working with information and images of other cultures.

The model illustrates that global events come to the attention of news workers through international news distributors, or they may be discovered and made discursive by Japanese journalists abroad.

Alternatively, they may be a combination of both. Incidences happen locally but are made available to an international marketplace or sphere. The ability to gain access to local sources through offices and correspondents around the world is determined by the financial situation and policy of the news media. In the Japanese case, the investigated media have financial means and connections worldwide to develop their own stories. The national broadcaster is involved in a continuous process of negotiating and mediating international information to national audiences. The communication process is thus one of mediation in a dialogue of cultural reflexiveness.

Case – the French Nuclear Testing in Mururoa

The French nuclear testing was covered by media world-wide as a considerable international political event. News programmes reported about consumer boycotts spreading from Australia, New Zealand and Japan to Germany, Austria, Britain and Scandinavia. The regional resentment from Tahiti lead by independence leader Oscar Temaru and the condemnation of the tests by Australian Prime Minister Keating could therefore be interpreted as an economic attack by the countries in the Pacific region who wanted France out of the region.

In Japan, the news about the French Nuclear Testing concerned the actual event in Mururoa. But even more so, it provided insight into the *particular* complex and emotional issue of international diplomacy and the domestic policy of Japan as an anti-nuclear weapon country protected by the US 'nuclear umbrella'. The event was prioritised and received much airtime. On September 5, the day of the tests, NHK extended its News Seven programme with more than an hour of live reporting.[3]

In Denmark, the Prime Minister condemned the tests with the comment, 'It is regrettable', and the Danish Minister of foreign affairs raised the issue in the EU parliament. The Japanese Prime Minister likewise declared that the incident 'was regrettable' (*sore wa ikan*) in front of the cameras. However, rhetorical resemblances stopped here. While both countries are directly or indirectly protected by the US nuclear umbrella (Denmark through its Nato membership and Japan through post-Second World War military agreements) this was made clear in the Danish broadcast news, while the Japanese spokesman did not address the issue further. A Japanese Minister from the Sakigake Party protested against the tests through participation in peace marches in Australia. His activities were followed by the commercial station, which gave him a great deal of coverage and carried out a lengthy interview with him in indirect support of his anti-nuclear views. The Danish Stations covered their own politicians filing complaints with French diplomats and travelling to Mururoa to condemn the tests.

The themes and actors in the account of the event thus featured national elite actors representing national and media organisational political interests.

In Denmark, a main topic in the September 5 news was EU nuclear policies and the official stand on this issue within its member states. In Japan, the fact that the 50th anniversary of Hiroshima and Nagasaki almost coincided with the first Nuclear tests on the Mururoa Islands stirred revulsion against the incident. Sentiments and empathy with the Hiroshima and Nagasaki victims became the overarching themes of the Japanese public and media coverage. Hour-long presentations of the events were presented in the national news as an urgent matter. The issue was very *emotional* and the broadcast news reported accordingly. Although France is geographically distant from Japan, the Japanese people felt that nuclear tests ought to be stopped immediately. Most Japanese shared this feeling and this criterion carried much weight at both stations. The news was recognised as a priority at both the public service station and the commercial station studied; however, the approach and content of the news presentations differed. The journalistic practices and political stand of the public service and the commercial broadcast influenced news output. As expressed by one of the news producers:

In this respect you cannot say that news becomes global information. It depends on the theme, the journalist, the angle and the clips chosen for the presentation. The news is put together from many possible sources. In this case the news took a very Japanese form. (NHK, producer, interview, October 10, 1997)

The Japanese media took great interest in the issue as it appealed to a whole nation victimised by atomic bombs during the Second World War.

In comparison, there was very little coverage of the Chinese nuclear experiments. This may be due to the important economic and political relations with China. France in all respects is more distant and not much was at stake in terms of the foreign relations between the countries by presenting intensive emotional coverage. As a matter of fact, less than half a year after the massive criticism of France, Chirac was shown in the Japanese news shaking hands with the Japanese Prime Minister on an agreement to build a bridge together in Kyoto.

On location with Greenpeace – the global event

On September 5, TV Asahi and NHK news producers were on location to report on the tests. NHK carried out 'live' reporting from a Greenpeace ship close to the Mururoa Island where the tests were made. The TV Asahi news producer made a report standing on top of the French missiles in order to set the scene in a French environment. Both the TV Asahi and NHK reports were considered scoops – first come, first tell stories. The following elaborated on the considerations of the reporters concerning their coverage and set up of events.

The French had only invited national public channels and NHK was therefore automatically invited by the government. The TV Asahi crew was there by chance because the news producer had made connections to the Paris government himself and got permission.

Only NHK and TV Asahi were represented at the event, but as the programme director said, 'every story has its own roads'. There are many stories to tell and they can be told in many different ways. It was found that in this case, the different approach to reporting was due to different national cultural backgrounds, different organisational ideologies and different personal values of the news producers.

The invitation to go to Mururoa came about because the French government was concerned about negative publicity and wanted to make a promotion campaign to show that the tests were safe. The government wanted to show that all the Greenpeace stories were exaggerated and they tried to be as open as possible. France had invited only Pacific Rim countries: Japan, Australia, News Zealand and so on. No Western media were represented.

Perceptions of Greenpeace

Prior to the event, the TV Asahi programme director was sceptical of the Greenpeace activities and of the whole atmosphere of the organisation, which he described as an army. Although he had considered the possibility, he chose not to be in the middle of the action on the Greenpeace boat in Mururoa.

> Most of it was total rubbish with no scientific basis to it. I met one of the founders of Greenpeace on his boat in Papeete and interviewed him. The atmosphere on the boat was very like an army. Furthermore, the people's attitudes were: 'We are Greenpeace and we are cool'. But in reality, Greenpeace is not democratic. Even the members admit that it is not. (TV Asahi programme director, interview June 26, 1997)

He made his transmission from the top of the French missiles on a truck. The idea, which he discussed with his producer in the Tokyo office, was to explain the situation as objectively as possible without taking a 'Japanese emotional angle'. His intention was to cover questions such as: 'Why is this happening? Why do the French people believe in nuclear dissuasion? Why does Mitterand stop nuclear testing and why does Chirac suddenly say we have to do it again'. This was the initial step and idea of coverage.

Although he was fundamentally against nuclear weapons he found the Greenpeace style of protesting absurd. 'Those guys were so full of rubbish. It was unbelievable'. His production crew interviewed Greenpeace in Tahiti in Papeete and they did not find the members credible. He ended up *not* using the Greenpeace interview in the programme. He also chose not to go on board the Rainbow Warrior although he had the chance to do so.

While the TV Asahi reporter was very sceptical towards Greenpeace, the NHK news producers had a positive encounter. A few days before the test, the news producer was on board one of the Greenpeace rubber boats, the so-called zodiacs. He ended up being detained by the French navy but was able to make a call to the Tokyo office, and was thus able to make a report about the trip to Mururoa and give a description of the situation. The risk of detainment had been calculated into the preparations and supported at the highest level of the News Broadcast division.

The TV Asahi news producer boarded the Rainbow Warrior II in Papeete. The experience not only gave him insight into the tests. He also felt that he learned about Greenpeace: it gave him the chance to see what the members of Greenpeace think about nuclear testing and other issues. His image softened through closer acquaintance with them:

They were not eccentrics when I actually talked to them, they had very reasonable ideas. They share the work on the ship and are experts in their own fields. My impression was that a group of professionals got together and were working for the Greenpeace movement. I thought that they had very reasonable ideas and opinions. The impression we get from their activities is that they are extremists, but when you actually talk to them, they are not as extreme as you think. (NHK news desk, interview September 1, 1997)

Although and because the programmes were seemingly influenced by the stand of the news producers, the NHK news producer did not see any bias in being associated with Greenpeace and their protest action. The TV Asahi journalist did not feel that he was influenced by the French government invitation in his reporting. Both reports however greatly reflected their perception and political position about the deeds of the French government and Greenpeace, respectively.

The audience in mind

In the NHK newsroom, the event was not considered a particular French matter but an issue of anti-nuclear sentiments. The French nuclear tests overshadowed all other international events because of the Japanese historical past as victim of an atom bomb. In this sense, the subject was very urgent and the issue had many emotional aspects.

We are against nuclear weapons and we wanted to convey this message, which is an emotional matter for us. This is our broadcast perspective and it became our news criterion. (NHK, producer, interview, October 10, 1997)

NHK made reports on the French Nuclear test every day for a week with this angle.

TV Asahi also gave high priority to the French Nuclear tests and aired extensively for 10 days. The main initiator of the reporting was the programme director, the only foreigner and Swiss-born employee. He was not in favour of the tests, but he felt that the Japanese coverage and public reaction was emotional and out of proportion. Instead, he reported on the French political and public reactions from a French perspective. He deliberately tried to provide factual information about the background of the events and deliberately chose an angle which was *not* Japanese. The producer of the programme praised his effort and nominated his reports as some of the best in the Japanese media.

Professional scripts and models

As a public service provider NHK aims to deliver balanced and neutral news coverage. In the producer's words, NHK tries to make its news as 'objective as possible'. It was therefore not possible for the station to state openly that the French nuclear testing was an inexcusable (*ke-shikaran*) undertaking. Further, it was asserted that direct protests would interfere with diplomatic relations. Therefore, NHK showed the situation in France by making a direct broadcast from Paris in co-operation with the reporter there and clips from protests around the world. Reports from Hiroshima and Nagasaki illustrated the Japanese protests. From other locations in Japan reports were made of ordinary people saying that it was 'inexcusable'. This way, the NHK original message remained intact. 'The news still appeared to be objective but somewhere in there our subjectivity is included. It is not the NHK style to say up front that these tests need to stop and this approach is not necessary' (NHK producer). The underlying meaning, however, was expressed indirectly through Japanese people, who spoke out against the tests.

When asked how he managed to maintain a professional distance on location he said:

> For example, I am drinking coffee now. I can tell that this is coffee, because I am drinking it. Even if it is served as coffee and it looks like coffee, it may not be coffee. This is the difference between reality and truth. Journalists have to always ask themselves this question. In order to narrow down the gaps between reality and truth, we need to know facts. Journalists therefore have to collect as many facts as possible. (NHK news desk, interview, September 1, 1997)

But how did he keep a distance to the event while on board a Greenpeace ship? Was there no danger that he might become partial towards their views?

> Of course, journalists have to inform the general public what sort of organisation Greenpeace is, but at the same time, we have to report the fact that they are against nuclear tests and that they took

various actions because they wanted the French government to stop the test. It is important for journalists to present as many facts as possible to the Japanese public. From the facts, Japanese people would be able to draw their own opinions objectively, instead of us telling them what we think. It is very dangerous if journalists give their own opinions to the general public. (NHK news desk, interview September 1, 1997)

The news producer was entirely convinced of his capacity to be loyal to events and present them in a factual, objective way.

The TV Asahi news producer, on the other hand, related the difference between making news for Swiss TV and making news for the Japanese. He found that the agenda, first of all, differed greatly. Sometimes news that was big in the West did not get any attention in the planning sessions at the station. In the production of particular news items, especially concerning Europe, he often found that it was difficult to explain information which was very important for him as a European to a Japanese audience of which many viewers did not have any prior knowledge. In a report about the Swiss secret bank guarantees he started the transmission from the Jungfrau Mountain just to greet viewers from a setting well known to Japanese tourists. His choice of news items was sometimes very random, found simply by going on the Internet and looking up something interesting which he could then mold into a news report.

In sum, the NHK professional models and scripts for news reporting may reflect a perception of news as a 'mirror on the world' with the obligation to present objective facts. The news producer shows as many sides of 'reality' as possible in order to allow the viewers to get their own impressions and make their own decisions about events.

In comparison, the TV Asahi news producer views news as a ritually constructed communication of events. The news producer puts together a story through news communication forms. He presents issues to an audience that differs from his own historical cultural and emotional background.

Personal knowledge and values

The NHK news producer's point of departure in his reporting and his personal feeling about the case was based on the Japanese sentiment and inherited general knowledge about the bombings of *Hiroshima and Nagasaki*. Japan is the first country in history to have experienced

Lisbeth Clausen

the atomic bomb. Because of this experience, he said, Japan has a different feeling towards atomic bombs and nuclear tests than the rest of the world.

> But because of the emotional involvement in past experience, the Japanese cannot accept the nuclear test, regardless of whether it is the last one or whether there are more to come in the future. It was therefore natural that his feelings were different from those people representing other foreign news media in Mururoa, and of course *the Japanese emotional involvement differed from the rest of the world.* (NHK news desk, interview September 1, 1997, my emphasis)

While he was in Mururoa he had an experience that made his Japanese background become even more apparent. During a press conference about the success of the tests, he remembers:

> What was first on my mind was to know what his message was to those who were against the nuclear tests, including the Japanese and especially the people in *Hiroshima and Nagasaki*. His message to people in *Hiroshima and Nagasaki* was that this experiment was done to seek peace. I thought that the message flatly contradicted what he and his team had just done. I do not know how the Japanese interpreted his message, as I cannot ask individual members in the Japanese audience. (NHK news desk, interview September 1, 1997)

At any rate he felt very *Japanese* and different from the rest of the journalists there.

His journalistic experience includes several adventures in the front line of events but he does not have a personal agenda or life project outside of his profession that supports his idealism. His project is to be messenger and mediator of news. It was his first time covering news about the nuclear testing and in his own interpretation he did not have any personal attachment to the subject, except of course, sharing the Japanese sentiment and sympathy with the victims in Hiroshima and Nagasaki.

The Asahi news producer, on the other hand, expressed much knowledge of and interest in the issue. However, his view of the 'Japanese sentiment' was very sceptical.

> The Japanese were furious with the French. They sat outside the French Embassy for days. Japan is under the so-called 'nuclear umbrella protection of the United States'. The nuclear system of the United States exists because the Americans did some 1500 nuclear tests in the Nevada Desert and the Marshall Islands. (TV Asahi, programme director, interview June 26, 1997)

The programme director found the Japanese attitude plainly ridiculous in view of this bilateral military treaty between Japan and the United States.

> Nobody has mentioned the debate about the military system. This is a good opportunity for the Japanese to think. What is the defence system of Japan? If North Korea threatens and decides to drop a bomb on Japan; the US will drop a bomb on North Korea. Therefore Japan is a nuclear country, even if it does not possess nuclear weapons. (TV Asahi programme director, interview June 26, 1997)

The programme director found that the Japanese reactions were exaggerated, especially because of the fact that Japan is protected by the nuclear arms of the US.

> They went berserk with demonstrations (*demo*) outside the French embassy every day. The United States has done 1,500 nuclear tests, as a protection measure, which Japan does not mention. The French wanted to do 5-6 more tests. It is so emotional. (TV Asahi, programme director, interview June 26, 1997)

According to the TV Asahi news producer, the Japanese should take their opposition to nuclear dissuasion one step further and declare that they cannot go hand in hand with the US.

To sum up, while the NHK news producer covers the event from the emotional perspective of the people in Hiroshima and Nagasaki, his counterpart at TV Asahi deliberately does not cater to this part of Japanese sentiment in his reports.

Lisbeth Clausen

Summary at the different levels of perception and production

Global

At the global level of analysis it was found that the French Nuclear testing was presented differently in Denmark and Japan. The social and professional actors in the news stories represented different domains of historical, political and cultural knowledge and the final news output consequently differed according to the national cultural and political frame of reference in the two settings. It was found that the news about French Nuclear testing was aimed at political and social agents in a Danish or Japanese national context. The focus on geographic areas and the choice of news items and actors was influenced by the national positioning in the international economic and political community, as was the expression of national self-awareness in the news items.

National

In the considerations of the news producers, the viewers of the news were found to be important in the choice of angle. The imagined audiences were the targets of the news messages and consequently, the set-up and arrangement of news sequences was done in order to appeal specifically to national audiences. In cognitive terms, global information was framed to match pre-existing schemes of knowledge or models for world events for the Japanese audiences within their national framework of reference.

Organisational

At this level, the micro processes and 'mental model' of news producers showed how the meaning of events was negotiated on location and later with producers at the Tokyo office. Organisationally shared notions of the political framework and angle of the report were important at this level. It was found that the capability to work within the organisational framework of ideas (internalising company ideology), and scripts for good news coverage were important in the production of international news in two ways. First, *knowledgeable* staff were necessary to recognise and interpret what was happening at the event. Secondly, the use of prior knowledge and evaluative perceptions of events formed the final output.

It may be argued that while professional and organisational structures were imprinted in the news producers' work (professional mental

126

models) in important ways in order to shape news, news producers continuously reconstituted and changed these structures.

Professional

At this level, which is closely connected to the organisational level, the personal approach and strategies on location abroad were aimed at exploring the way preconceived ideas and impressions were dealt with in the situation of the event. It was found at this level of analysis that the internalisation of the institutional and professional values affected the strategies of production. The production of a specific news item from the planning to the final output was undertaken by individual news producers through negotiations with colleagues and superiors. The process of event production included the choice of themes, actors and visuals for the final output.

The study of *professionals* in action at this level provided insights into individual knowledge and considerations. Their personal attitudes, values and beliefs about the event had great impact on the angle and choice of sources. It was found, however, that internalised schemata about world events and professional practices would enhance individual influence on the production of news as each news producer was an *expert* in his field and the Tokyo producers and editors therefore allotted them authority status in the interpretation of events.

The study of a specific national broadcast news story – the Nuclear testing in Mururoa – provided insights into practices of international news production in media organisations as well as their perception of the audiences in mind.

In summary, the complexity and inter-relatedness of the different levels of influence on news content are obvious and a challenge to media scholars. The question of where to focus is paramount. Most studies, like this one, deal with some combination of levels. The focus here was the perception of events and production strategies of news producers.

The analyses at each level is not understood as hierarchical structural influences but as overlapping and interrelated.

Conclusion

In today's information society, the ability of news producers to negotiate a story successfully accounts for the success of national news stations to maintain their culturally integrative function. Audiences turn to their national TV stations to get information about world events.

Lisbeth Clausen

The present case exemplified how news producers first try to make sense of events for themselves by selecting, rejecting and seeking information that in turn is made available for consumption, perception and meaning production by the receiving audiences. This process of knowledge negotiation, the choice of words and visual scenery depended on personal experience as well as the ability to prioritise and contextualise information.

A synthesis of approaches in cognitive theory provided a theoretical framework for the study of perception and production of news. A model was proposed to demonstrate the dialogic process of meaning negotiation in the perception and production of global events.

The use of cognitive schema theory helped to break away from the categories often used to describe Japanese communication. Japanese cultural studies have tended to focus on differences, which has made Japanese cultural characteristics appear 'unique'. A cognitive approach such as the present one opens up for analysis of work strategies that do not take their point of departure in these conventional cultural categories and therefore opens up for new ways of describing cultural encounters in communication processes in their heterogeneity and complexity.

References:

Beamer, Linda and Varmer, Beamer; *Intercultural Communication in the Global Workplace.* New York: McGraw-Hill companies, Inc., 2001, 1995.

Clausen, Lisbeth; *Global News Production.* Copenhagen: Copenhagen Business School Press, 2003.

Cottle, Simon; New(s) Times. Towards a 'Second Wave' of New Ethnography". *The European Journal of Communications Research* 25 (1): 19-41, 2000.

Dahlgren, Peter; What's the meaning of this. Viewer's plural sense-making of TV news" in Paddy Scannell, Philip Schlesinger, and Colin Sparks (eds) *Culture and Power.* London, Newbury, New Delhi: Sage Publications: 201-218, 1992.

Fiske, John; Postmodernism and Television in James Curran and Michael Gurevitch, (eds) *Mass Media and Society*, 1996/1997.

Graber, Doris; *Processing the News. How People Tame the Information Tide.* New York: Longman, 1984/1990.

Hall, Edward; *The Silent Language.* Greenwich: Fawcett, 1959.

Hall, Edward; *Beyond Culture.* New York: Anchor, 1976.

Holden, Nigel and Søderberg, Anne Marie; Rethinking Cross cultural Management. *International Journal of Cross Cultural Management*, 2,1, 103-121, 2002.

Hjarvard, Stig (ed.) *News in a Globalised Society.* Göteborg: Nordicom, 2001.

Ito Youichi; "Mass Communication Theory in Japan and the United States", in William Gudykunst (ed.) *Communication in Japan and the United States.* Albany, New York: State University of New York Press, 1993.

Lisbeth Clausen

Ito Youichi; What Causes the Similarities and Differences among the Social Sciences in Different Cultures? Focusing on Japan and the West. *Asian Journal of Communication*, Volume 19 (2), 2000.

Jensen, Iben; *Interkulturel Kommunikation i Komplekse Samfund [Intercultural Communication in Complex Societies].* Roskilde: Roskilde Universitetsforlag, 2001.

Lasswell, Harold D; The structure and function of communication in Society, in Bryson (ed.) *The Communication of Ideas.* 1948.

Leininger, Carol; The alignment of global management strategies, international communication approaches, and individual rhetorical choices, *Journal of Business and Technical Communication*, 11, 203-228, 1997.

Lippmann, Walter; *Public Opinion.* NewYork: McMillan, 1922.

Robertson, Roland; *Globalisation, Social Theory and Global Culture.* London: Sage, 1992.

Samovar, Larry A & Porter, Richard E; (eds) *Intercultural Communication: A Reader.* Wadsworth Inc. (8th edition), 1997.

Weaver Warren & Shannon Claude E; *The Mathematical Theory of Communication.* Urbana, Illinois: University of Illinois Press, 1963.

Søderberg, Anne Marie, Annette Willemoes; (2. edition). *Sprog, kultur og kommunikation i den erhvervssproglige medarbejders perspektiv.* Copenhagen: Samfundslitteratur, 1995.

Van Dijk; T.A; *News as Discourse.* Hillsdale, NJ: Erlbaum, 1988.

Yan, Rue; Yin/Yang principle and the relevance of externalism and paralogic rhetoric to intercultural communication. *Journal of Business and Technical Communication*, 11, 297-320, 1997.

Yoshikawa, Muneo; The Double-Swing Model of Intercultural Communication between the East and the West, in Kinkaid (ed): *Communication Theory: Eastern and Western perspectives.* London: Academic Press inc. Harcourt Brace Jovanovich College Publishers: 319-329, 1987.

Notes

I would like to thank Professor Anne-Marie Søderberg for helpful comments on an early draft of this chapter.

---

[1] The project 'Corporate study of Foreign News and International News Flow in
the 1990s' is co-ordinated by Professor Robert Stevenson of the University of
North Carolina and Professor Annabelle Sreberny at Leicester University. A description of the project and a list of participants are available on the project web
site: http://www.sunsite.unc.edu/newsflow/

[2] Adapted from Clausen, 2003:63

[3] The extended hour programme about the nuclear tests is not included in the
quantitative study of the News Flow Project. It was not recorded in the original
material.

5

Mentality: A Neglected Field of Investigation in Intercultural Studies

HENRIK RYE MØLLER

Introduction

In recent years mentality has become a somewhat overlooked or neglected field in various research disciplines, e.g. history, sociology,
psychology and cultural studies. Mentality studies seem to have been
overtaken by more mainstream *identity studies* that do not necessarily
pay attention to the mental issues in people's 'hearts and minds', in
which the German sociologist Theodor Geiger located mentality,
when in the early thirties he advocated the scientific interest in the
field of mentality.

I prefer the term 'self' to heart and mind, but like Geiger I shall advocate the scientific use of mentality, because it can help differentiat-
ing the field of what is nowadays often very broadly conceptualised
solely as 'identity'. Although it is defined in numerous ways there is a
tendency to conceptualise identity as something that the individuals
are quite aware of and conscious about.[1]

But how do we describe the aspects of the human self that operate
on a more subconscious level? In my view mentality research can be a
useful way, simply because to a large extent its research field is the
subconscious or even the non-conscious. It will make possible a complex, differentiated and fine-grained description of individuals and
groups in a time characterized by cultural and social complexity.[2]

I will present two examples that in my opinion demonstrate the
relevance of paying attention to mentality aspects in a broad description of identity.

Henrik Rye Møller

I do not see mentality in opposition to identity as some researchers do.[3] I consider mentality a fruitful and therefore useful expansion of the field of identity, but the subconscious character of mentality makes it hard to 'prove' empirically, which may be one reason that many scientists prefer to avoid using it. When they do work with mentality there tends to be a lack of academic precision and coherence, so the study of mentality calls for more scientific attention and accuracy than has been the case so far.[4]

The 'scientification' of mentality is an academic challenge that I will try to take up in this chapter. Before turning to concrete examples, I will make my conceptualisation of mentality explicit. The argumentation for this definition will follow in the sections below.

> Mentality is an individual's or a group of individuals' disposition or potential for certain attitudes which influence and frame their individual and collective acts, behaviour and relations to the external world. This disposition or potential is based upon a long-term socialisation of an individual's genetic heritage and specific personal traits. Through the socialisation process mentality is collectively developed and individually embodied.

History of the mentality concept and its current status

The earliest scientific attempts to conceptualise the field of mentality that I am familiar with are the Danish philosopher Jens Kraft's observations on '*De vilde Folks Tænkemaade*' ('The savages' way of thinking'), dating back to the 18th century.

In 1921 the French anthropologist Lucien Lévy-Bruhl published his work on '*La mentalité primitive*' (English translation in 1923 '*Primitive Mentality*'). These early attempts worked in the anthropological tradition that perceived culture as an empirical category that could be observed, described and evaluated by an independent researcher, and the comparison was usually in favour of the researcher's own culture. In contemporary anthropology this position has been abandoned in favour of seeing culture as an analytical implication.[5]

Around the turn of the last century the French sociologist Émile Durkheim introduced the expression '*collective representations*', which refers to the mentality of a community of individuals. In the early thirties the German sociologist Theodor Geiger developed this concept further and defined mentality as '*a disposition of the mind and soul*' and the '*unmediated impact of life experience on the indi-

vidual[6] and he stressed the formless, floating and impressionist character of mentality.

The interest in mentality studies abated somewhat during and after World War II. Not until the late seventies did mentality experience a come-back, very much under the influence of the French 'Annales School', which concentrated mainly on mediaeval history and focussed on everyday aspects of life.[7] As the British historian Peter Burke formulates it, the history of mentality had the power to fill out the 'conceptual space', also named the 'third level', between the history of ideas and the history of persons.

> [W]e very much need something to occupy the conceptual space between the history of ideas, defined more narrowly, and social history, in order to avoid having to choose between an intellectual history with the society left out and a social history with the thought left out. (Burke, 1986: 440)

Mentality was seen as a discipline that, in the sense of Peter Burke, could soften stiff discipline boundaries. The interest among historians especially in Central and Northern Europe for mental issues grew remarkably in these years, and mentality was often the main thread in historical anthologies.[8] Some German historians focussed primarily on the 'common people'[9] or combined the history of the workers with a strong left-wing political ambition.[10]

Parallels to the German interest in mentality in the eighties could be found among mostly feminist historians in Scandinavia, whose main task was to examine the relevance of the history of mentality in connection with gender studies,[11] but the impact of this work on the research of the nineties and later was not very significant. The mentality studies of the eighties have underlined the importance of drawing on the societal context (e.g. politics) when the researcher considers the various factors that have an influence on mentality. That is one of the reasons why the influence of the so-called secondary socialisation will be stressed in the following.

Examples illustrating a specific mentality

I shall introduce two examples that in my view illustrate the need for mentality as an area of investigation.

The first example is taken from the empirical part of my Ph.D. dissertation (Møller, 2002), which consists mainly of interviews with

Henrik Rye Møller

Danish businessmen working in a Danish firm in Germany. These examples show how mentality has an impact on interactive situations, in this case in an intercultural context. They illustrate how mentality gives the individuals a disposition towards certain behavioural patterns and ways of conduct, e.g. a preference for certain roles when presenting themselves to others. The aim of describing the empirical findings is to demonstrate the relevance of the field of mentality in studies of human interaction and culture studies.

The following examples have been chosen from other researchers' studies on political culture in the unified Germany, especially in East Germany. These studies show that the East German political, social and cultural development has created specific contextual foundations for the socialisation process[12] of individuals. The development is not only limited to the GDR's history,[13] but reaches further back in history. The specific mentality caused by these socialisation processes has led to a disposition for other political preferences, which have influenced the formation of a specific political culture in East Germany. This should be of interest for studies of social, political and cultural science.

First example: Work culture

First a very brief presentation of my empirical work: I conducted the main part of my (semi-structured, qualitative) interviews in Germany in a Danish based firm known in English-speaking countries under the name 'Jysk Linen 'n Furniture'. My informants were young (mainly in their late twenties) Danish businessmen working at various managerial levels in the organisation and with job experience from both West and East Germany, which allowed comparisons between East and West. The interviews focussed on the informants' experiences during their cultural encounters with Germans at various locations in Germany.

The informants had experienced a general *fluctuation of spheres* in East Germany, the private sphere being work related (socializing with colleagues from work during leisure-time is common) and the work sphere being privatised (e.g. through involving one's family in business matters). The informants themselves were typically met with overwhelming hospitality and family-like openness, when they first came to East Germany. The informants generally evaluated this East German softening of the boundaries between work sphere and private sphere positively as a socially oriented mental trait, but also fairly negatively as a somewhat unprofessional attitude towards work.

It is therefore surprising that there is a quite significant contrast between the egalitarian tendencies just mentioned and the attitudes towards the superior in situations that are more closely related to the job itself. Some informants mentioned staff meetings with the manager as an example of this. The East German employee had a tendency to try to please the manager by spontaneously agreeing with him, by taking his standpoints, or by saying nothing at all. The roles that the East Germans put themselves into can be interpreted as expressions of a specific mentality grounded in a disposition for *hierarchical thinking*, resulting in obedience towards the presumed superior and in efforts to hide weaknesses, to try not to attract attention, etc. However, the goal of the Danish managers was to change attitudes, so that the East German staff were in charge of their own business areas, thereby taking over necessary responsibility and independently making the required decisions.

The informants reported a high degree of hierarchy between manager and staff, but among colleagues they observed many attitudes signaling equality: the willingness to cancel a day off in order to stand in for a sick colleague or the wish to share a personal financial bonus with other staff members who in the opinion of the bonus receiver should also be credited. The social understanding revealed in this *egalitarian attitude* applied not only to colleagues at the same level, but also to the firm as such. Several informants mentioned the very high commitment to the workplace, to colleagues and the firm's interests.

To summarize: three basic aspects are noted in connection with East Germans: 1) privatisation of work; 2) hierarchical thinking in relation to superiors; and 3) egalitarian attitudes towards colleagues.

I believe that the concept of mentality will help to explain these aspects in detail; as I explain in a later section, 'Analysing the interaction processes.'

Second example: Political culture

Another field that shows the need for a mentality-oriented approach is the political culture which can be observed in East Germany. Many observers have difficulties interpreting and explaining the specific East German voting pattern that still, more than a decade after the unification of Germany, separates it from the West German voting pattern.

The rise of this specific political culture reaches back in history. In the 19th century, and the tendency can be traced further back, the Eastern and the Western parts of Germany were divided mentally approximately where the river Elbe runs. One spoke of an 'East Elbian' and a 'West Elbian' attitude towards life, the East being influenced by more desolate landscapes dominated by farming and the West being influenced by dense population and more industry.

German literature is a source of stories about different mentalities in the East and in the West, most prominently represented in the writings of Theodor Fontane (1819-1898), who describes the absence of regional development and progressive elements in the East, which allowed the power of the ancient aristocracy to be maintained. This missing democratisation of course influenced the mental processes of the individuals living in the East,[14] but, although almost by definition authoritarian, the East Elbian aristocracy was guided by ideals of a fairly ordinary, non-extravagant life-style combined with social understanding towards the population living under its protection.[15]

This duality of the Prussian state, being authoritarian *and* socially conscious at the same time, which at the first glance seems paradoxical, is often referred to as the '*Janus-face*' of Prussia: military, hierarchical, suppressive, reactionary, etc. on the one side, but in its own specific way also humanitarian and tolerant on the other side. The ideals of the Enlightenment period were part of the double face of Prussia. The social aspects of the Prussian aristocracy that Fontane describes had their political continuation in the twentieth century through the dominant position of the Social Democratic Party in Prussia after World War I and until the Nazi liquidation of democracy and federalism in Germany in the early thirties.[16]

The GDR was to a large extent geographically situated on the territory of Prussia. These apparently contradictory Prussian features, authoritative thinking combined with a certain amount of social understanding, have quite distinctive continuation lines from Prussia to the GDR. I believe that the mental structures that among many other factors have led to specific voting patterns were latent in East Germany after World War II and they were reinforced and further developed by the GDR-society.[17]

What are these voting patterns, then, and how do they differentiate the East from the West? As can be seen from the election results, the two parts of Germany vote differently, and it can be argued that not only is the voting behaviour different, but the contents of the actual politics in regional organisations of the same political party also show East-West differences.[18] The so-called political landscape is also different in the two parts of Germany. The most obvious example of another political landscape is of course the existence of the Party of Democratic Socialism (PDS), the successor of the former communist party. The PDS gets around 20 percent of the votes in East Germany in most elections, whereas, with very few exceptions, it is non-existent in West Germany.[19]

I interpret these factors as strong indications of the importance of the secondary socialisation (impact of e.g. school systems and political life) for the development of mentality.

In sum, a presentation of the dominant political culture in East Germany shows hierarchical thinking running parallel to egalitarian aspects.

Theory: The conceptualisation of mentality

Introduction
Also in studies of intercultural communication the field of mentality is quite insignificant. Most studies that I am familiar with seem to limit themselves to the field of identity and to leave out mentality aspects.

A view on identity that has attracted much attention and recognition is the *negotiation perspective*, according to which an identity is not something that an individual possesses or chooses to have, but something that he negotiates in dialogue with one or more other individuals. Stella Ting-Toomey, who is one of the leading American theorists within studies of intercultural communication, has had a major influence on this perspective. In the so-called primary identities she distinguishes between group membership identities (integrating cultural, ethnic and gender identity), and personal identity.[20] This distinction is inspired by social group theorists in the tradition of Henri Tajfel and colleagues who describe social identity as follows: '*[E]very individual is characterized by social features which show his or her membership of a group or a category*' (Deschamps & Devos, 1998: 2), and personal identity is perceived as '*personal features or individual characteristics which are more specific, more idiosyncratic*' (ibidem: 2).

Basically I believe that parallel to all the identities mentioned mentalities can be found that are located on a more unconscious level. It makes sense to talk about an individual mentality and group membership mentalities that can be divided into various subgroups. So, in everyday use, one can speak about a specific individual's mentality ('I don't like his mentality'), a gender mentality ('He has a typical male mentality') or a national mentality ('I like the British mentality').

But mentality works over a long period of time and is characterized by inertia, and mentality is only partly something that the individual has influence upon. This makes it more difficult to speak about multiple mentalities in the way one often speaks of identity: today many people claim to have multiple identities. For example, inhabitants in European countries often stress their new supranational identity by the *self-labelling* claim 'I am a European'. The national identity can to some extent be individually and consciously chosen. A new identity can be the result of the reflected individual's rational thinking; it can be formulated by oneself. This does not mean, however, that identities are necessarily superficial. The identity e.g. as a mother can of course be very deeply felt, although it is identifiable as a result of conscious reflexivity.

Concepts of the 'self' and the impact of socialisation

I use the writings of the American social psychologist George Herbert Mead as a point of departure and combine them with the widely accepted psychological theory of primary and secondary socialisation, which I consider a relevant background for a definition of mentality. In his main work '*Mind, Self, and Society*' (1934), Mead states:

> Selves can only exist in definite relationships to other selves. No hard-and-fast line can be drawn between our own selves and the selves of others, since our own selves exist and enter as such into our experience only in so far as the selves of others exist and enter as such into our experience also. The individual possesses a self only in relation to the selves of the other members of his social group; and the structure of his self expresses or reflects the general behavior pattern of this social group to which he belongs, just as does the structure of the self of every other individual belonging to this social group. (Mead, 1934: 164)

Mead makes a substantial distinction between the 'I' and the 'Me' in his conceptualisation of the self. The 'I' is the unsocialised self, that is, the platform from which the self expresses own personal wishes, needs and dispositions meant to separate it from others. The 'Me' is the socialised self, which mainly consists of the attitudes of others that have been experienced since early childhood, first during primary and later during secondary socialisation and internalised in one's self.

To summarize, I see mentality as an embedded part of the self which is influenced by primary and secondary socialisation and therefore, in Mead's sense, more 'Me' than 'I'.

Let me illustrate how I conceptualise the development of the self through a drawing:

Figure 5:1

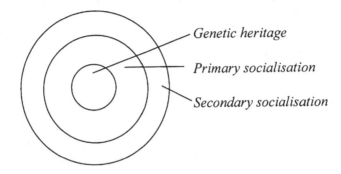

Human beings have certain biological and physiological features, i.e. *genetic heritage* transmitted from the parents that make up a natural core in the newborn child. How influential and how specific these genetic patterns are has been the subject of much genetic research for many years and will probably always be a matter of heavy scientific, philosophical or religious dispute.

Since we are no clones of our parents, a register of *individual traits* in the newborn child must exist parallel to genetic heritage and is as yet unaffected by the primary socialisation. The importance of these individual traits for the later development of the child's mental dispositions is also unclear, but cannot be ignored as a possible factor.

In social psychology the expression *primary socialisation* means the care, the upbringing and the development of psychological processes that occur in early childhood usually in a family. *Secondary socialisation* takes place in societal institutions or other societal connections (kindergarden, school, further education, mass media, political life, etc.) that continue, replace or supplement the influence of the family (Berger & Luckmann, 1966: 154).

The external influence through primary and secondary socialisation is *automated, internalised, embedded* and *incorporated* on a long-term basis. They appear and can be decoded in face-to-face situations through interaction, role playing and body signals (which would apply to my description in the above section 'First example: Work culture') or in analysing the behavioural patterns in larger groups or populations (which is relevant in the above section 'Second example: Political culture').

Henrik Rye Møller

Concepts of the habitus

A frequent reaction from people who hear about my understanding of the concept of mentality is the question of whether this is the same as or resembles the concept of *habitus*. My answer would be that it depends on the definition of habitus. It does resemble the way habitus is used by the German sociologist Norbert Elias, in whose view habitus *"refers to those levels of our personality makeup which are not inherent or innate but are very deeply habituated in us by learning through social experience from birth onward – so deeply habituated, in fact, that they feel 'natural' or inherent even to ourselves."*[21] This description covers my position quite well: mentality is something that, through socialisation, individuals have *habituated* ('habituate' in its original sense of 'to get used to') or embedded so intensely that they feel it existed right from the very beginning. Actually, Elias sometimes uses the word mentality parallel to habitus, which illustrates that the choice of term is often a matter of taste. The important thing is of course what lies behind the definitions and concepts regardless of the chosen terms.

My understanding of mentality is also inspired by the French sociologist Pierre Bourdieu's notion of habitus, but it differs from his definition with regard to the attribution of habitus to class aspects. Bourdieu defines his conception of habitus as follows:

> The habitus is both the generative principle of objectively classifiable judgements and the system of classification (principium divisionis) of these practices. It is in the relationship between the two capacities which define the habitus, the capacity to produce classifiable practices and works, and the capacity to differentiate and appreciate these practices and products (taste), that the represented social world, i.e., the space of life-styles, is constituted ... The habitus is not only a structuring structure, which organizes practices and the perception of practices, but also a structured structure: the principle of division into logical classes which organizes the perception of the social world is itself the product of internalisation of the division into social classes. (Bourdieu, 1984: 170)

I would argue that mentality is much more than the division into social classes and therefore should not be limited to that. Class aspects are *one* possible perspective, but they themselves are no basic characteristic of mentality. I even see mentality as a possibility to describe what is common to people of a certain community in spite of class diffe-

142

rences. I see this idea displayed in the works of other mentality theorists as e.g. Norbert Elias and various 'Annales School' historians. In his major works *The Civilizing Process* and *The Germans* (Elias, 1978 and 1996). Norbert Elias describes and interprets the development of everyday life and everyday manners, ways of conduct and interaction in the nineteenth and twentieth century. Among his fields of investigation were table manners and non-verbal body and facial expressions that have been embedded and incorporated in people over a longer period of time and passed on from one generation to another.

Elias's examples correspond very well to some of the major topics dealt with by mentality historians (see the section 'History of the mentality concept and its current status') and they also support a statement by Jacques Le Goff from the 'Annales School' that the history of mentality focuses on trivial, everyday and even automated behaviour that unites Ceasar and his warrior, Saint Louis and his peasant, and Columbus and his sailor (Le Goff 1974: 80).

Methodology: identification of mentality

The identification of mentality is not possible in a direct way, since the individuals themselves or people around them have no direct access to the mental core outlined above. Therefore mentality has to be traced indirectly and in the following I suggest some possible ways to do the analysis.

Analysing the interaction processes
One possible way of analysing, which refers to my first group of examples above, is to observe the interaction process that takes place when individuals engage in cultural encounters. My perception of interaction is covered by Alfred Schütz's definition:

> Interaction is the process of mutual awareness of signitive-symbolic signs – words, body and face movements, artifacts, and virtually anything that symbolizes meaning. These signs constitute a "field of expression" of an individual; and as they are mutually read, individuals begin the process of constructing a sense of intersubjectivity (Turner, 2002: 10).

I regard Schütz's accentuation of 'body and face movements' as a very important aspect of the identification of mentality which ought to be investigated in future research.

Henrik Rye Møller

In the interaction process it becomes clear that there are some fundamental traits that unconsciously influence the conduct of the individual. They are *'formulated'* and become *'visible'* through verbal and nonverbal signs and thereby made accessible for analytical purposes.

If due to practical or other reasons actual observation is not possible (as in the case of my interviews), the researcher could make his analysis on the basis of the interacting persons' accounts of the cultural encounters. Whether the researcher himself observes or he uses descriptions by the interacting parties as his analysis material, his conclusions will be based upon interpretations of the analysis.

In the analysis and interpretation process the researcher can draw upon the methodology that is commonly accepted within the field of qualitative[22] research dealing with interaction regardless of the concrete research field.

But mentality research must look for *additional* research methods; because its ambition is to approach the very core of oneself – or rather *one's self. Role-taking theory* could be such an additional method.

Role-taking

The sociologist Erving Goffman claims that in the interaction processes we reveal our selves in acting, in filling out the roles we have chosen to play in order to show the other party, our audience, our best performance. In his theory of human behaviour he uses the metaphor of a theatre as his point of departure. At a performance on a stage the actors try to convince the audience of the seriousness of their role-filling, he explains. Goffman's point is that in spite of the somewhat artificial choice of roles the performers try to act as naturally as possible, so that in the interpretation of the audience their performance is seen as the real character of the performer, i.e. the individual.

In his work *'The Presentation of Self in Everyday Life'* Goffman writes:

> When an individual plays a part he implicitly requests his observers to take seriously the impression that is fostered before them. They are asked to believe that the character they see actually possesses the attributes he appears to possess, that the task he performs will have the consequences that are implicitly claimed for it, and that, in general, matters are what they appear to be. (Goffman, 1990 [1959], 28)

In this quotation Goffman expresses the view that the role-filling reveals the actual attributes of the role-taking individual. As I see it, the roles we play are reflections of the 'self'. Of course such a methodo-logical approach needs further development, but it seems to be a fruit-ful way to analyse and interpret the studies of some other researchers who have investigated role-taking in a German context.

These studies show a clear tendency that East Germans identify with their role; they pick a role that is close to their selves. This con-clusion is supported by the observation that East Germans find it diffi-cult to shift roles in a work-related context. Other researchers have observed the same phenomenon, for instance in the way people be-have and present themselves at job interviews, which has been pointed out by the linguists Auer and Birkner in various papers.[23]

Another study argues that West Germans seem to be better at pre-tending and showing off in order to 'sell themselves' better, in other words to pick a role and play it well. As mentioned by sociologists Antos and Kühn, there is a difference in what they label 'life-style'. East Germans tend to keep a low profile in larger groups and they show this in the way they dress and speak. *"Self-importance and va-nity are considered ridiculous. The majority of East Germans do not want to appear better than they really are."* (Antos & Kühn, 1999: 35)

These studies demonstrate how role-taking can be interpreted as specific mentalities that are categorisable as a kind of stereotyping.[24] In the case of these two studies two stereotype categories would be 'honest' and 'unpretentious'. The stereotypes are, like mentality itself, usually quite stable, but not static. The negotiation perspective on cul-ture that I mentioned above takes its point of departure in the relation-ship between the stereotypes that a person has about himself and those that others have about him. In other words: this perspective accentu-ates the dynamics that arise in the combination of self-images and self-definitions with ascriptions made by others (Vaara et al, 2003: 64).

Analysing political culture
In the section 'Second example: Political culture' I made a brief com-ment on the voting pattern in German elections, which show some East-West differences with regard to voting habits and preferences. A closer study of the interpretation of the political principles and con-tents in the established parties also indicates that there are certain ba-sic differences between the East and the West, and I believe that to some extent they are expressions of mental characteristics. The Social Democratic Party (SPD) is an example of this.

The former prime minister in the East German state of Saxony-Anhalt, Reinhard Höppner, argues for a comparable development between the citizens' network relationships in the former GDR and the social 'we'-orientation[25] among citizens in the Eastern part of the united Germany:

> The GDR-slogan "From the 'I' to the 'we'" did not pass the East Germans without leaving traces. While individualism prevails in the West, many people in the East quite naturally ask: how can *we* solve this or that problem? It is a feeling of solidarity, which arose under the pressure of a dictatorial society, but which over time also has become voluntary.[26]

According to Höppner and other observers of German politics, these regional differences in the programme contents and the pragmatic activity of political parties can be explained through different mentalities that are highly influenced by secondary socialisation aspects.

If we take the example provided by the PDS it is quite obvious that the 'we'-identification is used as a way of setting up boundaries and segregating between 'we' and 'they', but also as an integrating factor within the 'we'-category to recreate and further develop the feeling of mutual closeness and interdependence. The PDS-demand for 'justice' ('Gerechtigkeit') for the East Germans in the united Germany expresses an egalitarian claim that I interpret not only as PDS-rhetoric but as something very typical for the entire East German political culture.

Does the analysis, then, also show the apparently paradoxical combination of East German egalitarianism and hierarchical thinking? In my view, it does. Political observers argue that East Germans tend to have a preference for strong political leader types. This can be seen e.g. in the nomination of political candidates on a regional level,[27] and it corresponds with an East German tendency to favour political parties on the extreme right or the extreme left – or not to vote at all which to some extent can be interpreted as a rejection of the democratic system. Opinion polls show that East Germans generally are less dedicated to democracy and freedom in the Western sense than West Germans.[28]

These findings are further indications of the existence of different political cultures in East and West Germany, which are influenced and at least partly explainable by different mentalities that have developed in different contexts of socialisation.

Perspectives

My aim with this chapter was to argue for the reintroduction of mentality as a field of investigation in order to make possible a differentiation of cultural studies on identity. I wanted to demonstrate how an awareness of the unconscious in the human mind could contribute to a differentiated, fine-grained and nuanced description of individuals and groups of individuals.

My conceptualisation of mentality draws upon various scientific disciplines: the essentialist perspective on generic heritage, social psychology, sociology and history (mainly constructivist perspectives), and my approach can be categorised as moderate constructivism.

I have outlined some thoughts and ideas about the theory and methodology of mentality research, and I hope that fellow researchers will join a scientific discussion about the possibilities and limitations of the presented field.

Finally, I see a promising perspective in using mentality research in a practical or commercial context. Internationally operating firms could probably benefit from the field of mentality in a practically applied form. I believe that awareness and knowledge of similarities and differences in mentality could be useful for businessmen when planning their sales and communication strategies in an intercultural context.

Henrik Rye Møller

References

Antos, Gerd & Christine S. Kühn; One Germany; United but still divided? Verbal and non-verbal approaches. In Karlfried Knapp *et al.* (eds), *Meeting the Intercultural Challenge*. Berlin: Verlag Wissenschaft und Praxis, 1999.

Auer, Peter; How to Play the Game: An Investigation of Role-Played Interviews in East Germany, *Text* 18, 1, 1998.

Berger, Peter L. & Thomas Luckmann; *The Social Construction of Reality*. New York: Penguin, 1966.

Birkner, Karin; *Ost- und Westdeutsche im Bewerbungsgespräch. Eine kommunikative Gattung in Zeiten kommunikativen Wandels*. Tübingen: Niemeyer, 2001.

Bourdieu, Pierre; *Distinction. A Social Critique of the Judgement of Taste*. London: Routledge, 1984.

Burke, Peter; Strengths and Weaknesses of the History of Mentalities, *History of European Ideas*, 7, 5, 1986.

Burke, Peter; *The French Historical Revolution, The Annales School, 1929-89*. Cambridge: Polity Press, 1990.

Bøttzauw, Ole *et al.* (eds); *Kultur, mentalitet, ideologi*. Århus: Den jyske historiker 29-30, 1984.

Craig, Gordon A.; *Das Ende Preußens*. München: Deutscher Taschenbuch Verlag, 1989.

Deschamps, Jean-Claude & Thierry Devos; Regarding the Relationship between Social Identity and Personal Identity. In Stephen Worchel *et al.* (eds), *Social Identity. International Perspectives*. London: Sage, 1998.

Dinzelbacher, Peter (ed.); *Europäische Mentalitätsgeschichte*. Stuttgart: Kröner Verlag, 1993.

Elias, Norbert; *The Civilizing Process*, Vol. 1: *The History of Manners*. Oxford: Blackwell, 1978 [1939].

Elias, Norbert; *The Germans: Power Struggles and the Development of Habitus in the Nineteenth and Twentieth Centuries.* Oxford: Polity Press, 1996 [1989].

Fontane, Theodor; *Effi Briest.* Frankfurt/M: Verlag Ullstein, 1974 [1895].

Fontane, Theodor; *Wanderungen durch die Mark Brandenburg.* München: Nymphenburger Verlagsanstalt, 1979 [1862-1882].

Frederiksen, Inge & Rømer, Hilda (eds); *Kvinder, mentalitet, arbejde.* Århus: Århus Universitetsforlag, 1986.

Geiger, Theodor; *Die soziale Schichtung des deutschen Volkes.* Stuttgart: Ferdinand Enke Verlag, 1932.

Goffman, Erving; *The Presentation of Self in Everyday Life.* London: Penguin, 1990 [1959].

Hall, Stuart; Cultural Identity and Diaspora. In Jonathan Rutherford (ed.), *Identity. Community, Culture, Difference.* London: Lawrence and Wishart, 1990.

Höppner, Reinhard; *Zukunft gibt es nur gemeinsam.* München: Blessing, 2000.

Kroll, Frank-Lothar; Das Janusgesicht Preußens. *Berliner Lesezeichen* 6-7, Edition Louisenstadt, 2001.

Kuczynski, Jürgen; *Geschichte des Alltags des deutschen Volkes.* Berlin: Akademie Verlag, 1980.

Kvale, Steinar; *Interview.* København: Hans Reitzels Forlag, 1994.

Le Goff, Jacques; Les mentalités. Une histoire ambiguë. In P. Nora (ed.), *Faire de l'histoire,* 3, 1974.

Lemert, Charles & Ann Branaman; *The Goffman Reader.* Malden, Mass.: Blackwell, 1997.

Henrik Rye Møller

Lüdtke, Alf (ed.); *Alltagsgeschichte. Zur Rekonstruktion historischer Erfahrungen und Lebensweisen.* Frankfurt / New York: Campus Verlag, 1989.

Mead, George Herbert; *Mind, Self, and Society.* Chicago: Phoenix, 1934.

Mennell, Stephen and Johan Ghoudsblom (eds); *Norbert Elias: On Civilisation, Power, and Knowledge. Selected Writings.* Chicago: University of Chicago Press, 1998.

Møller, Henrik Rye; *Østtysk mentalitet efter Murens fald - set med danske øjne.* København: Copenhagen Working Papers in LSP, 2002.

Qvortrup, Lars; *Det hyperkomplekse samfund.* København: Gyldendal, 1998.

Raulff, Ulrich (ed.); *Mentalitäten-Geschichte. Zur historischen Rekonstruktion geistiger Prozesse.* Berlin: Verlag Klaus Wagenbach, 1987.

Schultz, Majken; *Kultur i organisationer – funktion eller symbol.* København: Handelshøjskolens Forlag, 1990.

Sellin, Volker; Mentalität und Mentalitätsgeschichte, *Historische Zeitschrift*, 241, 1985.

Søderberg, Anne-Marie; Do National Cultures Always Make a Difference? In Torben Vestergaard (ed.), *Language, Culture and Identity*, Aalborg: University Press, 1999.

Ting-Toomey, Stella; *Communicating Across Cultures.* New York & London: Guilford Press, 1999.

Turner, Jonathan H.; *Face to Face. Towards a Sociological Theory of Interpersonal Behavior.* Stanford: Stanford University Press, 2002.

Vaara, Eero, Anette Risberg, Anne-Marie Søderberg & Janne Tienari; Nation Talk. The Construction of National Stereotypes in a Merging Multinational. In Anne-Marie Søderberg & Eero Vaara, *Merging Across Borders. People, Cultures and Politics.* Copenhagen Business School Press, 2003.

Vester, Heinz-Günter; *Kollektive Identitäten und Mentalitäten. Von der Völkerpsychologie zur kulturvergleichenden Soziologie und interkulturellen Kommunikation.* Frankfurt am Main: IKO – Verlag für interkulturelle Kommunikation, 1996.

Henrik Rye Møller

Notes

[1]   An example is Stuart Hall's concept of identity or identities as a constant, productive process of self-positioning in relation to others. Hall, 1990.

[2]   As described e.g. by Qvortrup, 1998.

[3]   E.g. Vester, 1996.

[4]   Sellin, 1985.

[5]   For an overview, see Søderberg, 1999.

[6]   Geiger, 1932, 77. Geiger strongly opposed the national socialist ideas of "the people's soul" and the Nazis forced him to leave Germany in 1933 for racial and political reasons.

[7]   For further reading, see e.g. Burke, 1990.

[8]   Examples of anthologies are Ulrich Raulff's *'History of Mentalities'*.(Raulff, 1987) and Peter Dinzelbacher's *'European History of Mentality'* (Dinzelbacher, 1993).

[9]   As e.g. Alf Lüdtke in his *'History of Everyday Life'* (Lüdtke, 1989).

[10] E.g. in Jürgen Kuczynski's *'History of the Everyday Life of the German People'* (Kuczynski, 1980).

[11] See e.g. *'Women, Mentality, Work'*. (Frederiksen & Rømer, 1986) and *'Culture, Mentality, Iideology'* (Bøttzauw et al, 1984).

[12] See the section "Theory: The conceptualisation of mentality"

[13] *GDR* is an abbreviation of *German Democratic Republic*, the East German socialist state that existed between 1949 and 1990.

[14] E.g. a pre-democratic institution like the duel survived in the East Elbian area, although it was officially forbidden all over Germany. The duel is described in Theodor Fontane's novel *'Effi Briest'* (Fontane, 1974 [1895]).

[15] See e.g. Fontane's *'Wanderings in the Brandenburg County'*. (Fontane, 1979 [1862-1882]). Also see Gordon A. Craig's *'The End of Prussia'* (Craig, 1989).

[16] For details see Frank-Lothar Kroll's *'Prussia's Janus-face'* (Kroll, 2001).

[17] The Nazi regime (1933-1945) caused another reinforcement of the authoritarian side.

[18] See Møller, 2002, 85-98 for a detailed presentation and discussion of this theme.

[19] In the general election to the *Bundestag* in 2002 the PDS got 16.8% of the votes in East Germany and only 1.1% in West Germany. Other remarkable results: The Green Party: 4.8% (East), 9.5% (West). The Conservative-Christian Union: 28.3% in East Germany, 40.9% in West Germany.

[20] Ting-Toomey, 1999.

[21] From the introduction to Norbert Elias in Mennell & Ghoudsblom, 1998.

[22] E.g. Kvale, 1994 and Schultz, 1990.

[23] See e.g. Auer, 1998 and Birkner, 2001.

24 Stereotyping as *"reconstruction of widely held images of oneself and the other"* (Vaara et al, 2003: 61).

25 For a discussion of the category "we", see Gustafsson's section "The first boundary: The 'we's' and the otherness" (Gustafsson, this volume).

26 Quotation from an interview with Höppner in *'Die Zeit'*, 29 July 1999, my translation. His ideas are further developed in his book *'Future must be a united project'* (Höppner, 2000).

27 See Møller, 2002: 96.

28 See Møller, 2002: 86.

6

Textual Boundary Explorations: Positing Self and Other as actors in global charity

JAN GUSTAFSSON

Introduction

The aim of this contribution is to explore a basic problem of interculturality: the mechanisms of identity and alterity construction. These mechanisms will be studied on the basis of the theoretical background of semiotics and within the context of Danish development aid.

The field of interculturality that this chapter deals with – the construction of images of a cultural self and Other – has been the object of multiple studies, especially within the disciplines of sociology and anthropology. In the last decades, a still more general theoretical tendency has been to see identities as *symbolic* and *relational* constructions, depending on *boundaries* as markers of difference (cf. Jenkins, 1996 & 1997, Anderson, 1983, Barth, 1969). According to this position, the identity of a community does not depend on a kind of essence (whatever the character of this), but on the fact that its members share a certain idea or image (or a series of signs) of it. Such an image of the community will have the character of an 'us'/'we', which by dialectical and linguistic logic must be related to some 'Others', a 'they'/'them', independent of the specific character of the community (national, ethnic, religious, gender-related, etc.). Furthermore, the image of an 'us' *vis-à-vis* the 'Others' is sustained by an idea of a boundary between the groups. Such a boundary can be perceived as being of spatial, temporal or any other character, but its basic function is symbolic: it marks the line that separates 'us' from 'them', whatever actual differences may exist between the groups. In the words of Barth

(1969), it is the 'boundary that maintains the group, not the cultural stuff it encloses.'

I believe that semiotics can account coherently for these important theoretical trends. In the following, I intend to give an idea of some of the possibilities semiotics offers for the study of culture and interculturality, first very shortly in the form of some general proposals, and next as a more specific outline of a number of concepts.

This theoretical outline will contain a discussion of some theoretical and methodological proposals for the study of texts as a fundamental aspect of culture and interculturality. The general theoretical and methodological concepts that will be introduced are: text, context, semiosphere, boundary and translation. As more specific tools for the textual analysis I will propose the concepts of deixis (especially related to pronouns), metonymy and metaphor, and space, time and actors as elements of a narrative. The theoretical outline will be followed by a case study, in which a specific text – published by a number of Danish NGO's – will be analysed with respect to its constitution of cultural self and Other. By way of conclusion, some theoretical, semantic and ethical implications of the textual constitution of self and Other will be discussed.

Semiotics and culture

The theoretical background of semiotics offers three basic levels of contributions to questions of culture and interculturality:

- A first level would imply a proposal for a philosophic anthropology, based on the idea of sign and sign functions as a basic epistemological and even ontological feature of humanness. The main theoretical contribution in this sense is the semiotics of the American philosopher C. S. Peirce (1839-1914). The work of Peirce has been present in the North American philosophical and semiotic tradition (especially in pragmatic philosophy), but in recent decades his pragmatic and dynamic semiotics have gained ground in European and Latin American semiotic circles and enjoy general academic respect. Among more recent contributions to semiotic anthropology are the works of Antonio Ponzio (1990) from Italy, and Kaja Silverman (1983) from the USA. The German philosopher K. O. Apel (1994 & 1998) has reformulated the idea of a 'philosophic' or 'transcendental' semiotics, analysing Peircean semiotics in the context of the linguistic and pragmatic turn of the 20th Century.

- A second level could point at more specific theoretical proposals for where and how to 'find' and study 'culture', in the double sense of something that is common for all humans and something that is specific for distinct human entities, such as actual communities and individuals. The ideas of text, context, semiosphere and boundaries and translations are essential to this level. Some of the most important contributions are those of the Russian thinkers Mikhail Bakhtin (text, dialogue) and Yuri Lotman (context, boundary, semiosphere).
- A third level would deal with a number of more concrete theoretical and methodological instruments for cultural analysis, which within the broader theoretical context always has as its object a 'text' (defined broadly as any meaningful collection of signs). A great number of concepts originally belonging to linguistics, rhetoric and semiotics are pertinent at this level, including those of linguistically inspired narratology.

The theoretical outline that follows will deal mostly with concepts belonging to the second and the third level.

Theoretical outline

In this section I will propose some theoretical and methodological elements for the analysis of the case. These elements are situated at two levels, namely a general theoretical level based on the axis of the concepts text, context, boundary and translation, and a more specific theoretical and methodological level of proposals for textual analysis inspired by linguistics and narratology.

Text and context

It has been mentioned that signs and the sign-function (semiosis) are basic elements of human existence, according to a (Peircean) semiotic approach to culture. The semiosis or sign-function, however, is not a question of processing isolated signs, it implies *text*. It does so because any production or reproduction of signs requires a joint labour of various signs – some explicit and some implicit – that together form a text.

Jan Gustafsson

A simple reading of, say, an ideographic sign indicating that smoking is prohibited, requires the ability to understand and reproduce various sets of norms, prohibitions and interpretations, which are all 'texts' in the sense of being coherent or meaningful sign-structurations with a certain permanence and repeatability. Whether a smoker or a non-smoker, any 'reader' of the sign will under normal circumstances be able to evoke a lot more than the immediate intention of the sign (the prohibition), such as formerly read or heard 'texts' about the danger of smoking, or discussions about the convenience of general prohibitions, or images of smokers claiming the right to enjoy tobacco in public spaces etc. Although more implicit than explicit in most cases, the actual reading of a simple sign implies the 're-actualisation' of a number of texts of a certain permanence. This permanence, however, need not imply that the texts are materially recorded in some form (e.g. on paper or electronically). It means only that the texts have a presence in a given culture as something known and meaningful to its members as a *context* in which they live and act. So, a text is not necessarily bound to written language or even to language (although language as writing, talk and thought is undoubtedly the most important text-form). Texts might consist of images or other non-linguistic signs, and they might be purely mental. In this sense, the so-called oral myths of cultures without writing are also to be considered 'texts', as is also the case with 'beliefs', 'religion', 'ideology' etc. The partly or totally mental, as well as non-linguistic character of some texts does not mean, however, that they are not empirical: the strength of the 'textual approach' to culture is that – although seemingly quite abstract – it deals with empirical phenomena, like for instance the kind of phenomena that have been the objects of anthropology and ethnography.[1]

Permanence and repeatability are closely interrelated phenomena. Permanence depends on the ability of the members of a culture or community to reproduce (repeat) a certain textual meaning. The actual reproduction, however, cannot be a simple 'repetition': the circumstances of the reading of a sign or any other reproduction of meaning are always up to a point contingent and unique, depending on factors like space, time and the history and *horizon* or life-world of the producer and receiver of the message. To say that a text is repeatable should thus not lead to the idea of an identical repetition in every reading or reproduction of it.

In the same way as the idea of sign logically leads to that of text, text is closely connected to *context*. A text, of whatever type cannot be produced and reproduced without context, an idea already implied in the argumentation above about signs and texts. In a general sense, context is the space, the time, the code(s), the actors and the 'co-texts', including the concept of 'genre' of any semiotic or textual function. To take just one example, a casual encounter between two persons and the possible outcome(s) of it will depend on the context in the literal sense of the texts that determine the meaning of the space, the time, the possibilities and roles of the actors etc. We 'know', i.e. we can reproduce the cultural texts of what to say or do (and not do) at the bus stop, at a reception or, say, on a battlefield. Any kind of text, whether in the most narrow or in the broadest definition of the word, is embedded in other texts, in the most concrete as well as in the most abstract and broad sense. A newspaper article depends on the textual space of its production and reproduction – i.e. the actual 'paper' – in its printed or electronic version. It depends also on what has been written already in the same newspaper and other media on the given subject. Furthermore it depends on general and specific 'codes' and rules for journalistic genres, the style and editorial 'line' of the paper, and in an even more general sense, it depends on different national and international contexts (see also the chapter by Clausen, this volume). Context, thus, points into space as well as time. A newspaper article about an event in a foreign country will relate in space to other articles on similar themes and to the textual space of the paper as a whole. In a further sense, it relates to the whole context of a 'foreign' or international space, implicitly or explicitly related to 'our' national space. In time, such an article must refer to former texts about the same or similar events, and in a wider sense, to the whole temporal construction of events as such (e.g. as a narrative) or to the temporal ideas of 'home' and foreign space.

'Genre' is a contextual space that implies both space and time, as well as 'code' or 'rules' for textual production and reproduction. Any text will relate spatially to other contemporary texts belonging to the same genre, to earlier – and to potential future – texts, as well as to the formal or informal rules for the production and interpretation of the given genre. A boxing match has rules and codes, not only for the physical 'dialogue' between the combatants, but also for what the public might say, do and think. An elegant hook might recall the hook of some mythical fight, the style of a young promising middle-weight fighter might recall that of a Sugar Ray Leonard (or Robinson), and the most eagerly awaited fights create their own global context of lunch table discussions, conversations in bars and pubs, innumerable newspaper articles, sales and resales of entrance tickets etc.

Jan Gustafsson

The concept of 'context' as here proposed exploits the two common 'dictionary' senses of the word, i.e. as the (verbal) text surrounding a word or a passage giving meaning to this word or passage, and as the 'surrounding conditions' for a given phenomenon. These meanings are not eliminated, but should rather be seen as a point of departure for the theoretical concept. The common sense use helps the understanding of the theoretical meaning: 'context' is understood as the 'surroundings' for 'text' in its narrow sense of verbal text as well as the surroundings for any other kind of human activity. But any such activity is, according to a semiotic idea of culture, also 'textual' in the sense of necessarily having a symbolic or semiotic – i.e. 'textual' – dimension. In this way, the combination of the common sense of the word 'context' with a broad idea of 'text' points towards the basic idea of the theoretical concept, namely the textual or semiotic 'surroundings' or 'sphere' for any 'text', or in other words, the semiotic dimension of any human social phenomenon. Text and context are, thus, in a close relation of contiguity: the borders of the text have contact with and depend for their meaning on the context, which rather should be in plural, because context is a phenomenon of multiplicity and complexity, of innumerable boundaries crossing each other, as shown in the examples mentioned above.

Semiosphere, boundaries and translation

The word 'sphere' has been used as a quasi synonym for 'context', in the sense that the context is the spatial and temporal 'sphere' that surrounds and gives meaning to a semiotic event, i.e. a text. In order to define a context as cultural and semiotic space, Lotman has coined the term 'semiosphere', defined as 'the whole semiotic space of the culture in question' (Lotman, 1990: 125). This semiotic space is 'the result and the condition for the development of culture' (ibid.). Lotman stresses, thus, the semiotic dimension of culture and defines the semiotic (or textual) 'space' of a given culture as a 'semiosphere'. Although a seemingly very abstract and not easily applicable concept, the idea of semiosphere presents some advantages in relation to 'culture'. First and foremost, it stresses a specific and basic human phenomenon, the use of signs, while 'culture' (and consequently interculturality) tends to be a constant object of different (and often contradictory) theoretical and methodological approaches. Secondly, 'semiosphere' indicates a specific (and basic) empirical aspect of 'culture', namely its textual dimension. Accepting with Bakhtin (1997) that the object for the human sciences is the 'text', the idea of the semiosphere turns out to be a useful concept for the study of culture as a basically semiotic phenomenon, whose empirical manifestation is text in whatever form it might appear. The quotations show that Lotman, although persistent in a semiotics of culture, avoids a total identification of the concepts 'semiosphere' and 'culture': 'semiosphere' indicates the specific textual and empirical dimension of the less definable idea of 'culture'.

The relationship between 'context' and 'semiosphere' is of a contiguous and hierarchical character: while a 'context' can be the (textual) surroundings of a given textual manifestation at any level, the semiosphere pertains to a higher and more general (and therefore also more abstract) level. In its most abstract sense, the semiosphere represents existence and possibility of semiotic activity, of textual production, and on a more specific level, a semiosphere is the general context for a certain type of textual production. The semiosphere for boxing is, in principle, the sum of texts on boxing and the condition – i.e. possibility – of talking, thinking and writing about boxing. The national semiosphere of any nation state is not only the geography, jurisdiction or inhabitants of a given country, but basically the condition for the production of any 'national' text as well as the sum of such texts. In this sense, the idea of a 'national' text is of course not limited to images or spoken, thought, or written text about the nation, but any semiotic phenomenon in which nationality or 'nationness' takes part as an explicit or implicit aspect.

Summing up, one might define the semiosphere as a 'context of contexts', meaning that any semiosphere consists of an infinite number of smaller contexts or 'spheres' related to each other in different degrees (thematically, generically etc.) This implies that the semiosphere is crossed by innumerable boundaries (cf. Lotman, 1990: 125ff.). These boundaries are limits between texts and contexts, but this does not imply that any text or context is to be seen as an autonomous entity: meaning is a semiotic phenomenon constituted by relation. The production and reading of a sign (text) depends on differentiation, and differences establish and are established by boundaries. This means that the boundary is a phenomenon of relationships and the precondition for meaning. This can be illustrated by returning to the two previous examples, a newspaper story and a boxing match. In the physical space either of these two semiotic events is isolated from similar events as well as from 'texts' that are different. Spatial boundaries indicate the place of one text *vis-à-vis* others – that are different, but alike – within the physical space of the paper or the electronic 'page', and an 'outer space' belonging to different contexts. In a similar way, physical space boundaries indicate the exact geography of the fight itself, the place of the referees, of the public as well as the outer space of 'non-boxing area'. Temporally, the journalistic genre is limited by date, but this limit creates an evident relation: we read a story in relation to what was said about the same subject yesterday or the day before, and also with an expectation as to what tomorrow might bring. Something similar happens to the match, but the most important temporal boundaries in relation to boxing are those dividing the progression of the process of the match itself. The division into rounds and intervals (breaks) is a meaning-giving boundary construction. Each round is differentiated from the others, it can be won or lost by a fighter and it can be evaluated differently by members of the public or by the several referees, and they can be discussed one against another as arguments in favour or against the boxers. At the same time, the rounds indicate a series of inner boundaries in the progression of the event, whose outer limits are the beginning and the end.

The idea of boundary as a constitutive and meaning-giving basic element of text production, leads to the relevance of another important concept: *translation*. The idea of boundary implies a creation of meaning across limits. This creation of meaning is what I term 'translation', following Lotman (1990). Lotman also states that 'the elementary act of thinking is translation' (ibid: 143), indicating the idea of translation as the basic semiotic mechanism.[2] Translation is, thus, the possibility and capability of moving from one meaning, text or context to another, understanding each of these in the relation to the other. This also means that the idea of dialogue relates to the concepts of boundary and translation. According to Lotman (1990: 143), the 'elementary mechanism of translation is dialogue' in the sense of 'alternating directions of the message-flow' between different semiotic structures. Without denying the validity of this statement, I would prefer to invert the idea that says that translation is the elementary mechanism of dialogue. The Bakhtinian idea of 'dialogue' corresponds to a general ontological and epistemological principle, according to which language as well as individual and collective human existence, is to be seen as a constant spatio-temporal 'dialogue' between words, texts and identities (cf. Holquist, 1990). Translation, as I see it, is a general mechanism of this principle. The re-contextualisation of 'translation' as a basic and general concept in a semiotics of culture offers interesting theoretical and methodological possibilities. In the analysis below, I shall try to exemplify how boundary construction and meaning-translation are two indivisible phenomena in the semiotic process.

Semantic-structural elements of textual meaning-production

In this paragraph I intend to proceed to a more specific level and show some important semantic and structural elements that contribute to the production and construction of textual meaning. That these mechanisms are seen as 'structural' and 'semantic', means that they are considered generalised phenomena of certain genres of text that tend to structure the possibilities of meaning. Such mechanisms will necessarily operate at several levels, basically *within* a given text (where they are given and can be studied as empirical manifestations), *between* this given text and other actual texts to which the given text is related (for instance, thematically or by genre) and finally, between the actual manifestation in the given text and a more general level of a relevant semiosphere. Such a more general level could be a 'national' semiosphere, a thematic semiosphere etc.

The mechanisms here presented may appear in any textual genre. Nevertheless, in this case the interest lies basically in non-fictional texts,[3] like the text that will be used for the analysis.

The list of mechanisms in this chapter is not exhaustive, but I believe it includes some of the most important in cultural-textual analysis. The following mechanisms will be discussed:

- The deictic function that frequently indicate collective-cultural meanings, such as 'we', 'here', 'now', i.e. actors, space and time.
- Metonymic and metaphorical functions.
- The narratological functions of time and space and actors, especially the structural constitution of the different actors of the text and their mutual relations.

As stated above, these elements and mechanisms might be present on very different levels, from the most manifest level in a specific text to a completely abstract presence of a very general context. This also means that it can be possible to see a given mechanism as an implicit (or 'invisible') element of a given text. The elements mentioned will be studied on a semantic and pragmatic level, i.e. on the level of textual production and reception, and also as an intra-textual mechanism of syntactical structuration and semantic expression. It is important to stress that all these mechanisms are boundary phenomena in the sense of being present on different levels, and creating meaning not only within a given level (for instance in the reading of a given text), but between levels, translating from one level to another.

The basic cultural boundary and the deictic function

According to Lotman (1990: 131) the basic cultural boundary is the one that divides the world into 'our internal space' and 'their external space'. The 'boundary can be defined as the outer limit of a first-person form' (ibid). This means that words like 'we', 'here' and 'now', called deictics[4] (cf. Benveniste, 1971 and Ducrot & Todorov, 1995), play an essential role in any form of collective or cultural identification. A 'we' indicates the idea of a community to which the speaker(s) belong(s). Such a community might be completely circumstantial and transient, as for instance the case of two unknown persons who, due to circumstances, enunciate a 'we', as described very interestingly by Schütz (1980). But a 'we' can also be of a generic character, designating a more or less formalised community of a political, religious or other character, like a national 'we' of formal and informal text forms. In the first case, we are dealing with an authentic deictic function in the sense that the 'we' refers to a limited number of specific persons. In the second case, the deictic function is partly an ideological or pseudo-function, in the sense of being an abstract reference implying general characteristics of maybe millions of persons. For this reason, the cultural 'we' cannot be as purely deictic as the singular 'I' or 'you' of discourse, as analysed by Benveniste (1971).

A 'we', however, will always imply a certain 'context', i.e. a certain amount of text(s) produced by and producing the given 'we'. A 'we' consisting of two persons waiting at the bus stop is produced by texts such as the time schedule and the knowledge of a system of public transport, and it might produce texts like 'we'll have to wait another while' or similar phrases. On the other hand, a national or ethnic 'we' produces and is produced by an infinite number of texts constituting a semiosphere. That a 'we' is contextualised and might be constituted by and constituting a semiosphere does not mean, however, that context and community are identical phenomena. A context or semiosphere is a phenomenon given independently of the idea, will or conscience of the persons belonging to it, while a community is an ideological phenomenon depending on the idea and will of at least a part of its members. In this sense, one might say that what Benedict Anderson (1983) describes in his famous 'Imagined Communities' is – as the title indicates – the idea of the nation as a community, i.e. an ideological phenomenon, while other contemporary theorists, like Smith (1991), insist more on the contextual idea of nation.[5]

The third person, 'they/them', is the indicator of otherness. According to Benveniste (1971) the third person is not deictic, meaning that its reference is a question of more or less explicit contextuality. It is, so to say, a 'non-person' (cf. Benveniste, 1971 and Urban, 1989). From a cultural point of view, this statement is interesting, as it places the other in a secondary, or more exactly, *third* position as that or those that give meaning to the 'we' without having a 'real' reference, a possibility that will be discussed below in relation to the analysed texts.

Lotman only takes into account the first and the third persons of the personal pronouns as the basic cultural identity markers. This leaves the question of the function of the 'you'. As this problem implies fundamental discussions on the function of dialogue related to interculturality, it will only be possible to make a couple of short comments on the question: first, that the plural 'you' as well as the 'they' may imply abstract or ideological functions as reference to the cultural 'Other'. Second, that both imply a 'translation' regarding the 'we', in the sense of representing the otherness that gives meaning to the 'we'. Third, that the 'they/them', although constitutive of self and Other, obviously does not contain a dialogue *with* the Other. Fourth, that the plural 'you' is complex and problematic in character. Just as the 'we', it can have circumstantial as well as a generic reference. In relation to a first person pronoun, the plural 'you' can designate two or more specific others, as in phrases like: 'If you (children) take out the dishes, then we (the adults) will do the rest.' But in a phrase like 'Why can't you (children or young people in general) be a little more considerate?' the reference goes beyond the actual persons the sentence is addressed to, designating a whole class of people. This designation tends to function similarly to the generic 'we', and this has a series of implications, such as:

- It generalises in the sense of assuming a series of common features for the whole class of persons it comprehends, and assuming that these features are true in the specific case, i.e. valid for the person or persons the plural 'you' is addressed to.

Jan Gustafsson

- Although plural, the actual addressee might be a single person, as in an example like: 'You [Argentineans] are obsessed with psychology.'
- These functions tend to ideologise the use of the plural 'you', turning it into a mechanism of exclusion, related to the inclusive 'we'.

The deictic function is not limited to the personal pronouns. The actors expressed in the personal pronouns are situated in space and time (in a specific text and/or in a general context). This fact gives great importance to deictic indicators of time and space, of which 'here' and 'now' are the basic ones. In the same way as a 'we', a 'here' can indicate a simulated or pseudo deictic mechanism, referring not to the immediate space of the speaker, but to a generalised space, such as a national geography. In a parallel way to the 'we'-'them' pair, the 'here' implies the idea of an actual deictic function: 'Here' is 'our' space, the known and 'normal' space in opposition to an unspecific 'there', whose basic meaning is to confirm the 'here' and which needs further specification in order to refer to a given space.

Also the temporal situation is given by a contrastive deictic or pseudo-deictic function, namely of the word 'now', which refers to a more or less specific contemporary moment in opposition to a past and historic 'then', or – although less commonly – to an imagined future.

The deictic or pseudo-deictic functions of a 'we', a 'here' and a 'now' can be expressed more or less explicitly or implicitly in a specific text. In the texts to be dealt with in this contribution, the cultural deictic dimension will mainly be implicit. An example of an explicit use could be a sentence like: 'Here we don't do those kinds of things nowadays'. Depending on the context, such a phrase might have different meanings, but I suggest that a plausible reading would indicate the following 'translations': 'Here' means 'in our/my country', 'we' indicates the citizens of this country and 'nowadays' (or simply 'now') refers to the present, i.e. the epoch in which 'we' live. If such a reading is acceptable, it implies an interesting and important secondary and implicit reading: there are others, those who do not belong to the given 'we' defined by the 'here' and the 'now', who indeed do – or did – indulge in 'those kinds of things'. Furthermore, I believe that the unspecified 'those kinds of things' in such a reading probably would refer to some kind of 'barbarian' and 'uncivilised' habits. Such a reading coincides with Lotman's (1990: 131) indication of the 'outer' or 'other' space as 'chaotic' and non-cultured.

Displacement and condensation – metonymic and metaphoric functions

The rhetorical figures of metonymy, synecdoche and metaphor can also be seen as mechanisms of boundary and translation, within a given text as well as between the specific text and the contextual situation. Following Jakobson (1956), I do not distinguish between the specific rhetorical figures of metonymy and synecdoche, but rather between metonymic and metaphorical functions as basic linguistic mechanisms.

Traditionally, metonymy is defined as the substitution of a word or an expression for another according to a relationship of contiguity, such as the part for the whole, the container for the content etc., as in an example like: 'Let's have a pint'. In this case the quantity measure substitutes for the drink, meaning that the idea of beer is translated into an idea of quantity and vice versa. The metaphor consists in a substitution based on the principle of similarity. A word or expression is re-contextualised, giving new meaning to a phrase: 'The two shining stars of her face sent a glint of hope into the darkness of his sorrow.' In this example, 'stars', 'glint' and 'darkness' create a metaphorical system of meaning that enters the context of two persons in visual communication. But the 'translation' of 'stars' into 'eyes' and of 'darkness' into a feeling or a state of mind does not mean that these terms lose all their original meaning: the force of the rhetorical or poetic function of a figure consists in its capability for joining meaning from two contexts, i.e. in a constant movement of translation between contexts.

Although traditionally studied mostly as poetic devices, metonymy and metaphor permeate all human sign use. The important element in Jakobson's interpretation of the two is that they are not seen as specific and limited rhetorical figures, but rather as general linguistic functions. The displacement of linguistic signs on the basis of contiguity and similarity is fundamental for the dynamics of meaning (cf. Jakobson, 1956, Ducrot & Todorov, 1995).

This discovery can be extended to general functions of signification, whatever the type of sign or text. An example could be the 'case', as used for instance in journalism, teaching and academic research. The meaning of the case is not limited to the isolated situation; rather its meaning consists in being exemplary or a model. In this sense, the case is an image of a general situation gaining meaning from and giving meaning to similar and related situations. This means that such a text stands in a metaphorical and metonymic relation to what it represents, and that the two mechanisms function as intertextual or contextual systems of translation. An example could be a photograph of a child from the Third World representing not herself, but Third World children as such. In this case, the actual child is a metaphor for the suffering and poverty of the children of the Third World. At the same time, her situation is linked to others whose situation is alike, creating a sort of movement of translation from the actual child of the photograph (or rather from the sign as such) to others. In this case it is very difficult to distinguish the two functions, especially because they are interdependent. To discuss the function of contextual translation of a case like this, it could be useful to take into account the ideas of *condensation* and *displacement*, related to metaphorical and metonymical mechanisms, formulated by Lacan (1966, 1968), who develops Jakobson's and other semiotic theories (especially Saussure's). According to Lacan, the metaphorical function implies a condensation of meaning, while the metonymy displaces meaning. Although this chapter does not intend a Lacanian or psychoanalytical reading of the given objects, the two concepts suggest interesting possibilities of the reading of the specific signs of the Other. The child *condensates* meaning, maybe in her gaze, expressing the whole identity of the Other, and simultaneously she *displaces* the meaning away from herself and the sign vehicle (signifier) that represents her – the photograph – proposing a reading of the whole, generalised Other who, being this radical Other, gives the 'us' its own meaning as a differentiated cultural self.[6]

The elements of a narrative: Space, time and actors

Another important element of a great number of texts (maybe a majority) is what could be termed its narrative elements. Although the study of narratives is mainly an interest related to fiction, in recent decades the study of narrative elements of texts has become an essential part of various currents of social and human sciences. Ethnography, anthropology and cultural sociology in particular have witnessed a rapidly increasing interest in narrative aspects of experience, representation and research. This does not imply a 'fictionalisation' of these disciplines, but rather a recognition of the fact – or more correctly, the theoretical standpoint – that human texts of all kinds tend to be constrained in their structuration and meaning potential by certain basic features of cognition that can be expressed as narrative or epic-narrative elements of textual production.[7]

In order to find useful theoretical and methodological elements for the study of the narrative dimension of texts, I propose some elements of formalist and structuralist inspired narratology, developed originally by Propp, and later by Greimas, Genette, Bremond and others. Although developed mainly on the basis on and for the study of epic and narrative fiction, I believe it worthwhile to re-contextualise some of the theoretical and methodological proposals of narratology in the study of non-fiction, as proposed and done by several theorists, especially in the last two decades (cf. Bal, 1990). I believe there are two principal reasons for the relevance of such a proposal: first, that narratology offers a series of theoretical and methodological instruments for analysis that have proved to give interesting results in the reading of fiction, and such instruments might prove equally valid for the study of texts that claim a non-fictional status (cf. Bal, 1990). Second, that if narrative schemes are basic for human epistemology and communication, it could be suggested that narratological models to some extent account for certain ways of modelling human (i.e. cultural) representations of the world. When Ricoeur (1994: 120) states that '*a logic of possible narratives is simply a logic of action*' (my translation), he is suggesting, I believe, the existence of an ontological and epistemological reason for the use of narratives in human representations.

Some aspects of narratology and structural approaches to fiction have been the object of criticism, especially during the decades of the eighties and the nineties. A strong point of such criticism has been that actantial models and some other structural approaches were not able to account for the complex reality and interpretative possibilities of aesthetic representations. I believe such critical standpoints to have been important for the development of textual analysis. On the other hand, I also believe that if the narratological models in part have failed to account for the complex textual reality of aesthetic representations, they might help to point to important mechanisms for the creation of meaning in other text types, where the narrative model or element is not a conscious aesthetic choice, but a 'discursive mode which affects semiotic objects in variable degrees' (Bal, 1990: 730). This also means that underlying and unconscious narrative discursive modes can participate in *ideological* perceptions of social life. In the present case, my hypothesis is that implicit epic-narrative structures tend to form and perpetuate the cultural self and Other in certain pre-conceptualised positions that not only are images or signs of mutual others, but also contribute to maintaining the actual patterns of interaction, i.e. the social, political and economic relations between the actual individual and collective actors.

According to most contemporary narratological approaches, the basic elements of any narrative – as well as any other 'thing' that happens (i.e. an actual event, a performance or a dramatic play)[8] – will be the two dimensions of *space* and *time* and the *actors* to act in these. Regarding the first elements, these are normally considered and studied as intra-textual phenomena, due to the traditional narratological view of the text as an autonomous and self-sufficient object of study. But, when seeing structural-semantic text features as boundary phenomena moving between the actual given text and its context(s), it can be relevant to distinguish between an internal constitution of time, space and actors of a given narrative and the relation between these and the contextual spatio-temporal constitutions of self and Other (in this case) of a given semiosphere.

In the case of the actors, the principal question is not the specific characteristics of the individual actors, but the *relations* between these. A well-known contribution to the study of relations between actors is the actantial model of Greimas (1973; Barthes *et al.*, 1994; Bal, 1997), which establishes six basic 'actantial'[9] functions, namely the following: *subject, object, giver/sender/power, receiver, helper, opponent.*[10] Depending on the type of narrative, these actantial functions can be fulfilled by different types of actors, of which individual subjects (whether human or not) constitute only one. Institutions, natural or supernatural entities, collectives etc. are other examples. Also completely abstract phenomena might fulfil an actantial function. The object, for instance, is often an inanimate or abstract phenomenon, such as knowledge, love, wealth, liberty, or – say – the abolition of poverty.

The very designation of the different actantial roles indicates – as also mentioned above – that we are dealing with relational definitions. These relations have three basic characteristics, in the sense of being three relational axes. First, a subject desires an object – creating the relation or axis of *desire* or project. Second, a giver or sender gives the object to the receiver (corresponding to the relation or axis of *communication*), and third, there is a relation of *conflict*, in which the helper assists the subject (normally) in his project, while the opponent tries to impede it. As indicated, these different functions are abstractions and not necessarily corresponding to actual or personified actors of a narrative, and for this reason there might be coincidences of identity between different functions. A subject might very well be the same actor or person as the receiver. This is typically the case in a traditional love story, in which a hero (subject) struggles for and gains the love of another person (object). On the other hand, one actantial role might be fulfilled by more that one actor.

As is the case with time and space, the actantial relations are constituted (and studied) within the given text, but their meaning points outside the specific text: only insofar as the actantial roles of a non-fictional text can be identified with 'real' actors, can its status as a text about 'reality' be accepted (which, of course, does not imply that the readers of the text have to agree with its interpretation of such roles). Obviously, this point is crucial in the understanding and analysis of texts as producers and reproducers of identities.

The Text and the Context – Textual strategies for the production of 'us' and 'them'

In this section the analytical instruments presented above will be used for the reading of a text (including photographic images) concerning Danish development aid. The text is a brochure in tabloid format, published by a large number (46) of Danish NGO's. Its title is 'Verdens Fattigste' ('The Poorest of the World').[11] The brochure consists of eight pages, each with one or two photographs and two to four small, easily read verbal texts.

The brochure is part of a public campaign with the majority of the population as target group. This text, therefore, can be found in different public places, such as libraries, educational institutions and others, and has been distributed in the streets of major cities.
This establishes a broad, national context for the textual production and reproduction, with good possibilities for the study of the constitution of relational identities. The objective is not to make an exhaustive analysis of the text, but rather to show some main points of interest for a more or less coherent construction of mutual identities in the context of aid.

The first boundary: The 'we's and the otherness

From the first page *Verdens Fattigste* establishes the general context it works in: their space and ours. Imitating the characters of a typewriter, the following text is written in the upper right-hand corner of the front page: '*Verdens Fattigste – Hvad Gør Vi?*' ('The World's poorest –

What do we do?'] (cf. www.verdensfattigste.dk). The text is coloured by a radical boundary establishing two immediate and opposed actors: the 'we' and the 'world's poorest'. The first, spontaneous reading of this 'we' is, I believe, an idea of an identity comprehending producer (and sender) as well as reproducer (and receiver) of the text. The producer and sender of the text is formally identified as the 46 NGO's and the people working in them. The immediate reproducer or receiver is the actual reader, i.e. any member of the 'Danish semiosphere' who by chance receives and reads the text. Furthermore, there is an intention of reaching a majority of the (Danish) population, meaning that the 'implicit'[12] reader is any resident of the country who can read (Danish). The text is thus inserted in an implicit context, which could be termed the 'Danish semiosphere'. This context gives further meaning to the 'we': it is not only circumstantial – in the sense of consisting of a more or less specific producer/sender and an actual reader – but mainly relating to a contextual situation of national identification. This idea is confirmed on the second page of the publication, which I propose to examine with some detail.

The second page displays three texts. One of these establishes itself as the most important for several reasons such as its length, typography and place. It consists of three columns of text with a photograph placed above. The image depicts the faces of two persons, both smiling, and looking at each other. If one reads from left to right, the first person is a very blonde, young white girl, and the other – equally young and smiling – a black girl. Between the two persons, in the middle of the photograph, the title of the article runs: 'We give aid at eye-level'.[13] Below the image, in the body text of this article, one reads that, 'In Denmark *we* have tried another solution that often has worked: *we* join together. *We* create cooperatives, business associations and groups of citizens' (my emphasis).[14] Toward the end of the article, another 'we' appears: 'If we only collaborate with the government in the capital, we will never reach the poor'.[15] An important question is whether the three 'we's of the article constitute the same identity. My hypothesis is that they are not completely identical, but that they cannot be totally separated either, and furthermore, that this partial indetermination is significant.

In order to argue for the constitution of different 'we's in the general text, I will turn to another article of the brochure. The article on the third page is entitled: 'Tell us your opinion.'[16] This sentence shows a dialogical structure with an 'us' and a (singular) 'you'. This 'you' evidently corresponds to the reader, who is invited to give her or his opinion by phone or e-mail. The 'we' ('us') of this context is thus opposed to the readers ('you'), and corresponds logically (and explicitly) to the sender/producer of the text, the ones actually engaged in development aid, in Denmark as well as 'out there', in the 'South' (on several occasions the general text refers to the poor or developing countries as the 'South'). Returning to the former text ('We give aid at eye-level'), one of the 'we's obviously corresponds to a general Danish identity, the identity of the 'national semiosphere'. In the statement 'in Denmark we have tried another solution' and 'we join together', the 'we' corresponds to the 'Danes' in general, and in this way the text re-constitutes a supposed identity of 'we Danes' in opposition to a certain otherness. This otherness, however, is not just any otherness – the difference is not of a specific national character (although it implies nationness), but rather it implies a quality of being rich or poor. This specific difference is even more explicitly stated in the text on page four, which says, '*We* can afford to give a constant percentage of our riches to the least wealthy people of the world. When *we* are getting richer in Denmark, the help to the poor people of the world should grow' (my emphasis).[17] So, the text clearly constitutes a (pre-supposed) 'rich', Danish 'we', a national identity (in the sense of 'community') of people with resources and more or less willing to give some of these resources to those poor of the 'South' who have not got access to riches.

The question of whether this 'we' is identical with the 'we' of the sentence, 'We give aid at eye-level', still remains. Above it has been suggested that the answer could be that of a significant ambiguity. I shall try explain how. Two different 'we's have been identified, namely a general, national 'we' and the text-producing and sending 'we', consisting of the NGO's engaged in development aid. In the sentence, 'We give aid at eye-level', the 'we' can – and probably should – refer to the 'we' of the engaged NGO's, but also to a more general 'we' of Danes engaged in or willing to accept the Danish assistance to the 'poorest of the world'. Such a 'synthetic we' is a logical necessity of the text and its context in a double sense. First, it is a result of the intentionality of the text: the sender-we must create a community with the reading 'you', and this community becomes a 'we' that is supposed to share the basic view of the text, i.e. that development aid at 'eye-level' is necessary for the 'poorest' and beneficial for both giver and receiver. This 'we' can be extended to a greater context of people potentially willing to accept these ideas (a 'we' that ought to comprehend a majority of the 'rich' Denmark). The 'synthetic' and partially indeterminate 'we' (covering producer, reader and a certain proportion of the population in general) is, thus, the result of the logic of the text's own dynamics: in order to do what is right, this 'we' has to represent both sender, receiver and a majority of the 'grand we', i.e. the Danish population.

Another important aspect of the 'we's of the text is that they are implicitly 'Danish' and as such constituents of the basic cultural boundary that delineates the 'us' and the 'others'. In the present case, this boundary is based on the 'giving' function: the 'we' has the resources, the duty and (potentially) the will to give to 'the world's poorest'. Other signs, however, reaffirm the boundary. Between these are, for instance, the phenotype of the persons (see below) and the space. The 'we' lives in and belongs to Denmark, and to the 'rich world', while the 'others' belong to 'poor world' and to the 'South' (the two most common spatial definitions of the otherness in the text).

Giver and Receiver – a pictorial narrative

As mentioned above, the text contains a photograph showing two young people looking at each other, with a text in between. If the photo is 'read' from the left to the right, the first person is the blonde girl (of whom also is seen part of the hand), and the black girl is the second, i.e. the 'other'. Whether such a reading is intended or not, is not the question; the point is that it is not only possible, but probable or even inevitable, due to the text placed in the middle of the image, exactly between the two persons. Without the text (and the context), the possible readings of the image would be much freer. But the text forces some elements into the interpretation: first, the semantic content of 'aid' or 'help' as the basic relation between the two persons, and second, a direction in the reading of image and text together going from the white, blonde 'Danish-looking' girl to the black Other. In other words, the 'aid' goes from left to right, from blonde to black, from 'us' ('Danes') to 'them'. There is a boundary between the two girls, but this boundary implies a translation from one to another: there is a relation in which one is 'giver' and the other is 'receiver'.

Although the text in the photograph is a decisive element for such a reading, the context is also important. The immediate context is the brochure, with its other texts and especially other images. There are a few photographs showing anonymous persons and scenes from the 'Third World', and there are also photographs of eight different individuals from countries in Asia, Africa and Latin America. These persons have names and in each case there is a text beside the image, providing a short narrative of this person's history and activity with the idea of giving arguments for why 'we' should help, and why this help should be given directly and at 'eye-level'. Regarding the phenotype (especially hair and skin colour) and in most cases also the clothes, these persons are marked with a 'difference'. This difference is evident with respect to the immediate context, i.e. images showing 'Danes' in the brochure, but also regarding a more general cultural context, according to which 'Danishness' or what is considered to be a typical 'Danish' phenotype is defined by blond hair and a white complexion, opposed to black hair and a dark skin. So, these contextual elements support the reading of the image of the two young people as symbolizing the basic and general idea of the whole text (i.e. the brochure, including verbal text and images) of the 'help' (development aid) as something going directly from 'us' to 'them' at an equalitarian and sympathetic 'eye-level'.

This points to the potential for a narrative reading of the photo. 'Narrative' in this sense primarily implies two elements: actors and temporality. Although some models for the analysis of narrative, such as the actantial model, might suggest a 'de-temporalisation' of narrativity, I agree with Ricoeur (1994) that temporality is an intrinsic and inseparable element of narratives of any kind and, furthermore, that this temporal dimension is the key for the ontological status of narrative. In other words, due to the temporal conditions of human existence, meaning must reflect temporality, which is what occurs in narratives.

A narrative analysis of the image of the two young persons thus implies the existence of actors as well as action. The 'reading' of these elements is contextually bound in a very clear way: due to the surrounding texts (and especially the one between them), an image of two young girls becomes a 'story' of relations between different identities in a global relation of economic transactions. The context also makes the ('racial') differences of phenotype – which in other contexts might have been insignificant or circumstantial – a significant element of the narrative. The context makes it possible – or even compulsory – to 'read' the white girl as the 'giver' and the black girl as 'receiver'[18] of development aid given 'at eye-level' (i.e. in a direct and equalitarian spirit, eluding bureaucracy and corruption). The narrative and temporal aspect makes it possible to 'read' something not 'visible' from the image, namely the act of giving and receiving.

Jan Gustafsson

Another consequence of the narrative reading of the image is that the two actors become 'archetypes'. Rather than two 'real' persons, they are representatives of a narrative scheme that appears as a representation of reality. The narrative interpretation of the image suggests a reading of the relations between the actors based on the 'communicative axis' of the actantial model (cf. above) as the essential relation of the narrative: the important event is that 'giver' or 'sender' gives 'aid' to the 'receiver'. These two classes of actors, however, are normally not the most important of a narrative. The basic axis of a narrative is normally that of 'desire', or of the relation between a 'subject' and an 'object'. There is no doubt that the whole text (the brochure) is penetrated by an 'object of desire'. The implicit object of the activities of these NGO's is to relieve and improve the situation of 'the world's poorest', i.e. to reduce poverty.[19] The 'subjects' for a narrative in which the object is 'reduction of poverty' could be the poor person(s) or community, but it could also be the giving entity. In this case both things happen. In the eight very short stories about 'fiery souls' from the 'South' (examples of individuals from different Third World countries who make a personal effort in the struggle against poverty), the 'subject' is the poor man or woman who becomes a kind of 'hero' of poverty. These heroes, however, are not narrators of their own stories, they do not become an 'I' or a 'we' – they remain 'others'. This otherness is stressed by external features (clothes and phenotype, as mentioned above), and by the contextual situation; in other words, by the fact that sender and receiver of the text partake of the same 'we' described above, a 'we' constituted by its opposition to the Other, the 'poor'. This means that, although occasionally protagonist and subject of a story, the 'world's poorest' tend to play a subordinate role in relation to the 'we', who thus becomes the main subject of the general narrative expressed in the photograph of the two young girls and in the context. This narrative is the story of the 'we' helping the Other, who syntactically and semantically is turned into an object: the indirect object who receives the direct object (the aid as such).

This analysis suggests an actantial model in which the narrating 'we' presents itself as 'giver' (and 'sender') and, as 'subject', i.e. protagonist, while the 'poorest of the world' fulfil the role of the 'receiver', and only becomes 'subject' occasionally, namely when the 'we' delegates minor narratives to the Other.

Text and power

The idea of a 'we' as 'giver' and 'subject' implies an important dimension of power. In relation to this it is interesting to recall that Bal (1997) proposes the term 'power' for the function of the giver (cf. above), due to the fact that the 'giver' or 'sender' in many cases has the actual power over the general enterprise. When we talk about 'giver', 'sender' or 'power' as elements of an actantial model, evidently we refer to theoretical and methodological abstractions, not to actual entities. The similarities between the roles of the actual text and those of the abstract model, however, cannot but strike us. There is no doubt that from a political, a juridical and, as this chapter tries to prove, a symbolic position, the 'power' is on the side of the giver. Although an abstract ethical and moral obligation to 'help the Other' might be claimed, the 'giver' will always have the right to determine when, where, to whom and how to give. Politically, there has always been a relation between certain priorities and the development aid. This has not changed in recent decades, when a traditional development perspective with focus on national economic production and accumulation has given way to another, in which local production and human, gender and children's rights are main priorities. When Danida (e.g. Jespersen *et al.*, 2002) claims the moral and political right (or rather duty) to stop any assistance to countries in which human or gender rights are violated, this seems not only acceptable, but necessary from a common sense moral, ethical and political point of view. But in this case, such a common sense point of view might obscure another (and maybe more important) aspect of the relations of 'global charity': the giver has power over the receiver, not only because s/he has the money in his/her pocket, but also because s/he represents a better society, not only economically, but also politically and morally. If it was not so, it would be a case of meaningless hypocrisy. Obviously I do not intend to discuss whether or not there are elements of hypocrisy in the political and moral commitments related to the development aid, i.e. if the donor countries of the 'West' actually are so 'perfect', or so much 'better', as to be able to claim such a right. What I intend to show is that the context of development aid as such implies a relation of superiority and inferiority – of 'master' and 'slave' in a Hegelian sense – and that the emphasis on a commitment to the 'poorest of the world', or to gender, children's or indigenous rights, does not alter this situation, however righteous these commitments are from other moral, ethical and political perspectives. Rather, this commitment stresses the superiority of the giver, whose power not only depends on the money, but on being 'better' when it comes to all kinds of rights.

In the text here analysed, the aspects of children's, gender and human rights in general are more or less explicitly manifest in different 'sub-narratives' like the stories of the 'fiery souls'. The idea of the 'we' as model – and thus superior – is seen in the introductory text already quoted: 'In Denmark we have tried another solution that often has worked... **In the** developing countries a lot of people have discovered the *same* trick (my emphasis).' Denmark and the 'Danish way' become examples for intelligent conduct that leads to good results. If the Other discovers our way, if s/he follows 'our path', the situation will improve. Despite the fact that this text tries to render a 'real' and solidary portrait of concrete persons from the Third World, it does (and probably can) not avoid depicting a relation of superior and inferior, partaking of a general scheme of interpretation of the actors, and, consequently, in the construction of self and Other as better and lesser, respectively.

Condensation and displacement

Metaphor and metonymy as intratextual and intertextual meaning-creating mechanisms have been mentioned above. In the last section, it was also suggested that the two actors (the young girls) are to be read as archetypical representations of a political reality, rather than two persons with a specific identity. This is the consequence of a narrative reading of the specific text – the photograph – situated on the boundary between itself – an intratextual reading – and its double context of the other texts in the brochure and the more general context of development aid. Without these contexts, the photographical 'text' could have a completely different meaning. Such a 'border-reading' of the text depends partly on metaphorical and metonymical mechanisms of intertextual boundary-crossings. When a photographic text depicting two individuals becomes the 'story' of a generalised political and economic phenomenon, which is what happens here, the specific persons, or rather, individual actors, are read allegorically as representatives of an intercultural narrative with certain relations between the 'us' and the 'others'. The individuals become a metaphor for the general, condensing the meaning of something else and something more than themselves. This 'translation' of the general into the specific implies a new meaning. The photographic text does not lose its capacity to generate a meaning of its own. The two girls read as metaphor for the relations between the 'we' and the 'them' mean also a re-reading of these relations as something direct and almost intimate, as development aid at 'eye-level' in an almost literate manner. This is the way the 'we' of the sender (the participating NGO's) wish to present 'our way' of development aid. This and the other photographs (each with its own little narrative) of the brochure constitute the expression of a *desire* of a more tangible, immediate and nearer world, in which 'we' can help the 'poorest of the world' at 'eye-level'. The condensation of meaning occurs when an idea of an intangible and possibly angst-producing global and distant phenomenon (extreme poverty and thousands of development aid projects) is translated into something so 'near', concrete and tangible as two individuals smiling at each other.

The photograph and the two girls acting as a condensed metaphor for the relations of millions or billions of people in a kind of *inwards* or centripetal movement, does at the same time point in the opposite direction. In order to make sense, the metaphor has to be read not only from the general context to the specific text, but also from the specific text (i.e. the photograph) 'back' to the general context. But this second movement is metonymical rather than metaphorical. Once the metaphor has constituted the two girls and their relation as an intercultural 'case' with a given meaning, the case or specific situation can, and will, be read metonymically to be representative of (millions of) other cases of similar relations. So, the reading of the blonde girl as a representative of the giving 'we' and the black girl as representative of the receiving 'them', requires a double movement from context to specific text and from the specific text back to the context. This movement is metaphorical in its *condensation* of context in a specific text (not necessarily related to this), and it is metonymical in its *displacement* of the meaning of the specific text toward the generalised context.

Meanings of Self and Other

By way of partial conclusion to the analysis, I will resume some basic semantic elements of the construction of the cultural self and Other as they appear in the textual and contextual situation here analysed.

The fact that we are dealing with a non-fictional text implies that the 'reality claim' (meaning that this text talks about 'our' and 'their' actual world) constitutes the basic boundary of this text. This boundary means that the text delimits an 'actual world of actors and relations'[20] of which sender and reader are part, and for which reason there is a constant relation – i.e. translation – between intratextual and extratextual worlds. In other words, there is a claim of identity between the actual text and the reader's (and producer's) life-world. To any reader (with the possible exception of those who perpetrate ideological criticism, textual semiotics or social constructivism) this is too elemental a logic to be questioned. But a textual analysis moving constantly 'on the edge' between the intratextual, the intertextual and the extratextual instances might reveal some specific mechanisms of this logic, and thus question that it is something naturally given and indisputable.

An important example of such mechanisms is the metaphorical and metonymical movement between the specific text as a 'case' and the 'outer dimension' of that which the text represents. Another example is seen in the realisation of the textual 'we', which – as discussed above – manifests itself in three different instances, namely: the actual sender or producer of the text (the NGO's), a 'we' comprising sender and reader, and a generalised national 'we' including the former two, as well as those Danes in general who participate directly or via taxpaying as 'good givers' of resources to 'the poorest of the world'.

The actantial reading of the text – with particular respect to the photograph and the sentence printed between the two persons depicted – shows a basic axis of communication moving with the reading, from left to right, with a giver and a receiver corresponding to the 'white' and the 'black' girl, respectively. This reading, supported by contextual readings (including an actantial logic and general ideas of the 'First' and the 'Third' worlds), shows a relation of power in this communication. One actor is superior and independent, and the Other inferior and dependent.

Furthermore, there is a double superiority of the 'we': on the one hand for being better and having more, on the other for the ethical and moral disposition to give. This specific text shows some different strategies of 'democratisation' of the development context and of the relation between 'giver' and 'receiver', but clearly these strategies are not sufficient to alter the basic semantics of both text and context, i.e. the idea of a superior and developed 'we' and an inferior, underdeveloped and poor 'them'.

The relational constitution of community

The preceding analysis shows that context and text presuppose and reproduce that cultural boundary which Lotman (1990: 131, cf. above) defines as basic. Here it is seen in one of its specific semantic versions, namely as a relation between 'giver' (or 'donor', which seems the most common expression) and 'receiver' in the context of development aid. This constitution is relational in more than one sense, first and foremost because it depends on the 'Other', who is not only 'significant'[21] but constitutive. This is obvious from the intratextual point of view, where the actors are mutually dependent: the story of giver and receiver implies an axis in which these two identities only can exist as parts of the relation. In this relation nothing is something in itself, neither giver nor receiver, neither the mediating object, the gift. Nothing, on the other hand, seems to impede the transposition or translation of this logic to a broader context of global relations and identity constructions: although seemingly a 'naturally' and evidently a historically given situation, the existence of poor and rich nations, of donors and receivers, constitutes a narrative potential for the production of images of cultural (e.g. national) self and Other.

Culture, interculturality and textual analysis

From a theoretical point of view, a principal intention of this chapter has been to show some possibilities of semiotic and textual approaches to cultural and intercultural phenomena, exemplified in a specific context of identity construction. Hopefully, the preceding pages have shown some of the theoretical and methodological possibilities of the concepts presented and applied in this chapter. These concepts, although presented as part of a general (Peirce-inspired) semiotic framework, are perfectly useable without taking such a framework into consideration. Some of these – *text, context, boundary and translation* – have the strength and weakness of being also (and for most people only) concepts belonging to general common sense. The strength is that they make immediate sense to most people, even if not trained in textual or cultural analysis, while the weakness lies in the fact that it can be difficult to take the important step of abstraction implied in the analytical use here proposed, even if this use only implies a development of the common sense use in a more abstract sense (which is the case). The other concepts – *deictics, metaphor, metonymy* and the elements of *narratology* – already have the status of being scientific tools belonging to linguistic and literary disciplines. In the context proposed, these concepts maintain their original status and meaning. Their re-contextualisation as tools of cultural textual analysis, however, implies the exploitation of certain aspects of these tools or concepts, and therefore a use or interpretation of them that might not coincide totally with their use in other contexts. Such a re-thinking of the concepts is necessary and should be stressed, in order to differentiate the textually oriented cultural analysis proposed from traditional text analysis. This re-thinking or re-contextualisation is partly based on the interpretation of the mentioned linguistic concepts in relation to the 'common sense' concepts also proposed. When metaphor, metonymy or actantial relations, for instance, are read as concepts that work on the *boundary* of the text, pointing toward other texts and contexts, they deploy capacities and potential not always exploited in more traditional text studies, remaining, nevertheless, true to their origin as semiotic or linguistic tools.

On the other hand, I believe it relevant to state that the previous discussions and analysis only represent a timid attempt to show the possibilities of semiotics and linguistics for cultural and intercultural studies. Peircean transcendental semiotics (cf. Apel, 1994 and 1998) combined with structuralist and post-structuralist theory and methodology, the linguistic tradition of the 20th Century, the contributions of Bakhtin and Lotman, as well as the philosophical traditions (Continental and Anglo-Saxon) developed on basis of the 'linguistic turn' constitute a potential for cultural and intercultural studies, whose exploitation probably and hopefully is only in its initial phase. To continue re-thinking Lotman's semiosphere (Lotman, 1990) with Peircean semiotics, Bakhtinian dialogism (cf. Bakhtin, 1997, Holquist, 1990, Todorov 1984 and others) and the linguistic traditions of Jakobson, Benveniste, Greimas, Bremond and others as basis for theory and methodology for the study of culture and interculturality is a task for the future.

Epilogue

For a short epilogue I wish to reconsider some of the conclusions of the analysis or rather some possible ethical, moral or political consequences of these. Obviously, the kind of analysis here proposed contains a critical aspect. To propose a reading of the text according to which a cultural self and Other are positioned as superior and inferior, respectively, implies a critique of fundamental ideological[22] aspects of the discourse analysed. In this case, such a critical dimension of the analysis seems to be directly opposed to some of the principal author intentions of the text, which is what happens, for instance, in the reading of the photograph of the two girls. While the author intention here denotes ideas of 'equality' – the two girls looking each other in the eyes and the verbal indication of 'eye-level' – I have nevertheless proposed a 'pictorial narrative' (cf. above) including contextual readings that point to a situation of 'power' in favour of the left side of the photograph, i.e. favouring the 'white girl'.

Any text contains an ideological dimension, but any text implies also, at least potentially, a dimension of *praxis*, i.e. some sort of practical engagement with the world (including other texts). One could say that any text is also an act. Being an 'act', a text implies – potentially – also an ethical dimension. Or, expressed in another way, a text is necessarily a *relationship* between human consciences (whether or not these consciences are conscious of such a relation),[23] and ethics is, in its most elemental sense, a question of relations between human beings. Nørgaard, in this volume, defines ethics – quoting Ricoeur – as 'aiming at the good life with and for others' (Ricoeur, 1992 quoted in Nørgaard, this volume). According to this definition (and probably most others), the text here studied has an evident and strong ethical dimension, partly because it deals with one of the basic problems for a majority of mankind, but even more because it deals with this problem as a relation between a 'we' not affected by the problem and a 'them' mostly affected. In other words, it deals with the 'aiming at the good life *for* others'.

The textual intention sees this 'good life for others' as the result of an extratextual praxis, i.e. as something the text talks about and that 'actual' (extratextual) actors put into practice. The textual criticism postulated above, on the other hand, is aiming at a 'textual practice' meaning that the implications about self and Other implied in the text are 'valid' in the sense of being an essential part of the relations between the 'we' and the 'they' presented in the text. Whether or not the textual and symbolic constitution of self and Other is also present (or even decisive) in the direct interaction between the 'poor' and the actors of the NGO's would be an object of other methodological approaches. But there is a basic paradox, consisting in the fact that the text assumes a positive ethical attitude of the NGO's as a 'giver' of the good life for others, while the criticism postulates a stance of superiority. An immediate interpretation could be that one part is wrong. For instance, that the critique of the ideological constructions of self and Other are mere academic exercises without any real importance for the actual interaction, which is where things really happen. Or, on the contrary, that the ideological assumptions of the symbolic constructions are decisive and that an actual praxis will always imply a relation of power, in which the Danish, European or 'Western' 'we' has power over the 'poor' Third World 'other'. In any case, the answer implies a pragmatic approach, i.e. not a denial of the theoretical paradox, but a denial or confirmation of the importance of the symbolic construction for the social praxis.

Another approach could be to accept the paradox as both a theoretical and a pragmatic reality and as the actual conditions for the social praxis of the global relations of development aid. This means that reality is that on the one hand there is an urgent need to redeem or relieve the situation of millions of individuals – seen as such or seen as collectivities – and on the other, that the actions in which the 'rich' engage to help the 'poor' cannot but imply a relation of power in its symbolic construction and in its social practice. The critical demonstration of the textual construction of a 'superior we' is not an answer to the ethical and moral questions that can be asked in relation to the practice of development aid – but neither is it a hollow academic exercise. I believe it to be an essential and necessary part of a discussion about one of the most important fields of intercultural communication in the world of today: the relations between 'rich' and 'poor' concern international politics and world security and moves billions of dollars and euros every year. As such, we are dealing with a case of interculturality that implies symbolic constructions as well as basic ethical and moral questions.

References

Apel, Karl-Otto; *Semiótica filosófica*. Buenos Aires: Editorial Almagesto, 1994.

Apel, Karl-Otto; *From a Transcendental-Semiotical Point of View*. Manchester: Manchester University Press, 1998.

Bajtin (Bakhtin), Mihail; *Estética de la creación verbal*. México D.F.: Siglo XXI, 1997.

Bal, Mieke; The Point of Narratology, *Poetics Today,* 11:4 pp. 727-753, 1990.

Bal, Mieke; *Narratology. Introduction to the Theory of Narrative*. Toronto: University of Toronto Press, 1997.

Barthes, Roland *et al.*; *Análisis estructural del relato*. México D. F.: Diálogo, 1996.

Barthes, Roland; *Mitologías*. México D. F.: Siglo XXI 1994. (English version: *Mythologies*, London: Grant & Cutler, 1980.)

Barth, Fredrik; "Introduction", in: F. Barth (ed.). *Ethnic Groups and Boundaries: The Social Organisation of Difference*. Oslo: Universitetsforlaget, 1969.

Benveniste, Emile; *Problems in General Linguistics*. Coral Gables: University of Miami Press, 1971.

Billig, Michael; *Banal Nationalism*, London: Sage,1995.

Bruner, Jerome; *Acts of Meaning*. Cambridge, Mass.: Havard University Press, 1990.

Chandler, Daniel; *Semiotics, the Basics*. London: Routledge, 2002.

Cobley, Paul; *Narrative*, London: Routledge, 2001.

Danida; *Facts and Figures*, Copenhagen: Danish Foreign Ministry, 2001.

Jan Gustafsson

Geertz, Clifford; *The Interpretation of Cultures*. New York: Basic Books 1993 [1973].

Ducrot, Oswald & Todorov, Tzvetan; *Diccionario enciclopédico de las ciencias del lenguaje*. México D. F.: Siglo XXI , 1995 (French edition from 1972).

Escobar, Arturo; *Encountering Development –The Making and the Unmaking of the Third World*. Princeton, N.J.: Princeton University Press, 1995.

Greimas, Algirdas; *Strukturel semantik*. Copenhagen: Borgen, 1973.

Gustafsson, Jan; "Figuras de la alteridad: visiones danesas de América Latina", in: Cristoffanini (Ed.), *Identidad y otredad en el mundo de habla hispánica*. México D.F.: Universidad Nacional Autónoma de México & Universidad de Aalborg, 1999.

Gustafsson, Jan; *El salvaje y nosotros – signos del latinoamericano. Una hermenéutica del otro*. Copenhagen: Copenhagen Working Papers, 2000.

Gustafsson, Jan; Semiotik – tegnenes leg i tekstens mønstre, in: E. H. Jensen og J. A. Olsen (eds), *Tekstens univers*. Århus: Klim, 2003.

Haslett, Moyra; *Marxist Literary and Cultural Theories*. London: Macmillan Press, 2000.

Holquist, Michael; *Dialogism – Bakthin and his World*. New York: Routledge, 1990.

Hymes, Dell; *Ethnography, Linguistics, Narrative Inequality: Toward an Understanding of Voice*. London: Taylor and Francis, 1996.

Jakobson, Roman; "Two Aspects of Language and Two Types of Aphasic Disturbances", in: *Fundamentals of Language*, The Hague: Mouton, 1956.

Jenkins, Richard; *Social Identity*. London: Routledge, 1996.

Jenkins, Richard; *Rethinking Ethnicity*. London: Sage, 1997.

Jespersen, Jesper et al; Menneskerettigheder, *Udvikling*, 3, 2002.

Lacan, Jacques; *Écrits*. Paris: Éditions du Seuil, 1966.

Lacan, Jacques & Wilden, Anthony; *Speech and Language in Psycho-analysis*. Baltimore: John Hopkins University Press, 1968.

Lotman, Yuri; *Universe of Mind. A Semiotic Theory of Culture*. London: Tauris, 1990.

Mead, George Herbert; *Selected Writings*. Chicago: University of Chicago Press, 1964.

Peirce, Charles Sanders; *Collected Papers*. Cambridge, Mass.: Harvard University Press, 1958 [1931].

Ponzio, Augusto; *Man as Sign. Essays on the Philosophy of Language*. Berlin: Mouton de Gruyter 1990.

Ricoeur, Paul; *Oneself as Another*. Chicago: The University of Chicago Press, 1992.

Ricoeur, Paul; *Relato: historia y ficción*, México, D.F.: Dosfilos Editores, 1994.

Schütz, Alfred; *Phenomenology of the Social World*. London: Heinemann, 1980 [1967].

Sebeok, Thomas; *Signs – an Introduction to Semiotics*. Toronto: Toronto University Press, 2001.

Silverman, Kaja; *The Subject of Semiotics*, New York: Oxford University Press, 1983.

Smith, Anthony; *National Identity*. Harmondsworth: Penguin, 1991.

Tvedt, Terje; *Bilder av 'de andre'. Om utviklingslandene i bistands-epoken*. Oslo: Universitetsforlaget, 1990.

Jan Gustafsson

Tvedt, Terje; *Angels of Mercy or Development Diplomats? NGO's and Foreign Aid*. Oxford: James Currey, 1998.

Urban, Greg; The 'I' of discourse, in M. Singer, B. Lee & G. Urban (eds), *Semiotics, Self and Society*, Berlin: Mouton de Gruyter, 1989

Verdens fattigste, edited by 46 Danish NGO's, Copenhagen (summary in English at www.verdensfattigste.dk), 2003.

Zizek, Slavoj; *The Sublime Object of Ideology*. London: Verso, 1989.

Notes

¹ I believe this textual idea of culture to have important elements in common with the semiotic-hermeneutic idea of culture as 'webs of signification' (cf. Geertz, 1973).

² The sign-process in itself (the semiosis) can be seen as a species of translation in the sense of being a reproduction of the meaning of a sign by another sign (the interpreter). Cf. Peirce, 1958. For an introduction to semiotics, see for instance, Chandler, 2002, Sebeok, 2001 or Gustafsson, 2003.

³ Although an interesting question with a lot of challenging perspectives for a semiotic-textual theory of culture, I prefer not to discuss the validity of such a classification or possible definitions of 'fiction' or 'non-fiction'. Consequently, 'fiction' and 'non-fiction' is here understood as *conventional* (in an exact and a general sense) definitions of genres.

⁴ The term implies that the word 'points at' someone or something, taking its reference from this 'pointing out'. A deictic word is thus supposed to have no reference in itself. For the same reason, Jakobson calls them 'shifters'.

⁵ Obviously, the intention is not to discuss different approaches to 'nationness' nor to propose another. The point suggested is just that from a textual-semiotic point of view an ideological and a historical approach to the nation-state are not necessarily incompatible, but rather two aspects of the question.

⁶ The example, although imagined, could be part of aid campaigns by 'Save the Children', Red Cross and other NGO's. Below, in the analysis of the NGO-text, I take up these functions related to a photograph.

⁷ The area has produced a vast literature related to different disciplines. See for instance, Bruner (1990), Dell Hymes (1996) or Bal, 1990. Also Ricoeur, 1994, offers some interesting perspectives.

⁸ A basic idea in narratology is that the structural elements of an epic or a narrative correspond to the elemental structures of language, especially the sentence (with a subject, an object etc.). Cf. Greimas, 1973, Ricoeur *et al*, 1994.

⁹ This terminology indicates clearly that 'actants' and 'actantial model' represent abstractions for certain generalised functions of narrative schemes, and not narrative 'actors' (persons, personified animals, animated machines etc.) as such (cf. Bal 1997).

¹⁰ 'Giver' or 'sender' seem to be the most common terms used in English (for the original French 'destinateur'). Cf. The Literary Encyclopedia (www.LitEncyc.com) *et al*. However, Bal (1997) prefers the term 'power', mainly because "'sender' suggests an active intervention... and this does not always apply". But Bal's proposal does indeed also imply the idea that the sender/giver/power in many cases is a powerful entity, which very often "has power over the whole enterprise" (ibid).

[11] The text will be referred to as "Verdens Fattigste", also in the bibliography.

[12] Some currents of narratology use the concept of 'implicit reader' to indicate a sort of 'ideal type' of reader implicated by the text and its communicative frame (cf. Bal, 1997, Ducrot & Todorov, 1995 and others). Although somewhat problematic, the concept helps to distinguish between the actual readers of a text and the abstract identity of an implied reader.

[13] Original text: "Vi giver bistand i øjenhøjde". I have preferred a literal translation because of the importance of the play between the different semantic possibilities of the expression"øjenhøjde" ('eye-level'). All translation of the brochure text are mine. The English summary of the home-page is quoted with the web-reference.

[14] Original text: "I Danmark har vi haft en anden løsning, der tit har virket: Vi slutter os sammen. Vi danner andelsselskaber, handelsstandsforeninger og borgergrupper".

[15] Original text: "Hvis vi bare arbejder sammen med regeringen inde i hovedstaden, når vi aldrig ud til de fattigste." The use of the two adverbs "inde" and "ud" (in and out) creates a further semantic implication of the capital as 'center' and the poor people as decentered.

[16] Original text: "Sig os din mening".

[17] Original text: "Vi har råd til at give en fast procentdel af vores rigdom til verdens dårligst stillede. Når vi selv bliver rigere i Danmark, skal hjælpen til verdens fattigste i vejret".

[18] The original or 'actual' circumstances of the photo and the 'real' identity of the two girls (who perfectly well could be friends of the same high-school or neighbourhood) is, of course, completely irrelevant for the interpretation of the image as part of the text.

[19] This objective coincides with the goals of the official organisation for development aid, Danida, whose 'overriding goal and guiding principle' is to 'reduce poverty' (cf. Danida, 2001).

[20] If the actual character of this boundary is ontological or epistemological or of any other kind is not the point here, evidently. The point is that the text claims a status as representation of reality, and representation as such is a (basic) boundary mechanism that translates between the vehicle of representation and that which is represented. From a semiotic or a constructivist point of view, the latter is logically part of the former.

[21] Jenkins (1997) uses the expression 'significant Others' (originally a concept developed by Mead, 1964, in order to account for aspects of primary and secondary socialisation) to designate those others who are particularly important for the construction of identity. Although Jenkins's concept is very relevant, I prefer the expression 'constitutive other' (at least in this context), because the

other is not just a circumstance that reinforces an existing identity construction, but the basic element in the given relational construction.

[22] The term 'ideology' is here used in the sense of 'hidden' assumptions and messages of a text, i.e. *not* as a conscient message of political, religious or similar character. As such, ideology is a dimension of the text – in principle any text, including those of criticism of ideology – to be revealed by a critical analysis. For discussions about ideology, see for instance Billig, 1995, Haslett, 2000 or Zizek, 1989.

[23] Bakhtin (1997: 297-8) stresses that the 'event in the life of a text – i.e. its real essence – develops on the frontier between two consciences, two subjects'.

Intercultural Ethics
A hermeneutic approach to ethics in intercultural communication

JENS LAUTRUP NØRGAARD

Introduction

In an increasingly globalised world, opportunities and possibilities seem to multiply and grow at an ever-accelerating pace. Restraints are overcome and human freedom – of thought as well as of action – is *l'ordre du jour*. Whether this freedom is a social fact or wishful thinking is not the issue here, but at least it should not be too controversial to claim that freedom of movement is experienced more readily today than ever before, and that modern man, relatively seen, is rather unrestricted by place. As a consequence, the freedom, since it means almost routinely leaving ones 'own' place and entering that of others, involves frequent encounters with the culturally different. One would intuitively think that being confronted with the cultural Other has consequences for the freedom enjoyed by the modern individual if the social aspects of such encounters is not to be neglected; freedom is so to speak modified by the Other.

As Fernando Savater states, ethics is concerned with the question of how to use freedom (Savater, 2002), a statement which we can paraphrase, then, into how we should use freedom seen in the light of the Other. This question is provoked by and arises in connection with the intercultural encounter among other conditions. The present chapter addresses this relation between interculturality and ethics, or to be more precise the question is 'does it make sense to talk about *intercultural* ethics?' Or, to go even further, one could ask if there exists something like an ethical dimension for culture. José Antonio Marina

Jens Lautrup Nørgaard

(Marina, 2002) uses the metaphor of navigation to describe the role that ethics plays in our life, and taking up this image, the present paper is a reflection on how to read the chart of interculturality. Just like navigation is basically a question of having a good and safe journey, cultural ethics is a question of good and 'safe' interculturality.

The rising interest in intercultural ethics, to which a growing number of publications on the subject bear witness, is probably part of a broader trend or even development in late modern (world) society. Øjvind Larsen describes modernity and the state of continuous 'moving on'[1] that characterises it, saying that 'the very characteristic of modern society (is) to be in a permanent and explosive state of moving on that eliminates all pregiven traditions and ways of understanding' (Larsen, 1991). 'The dynamic change of modern society', Larsen continues, produces 'many new ethical problems that haven't been seen earlier in history' (ibid). As an example Larsen points to the technological development and illustrates it by mentioning the question of abortion and the new technologies of manipulation of human embryos, which confront modern man with new and until now unknown problems. But also within a cultural frame, and therefore anthropological epistemology, we are confronted with new and surprising problems like globalisation and its resulting effects like interculturality. We do not wish thereby to maintain the claim that culture-meetings did not occur in previous epochs, but it characterises late modernity and globalisation as an inherent part of it that interculturality has become everyone's condition, and not only potentially, but as an intrinsic part of our daily life. Consequently we, the world society, have already established norms for encounters with people from other cultures, norms that without doubt are submitted to an ongoing debate,[2] completely in convergence with Larsen's idea of us being on a continuous journey, but nevertheless an interculturality discourse proper with its own reasons and positions.

The huge majority of literature on intercultural communication, be it instrumentally orientated or more theoretically reflective, has a normative perspective. Sometimes it is not explicit, but most literature on the subject of interculturality includes ideas about how to behave and what to do and not to do in intercultural encounters. Very often norms are determined by the objective goals held by the intercultural actors, or to put it differently, the assumption is that we should act in the way that seems to be the most rational in relation to our specific goals. Very often intercultural communication is explicitly defined as goal-oriented (see for instance Scollon & Scollon, 1995 or Ting-Toomey, 1999). But there is an idealistic side to the normative perspective too that criticizes ethnocentrism and stresses openness as a quality in itself. It is within this latter side of normativity that we could begin to speak of reflections on ethics in the intercultural field.

It is the ambition of the present chapter to contribute to a discussion about interculturality and ethics and thus contribute to the creation of a framework for understanding. In order to do so, we shall begin with an outline of a basic conception of interculturality as a point of departure from which we shall consider the ethical problem. Interculturality is defined here as a practical experience of understanding and not-understanding. Furthermore, and before entering the relation between ethics and interculturality, we shall establish a distinction between ethics and morals. Much debate on the question of culture and ethics and morals relates to the antagonism between relativist and absolute viewpoints, but it would appear that much of the confusion that seemingly is a natural part of the debate comes from not properly distinguishing the ethical problem from the question of morals.[3] The discussion of culture and ethics takes its point of departure in this distinction.

It follows from the specification of interculturality as praxis that an associated ethical aspect must be seen as a praxis-aspect too. So my aim is to link interculturality and ethics conceptually rather than to reveal unknown features of ethics as such. In other words, I do not expect there to be a special intercultural ethics in its own right, but I expect interculturality to present another window onto ethics. My interest in ethics in this specific context is closely connected to praxis within a limited epistemological area, namely that of interculturality. I do not intend to propose any model for understanding ethics as a co-constituent of society. On the other hand it is a basic assumption in the chapter that interculturality as praxis and as a function of globalisation has become a universal social dynamic, and consequently reflections on intercultural ethics can contribute to a broader understanding of late modern society as such.

Interculturality

The expansion of the research field of *intercultural communication* is remarkable, and notions on the subject are becoming commonplace and some maybe even trivial. The continuous maturing of the field implies increased focus on the grounds for studying human communication seen in the light of culture. There seems to be, however, some confusion over epistemological and ontological questions that concern the field. The status of basic concepts such as *culture* and *communication* often remains unclarified, as well as the relation between the concepts. One possible way to clarify the concepts of the field could be the radicalisation of basic points of departure, and the initiating concern in this chapter is, by choosing such a point of departure, to conceptualise intercultural communication as an interactive hermeneutical experience.

When we find ourselves in what we can call the landscape of interculturality, we are in a landscape of a paradox of understanding. We are constantly confronted with contours hitherto unknown to us, and we feel that while we are able to discover the shape of the land, we are still not able to establish a satisfactory and structured topography of the environment so as to feel at ease and not alert. The paradox of interculturality, in other words, is the paradox of simultaneous understanding and not-understanding. As often stressed in the vast literature the intercultural encounter is charged with communication difficulties; it is a broadly accepted basic assumption that there exists a communication 'mis-match' between cultures. Nevertheless, human relations also seem to offer an apriori basis for community and, therefore, communication. Communication, thus, in its sociological sense implies relationship and not the lack of it, and in that sense the topic here is rather *how* people relate between cultures than *if* they do.

Interculturality manifests itself in praxis; it presents itself as the practical problem of understanding. Consequently, the concept of interculturality is an abstraction that encapsulates the experience of the paradox of understanding versus not-understanding described above. In the scholarly field, choosing either of the two sides of that paradox as the leading principle is a frequent way to address the problem, and a way that produces two opposite possibilities of thinking the intercultural: one that stresses understanding and another that underlines the lack of understanding as a basic feature of the intercultural encounter.

On the one hand the problem of intercultural understanding is considered a practical, solvable task. Awareness of cultural differences is seen as a possible parameter in strategic action.[4] Intercultural communication as a scientific field is primarily interested in the instrumental side of insight. The reason must probably be sought in history; it is so to speak a hereditary trait since the scholarly interest in intercultural communication from its earliest days up till to day has a traditionally close linkage with operational motives emanating from business managerial interests, academic as well as organisational. The writings of social scientist Geert Hofstede is an overwhelming symbol of this marriage between analytical interest in a phenomenon and operational motivation.[5] Naturally, the interest in intercultural communication is not limited to a business context. We can find the theme in wider organisational and educational contexts, to mention but a few, but the linkage with operational motives is equally dominant in these fields, a linkage that grows problematic since it – almost unavoidably – implies a qualitative as well as quantitative reduction of culture. The wish for operational tools, however, is not in itself what is criticised here. What makes it problematic is the fact that the rationalistic and goal oriented paradigm to a large extent also dominates the qualitative and explorative attempts to describe and understand interculturality. For some years intercultural competence was a keyword; with its distinction between motivational, emotional and performative aspects it aspired to an encompassing approach to interculturality, which all the same, even in its most interpretative approaches, had an underlying instrumental bias.[6]

On the other hand, intercultural understanding is considered to be essentially impossible, since our life and world can only be meaningful within the framework constituted by the language-world of a specific culture. If we try to understand what is culturally different, our efforts will therefore be obstructed both by the limits of our own world and the diffuse, untouchable strangeness of the other world. The constructivist position is at the centre of this approach to interculturality, and just as it underlines our inability to leave our home-world and transcend its frontiers, it has a tendency to advise us not to judge what we (think to) see in the culturally different world, since we cannot and will never be able to understand its culture-specific truth, trapped as we are in our home-world.

A phenomenological analysis, however, of interculturality reveals the paradoxical two-sidedness of the intercultural experience. Culture can be illustrated by the phenomenological concept of horizon, which is the network of possible reference; thus we are talking about the horizon of our meaningful world. The horizon is like a sphere, and depending on the perspective we can talk about an inner and an outer horizon. Within the inner horizon lies our home-world. 'Home-world' does not mean fully expressed life-situation; on the contrary it is being expressed constantly and never finally. The home-world is continually being acquired, but since it lies within the inner horizon, which is characterised by possible reference, it will be an 'explication' of something already known (Held, 1994). The outer horizon is where that which cannot be anticipated appears. The unanticipated – the culturally different – is both enigmatic and approachable. It is approachable in its quality of being meaningful just like our home world, but enigmatic too, since it is another and inconceivable meaning. Although we interpret the meaningful signs of the other world as such, i.e. signs of significance, the specific meaning of those signs escapes our comprehension. What constitutes interculturality, then, is the very tension between understanding and not-understanding; interculturality is this paradox. It results in an ongoing and never terminated approximation of meaningful worlds, and this approximation brings us back to everyday life and its practical problem of understanding.

Hermeneutics invites us to consider meaning and understanding as the key concepts of this relation, and interculturality then as the meeting and mutual understanding of meaning. Understanding here, of course, should not be read in any ideological way, but merely as the idea of two meanings gaining a 'room' in each other's horizons of interpretation, a room that in the extreme initial form is reduced to the mere recognition of the existence of another meaning. This room that represents a fusion of horizons is constituted and reconstituted in interpretation, where we draw upon our tradition in questioning the cultural Other for 'his' meaning, just as he asks us for 'our' meaning. I draw upon H.-G. Gadamer's idea of fusion of horizons without claiming that Gadamer was primarily referring to interpersonal encounters. He illustrates his point with reference to the historicity of understanding, i.e. the meeting of past and present in the one person (Gadamer, 1990). Nevertheless, since the effect of history in understanding (*'Wirkungsgeschichte'*) is what communicates past and present, it is exactly the same mediator that makes possible the fusion of two persons' horizons. Interculturality, furthermore, is not just about understanding the different; being interpersonal it also requires grasping the idea of the different understanding us, so that a phenomenological analysis of interculturality must refer to inter-intentionality.

Intercultural hermeneutics should be seen first of all as a complementary perspective to the more praxis-oriented approaches to interculturality, while keeping in mind that its implications are relevant to every intercultural encounter. It is, however, a perspective that contains a critical distance to the essentialist ideas of culture that dominate the field of intercultural communication. In designating an epistemological role to the concept of culture, the hermeneutical approach underlines understanding instead of *mis*understanding.

Thus, the topic of the chapter is interculturality as openness of interpretation. This openness is fundamental and cannot be methodologised as a task-solving instrument, because method as reduction implies closing. This distinction is pivotal to the argument, and despite its radical scope less exclusive than it might seem. The distinction does not imply a complete abandon of the idea of method, and it does not insist on the deconstruction of any fragment of structure that is constituted in understanding. First of all it is a critique of the tendency to letting method be the *first* approach towards the cultural Other, a tendency that we find illustrated in the concept of intercultural competence. Method is not the way to avoid stereotypes, it is itself a stereotype, we can claim paraphrasing Gadamers point,[7] and as such it can be manifested in praxis as foreunderstanding and as the question to the Other. Consequently the critique is not directed towards intercultural praxis whether it is founded in methodological systems or not, but focuses on a conceptualisation of the intercultural problem that by use of method objectivizes the understanding of culture. Interculturality, therefore, has hermeneutical implications, but since it presents itself as a reciprocal hermeneutical experience, we must add a perspective of double intentionality to the interpretation. The reciprocal condition is described as the understanding of the Other as someone who understands me as I understand him.

The concept of reciprocal intentionality implies the idea, although mostly implicit, of ethics. Gadamer speaks of openness in interpretation as something to strive for, but never (at least in his magnum opus) connects any explicit ethics to understanding. In the intercultural relation, in which meaning is constituted in reciprocal intentional community, such openness must be answered, if we shall be able to talk of authentic reciprocity. Ethics must be seen in co-relation with the limitations of the hermeneutic praxis itself. The limits of intercultural hermeneutics must be sought in the borderland between linguistic meaningfulness and the pre-linguistic sphere, which we could vaguely describe as the bodily mood of security of the (not yet verbalised) order of things. Culture, as it seems, cannot be reduced to mere meaningfulness; it also includes the moods, the non-reflected habits, etc. The intercultural paradox of understanding and not-understanding, then, is not just a paradox for the time being, it is also a paradox because we recognise the limitations, and in recognition we try to put words to what we have no words for. I recognize that this will remain an infinite project, but also a project we must engage in ourselves in the light of the intercultural condition. Only because we meet the different do we become conscious of the existence of our moods and habits and of those of the cultural Other.

Ethics and morals: distinction and relationship

One of the main points and a basic foundation for the argument of the present chapter is a clear distinction between ethics and morals. The point of such a distinction is not to enter a philosophical discussion about that theme, but merely to specify concepts for analytical purposes. In much literature on the subject of intercultural communication, including the part of it that is especially dedicated to the issue of ethics, the distinction is not made very clearly, and mostly the difference in significance of the two terms is blurred – excusably one may add, since there cannot be said to exist any broadly undisputed definition of the two concepts and what distinguishes one from the Other. But we assume that cutting through and formulating an explicit distinction will bring us beyond some of the discussions that stand in the way of a stricter concept of intercultural ethics, the main discussion being that of the possible existence of moral universals or not. The distinction made here is based on the idea defended by Paul Ricoeur (1992, 2002), who argues a clear conceptual difference between the two notions, but also a strict interrelatedness of the two. Ethics, according to Ricoeur, concerns the wish for the good life, while morality concerns duty in the form of norms, obligations and prohibitions that gain universal character. Marina (2002), following the same path, distinguishes between two major projects for mankind, the project of happiness and the project of perfection. 'Among the projects created by intelligence there are two that surprise by their universal insistence and their utmost and distinct vagueness. I am referring to the project of being happy and to the project of reaching perfection' (Marina, 2002). The ethical aim is that of a good life, to be happy so to speak, while perfection is the endeavour of morals in separating right from wrong. Ricoeur synthesises the ethical 'intention as aiming at the 'good life' with and for others, in just institutions' (1992). In this chapter the focal part of the definition is the good life with and for others, while the last part of it remains in the background, not because it is considered unessential, but because it is primarily the intercultural and interpersonal encounter that defines our perspective.

The distinction established by Ricoeur and quoted in the following is foundational to this chapter, since it has the potential to clarify and thereby deepen the analysis of the intercultural aspect of the ethical. 'I propose to establish, without concerning myself about Aristotelian or Kantian orthodoxy, although not without paying close attention to the founding texts of these two traditions: *(1) the primacy of ethics over morality, (2) the necessity for the ethical aim to pass through the sieve of the norm, and (3) the legitimacy of recourse by the norm to the aim whenever the norm leads to impasses in practice* – impasses recalling at this new stage of our meditation the various aporetic situations which our reflection on selfhood has had to face.' (Ricoeur, 1992; my emphasis). 'In other words', as Ricoeur continues, 'according to the working hypothesis I am proposing, morality is held to constitute only a limited, although legitimate and even indispensable, actualisation of the ethical aim, and ethics in this sense would then encompass morality' (ibid). Ethics, then, can be categorised as a basic, pre-linguistic recognition – a grounding mood of community – which to become interpersonal and socialised must pass through a specifying and contextualising moral formulation, which is nurtured by the unformulated urge of ethics, but which is also modified and even altered by this urge. Through ethics we experience the borderland between pre-linguistic being and the meaningful world of language; we might indeed be able to put into words the demand that lies in ethics, but the claim as such comes to us from outside our language-world. The ethical wish for a good life is formalised and generalised in morality, which in its basic form is expressed in Kant's so-called categorical imperative.

The application of moral norms in specific situations leads to conflicts, or at least contains the potential of conflicts, due to the possible incompatibility of norm and situation, conflicts to which the moral norm itself has no answer. The norm, then, must be measured in view of the ethical wish whenever it leads to conflicts that can only be solved by recourse to a practical sense that takes the singularity of the specific situation into account (Ricoeur, 2002).

In Ricoeur's view ethics and morals, as concepts, are thus relatively sharply distinguished, but even though we can consider them separately for analytical purposes, praxis connects them closely so that we should rather speak of two aspects of the same phenomenon. Still, for the sake of conceptualisation we can radicalise our formulation of the relation between ethics and morality as a dichotomy. Ethics opens and morality closes. This fundamentally hermeneutic perspective on the issue of ethics and morals connects the two sides even though defending their different significances. The nature of our knowledge of moral

principles is hermeneutic and therefore a process, searching and interpretative. The moral principles are a meta-framework, which must be
actualised, in the specific facticity, and it takes its precise form according to the specificity of the situation. If for the sake of conceptualisation we were to radicalise this point of view, we could state that ethics
concerns my relation with the Other. Ethics moves in the sphere between the first and the second person. It is practically impossible to
relate ethics to the third person, at least considered without its moral
manifestation. The starting point for morality on the other hand is the
third person. Whenever it is imposed on the I and the Other and their
relation, it assumes an element of violence and lack of attention to the
uniqueness of the 'one' person and the 'one' situation.

Furthermore while ethics seems to be embedded in the interpersonal
immediacy, morality is embedded in culture. The moral principle is
always relative to time and place (Cook, 1999; MacIntyre, 2002). 'To
understand a concept, to grasp the meaning of the words which express
it, is always at least to learn what the rules are which govern the use of
social life. This in itself would suggest strongly that different forms of
social life will provide different roles for concepts to play.' (MacIntyre, 2002). Not only is the concretisation of the moral norm dependent
on society, but the very quality of moral concepts vary with the societal context (ibid). This does not imply that what is said in one socio-
cultural context about for instance justice is totally irrelevant to what
might be said about a seemingly similar concept in another socio-
cultural context – on the contrary. 'There are continuities as well as
breaks in the history of moral concepts', and between different cultures
we might add. 'Just here lies the complexity of the history' (ibid), and
of interculturality for that matter. We must accept moral relativism in
other words, since morality is bound to a context as the localised manifestation or formulation of the ethical claim. But moral relativism does
not mean that morality is untouchable. If we consider untouchable the
life-form and with it the morality of the cultural Other, we reduce him
to an object; he becomes the museum of indigenous life-forms. This
may well be motivated by a wish to protect him and respect him, the
point being that we must accept and not try to alter different life-forms.
Nevertheless, if the Other is to be constituted as just such another subject, the ethical claim must be that of engaging in contact, which
means engaging in a form of contact which leaves neither of the parties
untouched. The point is that accepting moral relativism does not mean
accepting any moral norm with reference to its different cultural context; in that case we might as well dispose of morality. Much rather

accepting moral relativism means recognising the initial and foundational otherness of the Other in the light of the inter-intentional dynamics in which our relation is constituted.

The ethical demand

This points to what the Danish philosopher and theologian Knud Ejler Løgstrup describes as the ethical demand. The ethical demand finds its basis in the fundamental social orientation of man, in consequence of which we depend on and are delivered over to one another. It follows from this social orientation and interdependence that I always, to greater or lesser extent, hold the life of the Other in my hands, and that I must take care of this life (Løgstrup, 1991). As stated above, ethics is taken to be a pre-linguistic given in this chapter; the encounter with the Other is before reflection, according to Levinas (2002). The ethical demand, thus, lies immediately in the meeting as the ethical dimension of openness, or we could say as a not yet stated question to the Other. This question holds both the ethical demand of myself, i.e. the claim to attend to the best interest of the Other, and the realisation of myself as the incarnation of the ethical demand to the Other, and as such I do not request ethical responsibility of the Other, but unwittingly I carry the demand into effect insofar as it concerns the Other. Nevertheless the ethical demand in itself is limited to the state of initiation. It is the question, although un-asked, which must be answered – it must be responded to, or we could say it must be situated, e.g. contextualised and therefore textualised. So even though the encounter with the Other is before reflection, it must subsequently be mediated through reflection to be accomplished and fulfilled. Following Gadamer (1990) we can state that one does not experience without the activity of asking, and we might add that one does not ask without producing experience. The point here is not that the universals find their actualisation in the particular, but that this dialectic relation is preceded by the ethical demand. In the intracultural encounter the ethical demand is answered by convention in the form of already established moral norms, but interculturality *per se* has no convention and therefore no ready-made answer. In interculturality one's own conventional answers are highlighted as insufficient, and that means at least two things. Convention to a large extent is unconscious and unreflected when we consider it a daily praxis, and it can be so because it covers all eventualities, or in other words: as long as the borderlines of convention are not challenged, it can remain relatively unconscious and be the custom that as medium facilitates our daily life-routines – which is presumably the very foundation of convention. Consequently, it is the incompatibility of convention and the situational facticity that we find in interculturality which throws light on answers hitherto fully satisfactory, but insufficient in the new context. Interculturality, thus, not only points to the different, but in pointing at the different it points at that from which the different is different. Becoming aware of our incapacities leaves us with the outspoken wish for answers, a wish, however, that in spite of the delimitations of known structures and categories must rely on these very structures as the sole resource in the search for fitting categories.

In terms of the ethical demand our search for explicit answers is seen in the perspective of the unspoken demand to take care of the other person's life. It becomes part of the answer that the Other is equally searching, and his searching crosses mine in the inter-intentional relation across cultural differences. The two-sidedness of intercultural ethics and indeed of ethics as such is a constitutive feature, and must not be neglected in favour of the relative one-sidedness that seems to be prevalent in for instance the ethics of Levinas, who almost reduces the I to a mirror of the pre-ontological ethical light that emanates from the Other requiring our unconditioned engagement in this Other. It might appear that the subordination that Levinas reserves for the self with regard to the Other is some kind of deconstruction of the self, and that it expresses an illusory idea of the possibility of suppressing oneself that is based in the erroneous ideal that the Other only can do justice to himself if he does not meet me, if he so to speak is spared the confrontation with me. It is difficult not to ask whether there can be an interpersonal relation under such circumstances, as the same must be true for the Other insofar that I for him am the Other, and the idea therefore most of all seems absurd.

The 'fact' that we are dependent and hence delivered over to one another lies in the 'fact' that the Other is not me, and, seen in the analytical light of the notion of culture, he is a cultural Other. Every individual being a unique cultural crossroads, the Other will always as a principle and to a certain extent be a cultural Other. This point that converges with the general idea that all communication in principle and to some degree is intercultural, leads to the assumption that the ethical demand and ethics as such in principle and to some degree refer to the condition of interculturality, and interculturality seen that way is one possible conceptual approach to human relations.

Ethics and cross-cultural universals

We may say that the topic of a global norm or what is often called cross-cultural ethics on a worldwide basis arises with globalisation. The matter of universal normative prescriptions is not the issue in this chapter at first glance. Supposedly there is a conceptual difference that divides the question of the existence of the cross-culturally valid and the question of the interculturally desirable. The question of cross-cultural ethics is led first of all on motivations of defining standards in the 'single world' which is a cultural consequence of globalisation, but in spite of its formal tone it is still based in the practical experience of interculturality. Indeed we must see the 'single-world' concept in the light of the intercultural experience and vice versa to understand what drives the quest for universals. Consequently, what renders ethics urgent not only as a philosophical problem, but as a daily claim, is the late modern condition of being in a globalised world and the subsequent condition of unstableness, a condition described by Zygmunt Bauman as 'liquid modernity' (Bauman, 2000). As I stated in the introduction, modern man is on the move and confronted with ever new and unexpected situations to which conventional norms have no answers. On the other hand globalisation is aware of itself and calculates the unexpected, contradictory as it may seem. The cultural vagabond, and that is in fact a fair description of us all in liquid modernity, has a certain categorical relation to the diffuse and constantly changing structures of late modern life, and therefore it is not contradictory to talk of cross-cultural ethics, neither in its initial unspoken ethical form, to be sure, nor in the structured and explicit norm, but the structure must be highly dynamic or fluid in the terms of Bauman. Intercultural ethics seem to presuppose a cross-cultural metanorm (Karmasin, 2002). This presupposition stems from another presupposition taught to us by anthropologists and other social scientists, namely that nothing is culture-free. The latter presupposition leaves place but for two possibilities, on one hand relativism and on the other imperialism, but is there not 'a place for cross-cultural ethics which is between relativism and imperialism?' (Karmasin, 2002). The statement that globalisation makes the idea of isolated cultures illusory (Beck, 2000) seems to be commonplace in the debate, and following this thought it appears obvious to claim the same for moral systems. But increasingly becoming members of the single world does not necessarily imply that we worship the same moral standards – on the contrary it would seem. We are undisputedly increasingly connected across spatial and temporal as

well as social borderlines, but connectivity is not necessarily proximity, neither cultural nor spatial (Tomlinson, 1999). What we can say,
though, is that nobody's moral canon is untouched nor untouchable in
the globalised single world. In fact it is exactly because the single
world on one hand does not mean the same world and on the other
hand insistently and continuously presents itself to us that ethics comes
to the foreground as a routinely experienced aspect of everybody's
daily life.

We have argued that interculturality is a (perspective on the) interpersonal relation that is founded in praxis. The ethical question in interculturality arises as a result of a radicalised and continuous actualisation of the limits of our moral norms. The norms that are challenged
concern both intracultural and intercultural affairs, and the very norms
about cultural units are challenged as well as the notion of culture itself. Culture is seen as phenomenon, 'meaning', an ontological category: humans are culture-bound creatures, or suspended in webs of
significance, in the words of Geertz (1973). Culture is seen as an analytical implication (Hastrup, 1989), that is the concept we use to describe cultural difference, that is differences between social groups'
life-world or understanding of life, as Løgstrup would put it. One ines-
capable result is the difficulties in referring to specific culturally defined groups. Whatever restriction one lays on the culture unit in order
to define it empirically and be able to relate to it practically, the definition lays itself open to justifiable critique: culture-related specifications
of groups – small or big – are intrinsically described in quite roughly
defined terms that, to greater or lesser degree, leave out the complexity
of real life and thus do no justice to the multifariousness of the phenomenon we call culture. Often it is the term 'national culture' that
triggers the debate, but this term is not qualitatively different from any
other specification.

If we are, however, to furnish an answer to the question concerning
the possibility of cross-cultural ethics, we must lean upon Ricoeur's
distinction to say that it is exactly in ethics that we must search the
cross-cultural dimension in the aim at the 'good life' with and for others, in just institutions. The project of happiness is in nature not ini-
tially determined by culture: it is not culture that makes us strive for at
good life, but since the ethical aim must pass through the sieve of the
norm, ethical praxis becomes culturally conditioned, and it is in the
moral structuration that liquid modernity's confusion strikes us. It is
here more than ever that we are led to impasses in practice and forced

to re-pose the question about the good life with and for others in the light of the ethical demand of taking care of the life of the Other.

Ethical and moral implications for the intercultural praxis

As repeatedly underlined, ethics is mainly about striving for the good life, and this is still true for interculturality. Intercultural ethics, then, is not in the first place about finding or establishing the norms for the good intercultural encounter: rather, it is about understanding how the intercultural circumstance influences our wish and quest for the good life. 'In modern society the individual is no longer able to find his or her local community. In modern society the individual is only confronted with himself or herself, when he or she tries to establish norms for action. In this perspective man is totally free, with no limits what so ever' (Larsen, 1991). As it is described here, this pseudo-freedom – a judgement that Larsen presumably would agree to – is an extreme and hopefully purely theoretical consequence of the liquidity of late modern society in a globalised world community. It implies a radical lack of social dimensions, and even the hyper-complexity and accelerated dynamics of social life in the modern world do not lead to the dissolution of sociality. Man is neither totally free nor without limits, but on the other hand the norms of practically any local community are endlessly dynamic; they are constantly on the move, we can say with an allusion to Larsen himself. One social consequence of this dynamic is increasing interculturality. Because of the dynamic conditions the immediate communities strengthen their role as norm-creating frames for the individual.[8] The greater community is partly fragmented. Interculturality is not exclusively the consequence of the fact that other cultures come to us; it is also a consequence of the diversification of our own socio-cultural environment. Late modernity's constant move is also a dissolution, not in the sense of disappearance of the elements of this sociocultural environment, but rather as the uninterrupted change from one form to another, resulting in 'liquid modernity'. We may refer to an interculturality coming to communities from the outside and to an interculturality coming from within cultural communities. But still these seemingly separate processes must be perceived as related aspects of the same cultural dynamic. Against the above mentioned pessimistic vision of freedom we can invoke a qualitative concept of freedom, which does not converge with an ideal of multiplicity of choices that in the end leads to a state of uneasiness, since one is bound by the imperative of having to choose, but nothing to choose from.

I am doing what I want and therefore I am free, and I fulfil my duty because I want to, states Marina (2002). It is in fact a concept of freedom that, in opposition to freedom of choice, is based on the narrowing down of choices to the one right choice, which is right because it is what I want. Freedom in this view is an experience of being at ease and not being confronted with any restraints or barriers; we can do what we want. If we see freedom in this light, it might in fact be based on one and only one possible choice: as long as that choice is perceived as the right and only good choice, the experience of being free to follow one's wish is intact. This basic qualitative, unreflected, and felt freedom is threatened in late modernity in the way described by Larsen. We can no longer be at ease and follow intuition; we are obliged to choose, because our standards are challenged by the culturally different Other. In that situation we must recur to ethics as the resource that will help re-establishing the unreflected freedom that we strive for. To be sure, we must obey the necessity for the ethical aim to pass through the sieve of the norm, and this is where interculturality becomes the lived paradox of understanding and not-understanding. But the normative dimension is also where the one person re-locates his or her community with the consequence that he or she is no longer solely confronted with himself or herself, when he or she tries to establish norms for action.

Intercultural ethics means acceptance of cultural difference (Karmasin, 2002), which means recognizing the Other as intercultural facticity. Maybe intercultural ethics should be seen in opposition to intercultural competence, the concept we have used as an illustration of another approach to interculturality. While the latter concentrates on efficiency in interaction, thus reducing the intercultural encounter to a rational problem-solving process, the former conceptualises the good interaction. This, of course, is a very much more complex affair, but taking into account that real life is infinitely complex the ethical point of view at least can be said to have a more holistic approach. The competence point of view with its focus on efficiency misses some basic points about interculturality as such, so that the ethical stance – despite its tremendous and possibly breathtaking complexity – is more appropriate after all. The formulation of an intercultural competence is in a sense paradoxical since it dissolves what it is designated to cope with. In the construction of competence we constitute culture, and intercultural competence becomes *intra*cultural morality. There is nothing unfortunate about that, but awareness of this point leads to recognition of the limitations of the very concept that was supposed to be our way out of the home world and beyond the intracultural horizon, in fact out of ethnocentrism. Evidently, we should not dismiss intercultural competence as a barren concept, even though we detect a risk that it can be misleading; but we must continuously break out of its frame if it is to be what it claims to be, *inter*cultural, which is of course ironic and, as already mentioned, paradoxical, but nevertheless it does make sense within the frames of the concept of interculturality seen as a paradox of understanding and not-understanding.

Where does this leave us? If set in an intercultural situation that involved the question of marriage and thus confronted with the problem, should I out of ethical considerations warn against an arranged marriage where such arrangements are the habit and the norm – I myself being from a culture where this is not the habit? If a member of a multicultural workforce, should I act on the offensive regarding my own social standards, or should I take a defensive attitude, or simply resign myself to an unpredictable interculturality that I cannot in any way influence? The possible settings are legion, and ethics does not help us, or at least it does not provide an answer to the specifics of the situation. And we can say neither yes nor no, or rather we should say that we are not able to indicate general guidelines for what standpoint to choose. This is the whole point, or put more precisely: I cannot invoke culture as an argument for whatever choice I will make. On the one hand I cannot refuse to relate to a specific case with reference to relativism, seeking absolution in the fact that I am not able enter the life-world of a foreign culture. On the other hand I must admit and make clear to myself that I lack the necessary social and cultural insight to constitute an overview that would justify my judgement. The basis of my practical wisdom is, at best, very limited – at least if I choose to see that base as a normative resource. Paradoxically, even though I cannot invoke my culture as an argument for my choices, culture remains my sole resource in finding meaning and answers.

Under all circumstances there is a certain inescapability that characterises ethics; it lies in the nature of ethical problems that once arisen they do not disappear, or in other words, once perceived we cannot pretend they do not exist. We cannot neglect the 'impasses in practice', and insofar the practice is intercultural the recourse by the norm to the aim of a good life is both provoked by and coloured by the cultural Other.

Jens Lautrup Nørgaard

Intercultural ethics and the professional sphere

In order to relate the notion of intercultural ethics to a field of practice, we shall end this chapter with some brief considerations about intercultural ethics in a professional context, and about what could be the status for such ethical awareness in professional life.

Management is one field of practice that has seen a growing concern for ethical topics, and managerial practices are increasingly influenced by ethical considerations. Business ethics, admittedly, is not first of all a concern for intercultural relations, but with globalisation comes a cultural aspect to ethics in the professional sphere.

The predominant perspective in managerial literature on the topic is a focus on the ongoing globalisation of business norms, and much attention is paid to the problem of the relation between global and local business norms. The organisational level is a very predominant analytical perspective in the sense that what is treated and discussed is the compatibility of structures, e.g. organisations, value systems, etc., at a suprapersonal level (Schneider & Barsoux, 2003; Weaver, 2001; Dozier, Husted & McMahon, 1998). Consequently, business ethics, insofar as it concerns cross-cultural practices, is aimed at formalised systems of integration, and cross-culturality is the thematic norm at the expense of interculturality. In convergence with what seems to be a broadly accepted practice, I choose here to define the cross-cultural as typically concerned with cultural structures at a comparative level and interculturality as typically concerned with intercultural encounter proper at an actor and praxis level.

The question of integration of culturally defined business norms is clearly justified, partly because '(a) presumption of culture-free ethics management is visible, for example, in the common advocacy and development of formal codes of business conduct by international agencies' (Weaver, 2001) and partly because '(p)ractices which are appropriate in one cultural setting may violate the established understanding of organisational and social life in another cultural context, resulting in a loss of legitimacy for the firm, and in hostility toward or the rejection of the very management practices which are presumed to harmonize and improve organisational life.' (ibid). Nevertheless, justifiable as it may be, it cannot stand alone because very often the analysis is limited to the comparison across cultural borders that are defined very roughly, and because insofar as it concerns itself with an actual process of integration it is seen almost exclusively from the structural perspective. But to fully grasp the structuration that doubtlessly takes place, we must see structure as only a part of a triangle of dialectically related aspects: structure, agents and praxis (Giddens, 1984). To properly discuss the issue of cross-cultural business ethics and its integration of structures, we must include agents engaged in intercultural praxis.

In our return to the agent and interculturality, once again, we must insist on the distinction between ethics and morals, and in the light of this distinction we must say that cross-cultural business ethics considered as scholarly reflection is mostly concerned with the integration of different moral norms. Furthermore the one-sided focus on the structure level has a tendency to avoid ethical immediacy in specific situations. What I advocate here, consequently, is mainly a clearer distinction of concepts; the relation between morals and ethics should be clarified and interculturality should not be taken for granted as a result of the cross-cultural analysis. No doubt, cross-cultural findings might very well shed light on what to be expected in the intercultural encounter, but still they cannot avoid the inescapability and insistence of the ethical claim and demand that raise with and within the intimacy of the intercultural situation.

With Nina Jacob (2003) we can define intercultural management as the management of diversity or 'of paradoxes, of ambivalences and ambiguities'. But where can we place intercultural ethics in the context of management? According to Deetz, Cohen & Edley (1997), '(r)ather than focusing on the individual as the site of ethics, we will suggest that the commercial business context is perhaps a more significant, productive and meaningful site for ethical discussion.' In opposition to this statement, it is the point in this chapter that the one place to focus when the question of ethics presents itself is precisely the individual. Rather than reducing ethics, intercultural or not, to corporate norms of good behaviour, we must trace the spring of the ethical urgency to individuals. Once again we must insist on a clear distinction between the ethical question and the moral question admitting also, as argued above, that the two questions must be seen in the light of each other.

In a way, intercultural business ethics – as well as business ethics as such – points towards the perceived boundaries between what is part of the organisational and inter-organisational normative and what is extrinsic to it. When business norms lead to impasses in practice which challenge our reflection, it is also, or maybe exactly, our reflection on selfhood which is challenged, and once again we must rely on the aim for the good life, unspoken as it is, in the ongoing search for answers.

Jens Lautrup Nørgaard

References

Bauman, Zygmunt; *Liquid Modernity*. Cambridge: Polity Press, 2000.

Beck, Ulrich; What is Globalisation, in David Held & Anthony Mcgrew (eds); *The Global Tranformations Reader*. Cambridge: Polity Press, 2000.

Cook, John W.; *Morality and Cultural Difference*. Oxford: Oxford University Press, 1999.

Deetz, Stanley, Deborah Cohen & Paige P. Edley; Toward a Dialogic Ethic in the Context of International Business Organisation, in Fred L. Casmir (ed.); *Ethics in Intercultural and International Communication*. New Jersey: Lawrence Erlbaum Associates, 1997.

Dozier, Janelle Brinker, Bryan W. Husted & J. Timothy McMahon; Need for Approval in Low-context and High-context Cultures: A Communications Approach to Cross-cultural Ethics, *Teaching Business Ethics*, 2, 1998.

Gadamer, Hans-Georg; *Wahrheit und Methode. Grundzüge einer philosophischen Hermeneutik*. Tübingen: J.C.B Mohr (Paul Siebeck), 1990.

Geertz, Clifford; *The Interpretation of Cultures*. New York: Basic Books, 1973.

Giddens, Anthony; *The Constitution of Society*. Cambridge: Polity Press, 1984.

Hastrup, Kirsten; Kultur som analytisk begreb, in Kirsten Hastrup & K. Ramløv (eds); *Kulturanalyse. Fortolkningens forløb i antropologien*. København: Akademisk Forlag, 1989.

Held, Klaus; Hjemverdenen, fremmedverdenen, den ene verden, in Dan Zahavi (ed.); *Subjektivitet og livsverden i Husserls fænomenologi*. Århus: Modtryk, 1994.

Hofstede, Geert; *Cultures and Organisations. Software of the Mind*. London: Harper Collins Publishers, 1991.

Jacob, Nina; *Intercultural Management*. London: Kogan-Page, 2003.

Karmasin, M.; Towards a Meta Ethics of Culture – Halfway to a Theory of Metanorms, *Journal of Business Ethics*, 39, 2002.

Larsen, Øjvind; Etik & sociologi, *Social Kritik*, 17, 1991.

Levinas, Emmanuel; *Fænomenologi og etik*. København: Gyldendal, 2002.

Løgstrup, K.E.; *Den etiske fordring*. København: Nordisk Forlag A.S., 1991.

MacIntyre, Alisdair; *A Short History of Ethics*. London: Routledge, 2002.

Marina, José Antonio; *Ética para náufragos*. Barcelona: Editorial Anagrama, 2002.

Nørgaard, Jens Lautrup; *Dansk-spanske erhvervsforhandlinger og interkulturel forståelse – en hermeneutisk tilgang til interkulturalitet*. København: Copenhagen Working Papers in LSP, no. 4, 2002.

Ricoeur, Paul; *Oneself as Another*. Chicago: The University of Chicago Press, 1992.

Ricoeur, Paul; Etica y Moral, in Carlos Gómez (ed.), *Doce textos fundamentales de la Etica del siglo XX*. Madrid: Alianza Editorial, 2002.

Savater, Fernando; *Ética como amor propio*. Barcelona: Grijalbo Mondadori, 2002.

Schneider, Susan C. & Jean-Louis Barsoux; *Managing across cultures*. London: Pearson Higher Education, 2003.

Scollon, Ron & Suzanne Scollon; *Intercultural Communication*. Oxford: Blackwell, 1995.

Jens Lautrup Nørgaard

Søderberg, Anne-Marie & Nigel Holden; Rethinking Cross Cultural Management in a Globalizing Business World, *International Journal of Cross Cultural Management*, 2002 vol. 2(1).

Ting-Toomey, Stella; *Communicating Across Cultures*. New York: The Guilford Press, 1999.

Tomlinson, John; *Globalisation and Culture*. Cambridge: Polity Press, 1999.

Weaver, Gary R.; Ethics Programs in Global Business: Culture's Role in Managing Ethics, *Journal of Business Ethics*, 30, 2001.

Notes

1. Larsen uses the Danish term 'opbrud' that refers to the action of "getting on one's feet and making ready to leave" (Nudansk Ordbog); this has no precise equivalent in English. The point for Larsen is that modern man never settles, he is always on the move or about to move on.

2. An almost too obvious example being the debates in many Western European countries about immigration and immigrants.

3. For an apt account of the discussion, see for instance John W. Cook, 1999.

4. Geert Hofstede's (1991) idea of culture as mental programming is paradigmatic. Although Hofstede's ideas have been the object of very strong criticism, he still has quite a few followers, and even more who in spite of their explicit criticism use his ideas as explanatory models. Probably we shall find the explanation for such astonishing success in the tempting reduction of cultural complexity formed by Hofstede's four dimensions. If one needs to explain cultural difference, Hofstede is at hand as a universal and operational tool. Through his work, Hofstede seems to have grown into a father-like figure, and the ways in which he is referred to within the field are worthy of Freudian analysis.

5. Søderberg and Holden (2002) offer a thorough discussion of different cultural paradigms in cross-cultural management and their implication for the conceptualisation of the meeting of cultures in professional life.

6. I have criticised the concept of intercultural competence for being reductive vis-à-vis the very phenomenon it intends to embrace, e.g. culture, by confusing culture with the tasks and goals held by the intercultural actors (Nørgaard, 2000).

7. It is a basic point which Hans-Georg Gadamer underlines from the very introduction of Truth and Method, that although methods are practical tools we should not be led to believe that method as such is the way to unbiased insight, since methods in them selves are foreunderstanding (Gadamer, 1990).

8. The subjective judgement can only be assured against pure arbitrariness by integration into a communicative community, and the character of such a communicative community is both institutional and random, Larsen states referring to Habermas (1991).

DATE DUE
